Praise for *It's All about the Land*

"Taiaiake Alfred is unafraid to question the status quo, but he is also fearless about putting his own beliefs to the test. This new book reflects his personal, political, and philosophical journey, and the evolution of his thinking along the way. It is powerful and important reading for anyone committed to nation building – both Canada's and the First Nations' whose lands we call home."

Catherine Clark, President, Catherine Clark Communications and Co-Founder, The Honest Talk

"*It's All about the Land* takes mainstream (often, good faith) assumptions and beliefs about reconciliation as seen and processed through a colonial filter and turns them on their head. Insightful, informative, and deeply thoughtful, this collection of essays will have you thinking differently about decolonization and what reconciliation – as currently advocated by the government – really stands for, within the limiting framework of contemporary colonialism. Ultimately, it asks all of us to do and be more."

Toula Drimonis, writer, columnist, and author of *We, the Others: Allophones, Immigrants, and Belonging in Canada*

"This book is a heartfelt testament to the evolution of Indigenous Resurgence, a concept that Taiaiake Alfred has dedicated himself to for three decades. With humility and gratitude, he acknowledges his past shortcomings and embraces the importance of inclusivity and unity. This courageous introspection reflects the transformative power of decolonization and the ongoing journey towards Indigenous liberation. *It's All about the Land* stands as a powerful testament to the strength and wisdom of Indigenous peoples."

Nicholas Galanin, Tlingit and Unangax̂, multi-disciplinary artist

"Taiaiake Alfred's series of reflections, essays, and interviews is as complex and rich as the Kanien'kéha meaning behind his name. Some may be surprised, given my position and our respective philosophical world views, that I count Taiaiake as a friend, but his work forces me to scrutinize and constantly question my actions and those of my government so as not to reproduce the horrific social experiment that has devastated Indigenous peoples. This is healthy for anyone in a position of authority. This book, however, is not limited to political or philosophical reflections: it shows both the personal and philosophical evolution of a man in two worlds evolving out of an image of himself he fought so hard to create."

The Honourable Marc Miller, Minister of Immigration

"In *It's All about the Land* Taiaiake Alfred speaks powerfully, and at times discomfortingly, to the challenges Indigenous people face across the globe. The charting of

Alfred's developing thought and how he has changed perspectives over time is one of this work's most liberating contributions, showing that none of us is ever 'locked in' to the way we thought about things. This is a book for our time and an enormous contribution to the Indigenous struggle, both challenging and energizing in its core commitment to what we call 'country' as the life source of all that we do and all that we are."

Craig Ritchie, Dunghutti, Chief Executive Officer, Australian Institute of Aboriginal and Torres Strait Islander Studies

"As a strong Kanien'kehá:ka (Mohawk) activist, Taiaiake has moved through and influenced Indigenous movements all over the world, but the concept of Indigenous Resurgence is rooted in the culture, laws, and resistance of our people. The essays and speeches in this book prove it, proudly. In reflecting fearlessly on his own journey and the lessons he has learned as a leader, educator, and scholar, he shows the way for anyone who is committed to decolonizing themselves and becoming a stronger force for positive change for our people. *It's All about the Land* is essential reading for anyone who wants to understand the injustices Native people live under and what we should be doing about it."

Grand Chief Kahsennenhawe Sky-Deer, Mohawk Council of Kahnawà:ke

"I nodded repeatedly as I read this book. I know its hard central truth, that 'it's all about the land' and the Indigenous collectivism it enables. Land is where we anchor and sustain as Peoples. Taiaiake Alfred tells us that learning in/with our homelands will strengthen our will to defend those lands. He also provides a hard truth for Canada: 'Reconciliation' is a totally non-Indigenous affair. It is non-Indigenous people who must learn and accept Indigenous governance. I suspect increasing numbers of non-Indigenous people are ready to hear Taiaiake Alfred's message."

Kim TallBear, Sisseton-Wahpeton Oyate, Professor of Native Studies and Canada Research Chair (CRC) Tier 1 in Indigenous Peoples, Technoscience, and Society, University of Alberta

"Taiaiake Alfred is synonymous with Indigenous sovereignty. This timeless book must be read by the young people to jolt their hearts into action and to remind the older, complacent leaders that the fight is not yet finished. The controversial Taiaiake doesn't speak with forked tongue, he speaks truth to power. His words make some uncomfortable and that is good and that is powerful. In order to stop feeling discomfort, one must act. This book tells us what we need to do to be part of the Indigenous Resurgence. It's all about the land. For us women leaders, it has always been about our most important resources: our children and our land. Long after Taiaiake has passed into the Spirit World, his voice will echo through time. He will be an Ancestor that those Indian Warriors not yet born will speak of."

Mary Teegee (Maaxw Gibuu), MBA, Gitxsan Carrier, Takla Nation; Executive Director of Child and Family Services at Carrier Sekani Family Services; Chair of the BC Indigenous Child and Family Services Directors

Forum; BC Representative on the National Advisory Committee on First Nations Child and Family Services Reform; BC Representative on the First Nations Child and Family Caring Society of Canada; and President of the BC Aboriginal Child Care Society

"Outstanding! Taiaiake Alfred provides critical elements of decolonization visioning in *It's All about the Land,* directly confronting the hegemonic power of the Canadian colonial paradigm. He frames this from an Indigenous perspective as the 'colonial problem,' resulting in a radical shift in developing the authentic Indigenous strategic goals of reclaiming identity, cultural resurgence, and nation building – and at the center of all of that is land recovery."

Sakej Ward, survival expert and Mi'kmaw warrior

IT'S ALL ABOUT THE LAND

COLLECTED TALKS AND INTERVIEWS ON INDIGENOUS RESURGENCE

TAIAIAKE ALFRED

Edited and with an Introduction by Ann Rogers

ÆVO UTP

Aevo UTP
An imprint of University of Toronto Press
Toronto Buffalo London
utorontopress.com

Photos courtesy of Taiaiake Alfred

Publication cataloguing information is available from Library and Archives Canada.

ISBN 978-1-4875-5283-1 (paper)
ISBN 978-1-4875-5775-1 (EPUB)
ISBN 978-1-4875-5358-6 (PDF)

Printed and bound by CPI Group (UK) Ltd, Croydon, CR0 4YY

Cover design: Val Cooke
Cover images: (photograph) Taiaiake Alfred; (background) iStock.com/mustafaoncul

We wish to acknowledge the land on which the University of Toronto Press operates. This land is the traditional territory of the Wendat, the Anishnaabeg, the Haudenosaunee, and the Mississaugas of the Credit First Nation.

University of Toronto Press acknowledges the financial support of the Government of Canada, the Canada Council for the Arts, and the Ontario Arts Council, an agency of the Government of Ontario, for its publishing activities.

Canada Council for the Arts | Conseil des Arts du Canada

ONTARIO ARTS COUNCIL
CONSEIL DES ARTS DE L'ONTARIO
an Ontario government agency
un organisme du gouvernement de l'Ontario

Funded by the Government of Canada | Financé par le gouvernement du Canada | Canada

This book is dedicated with admiration and deep gratitude and love to my Mom and Dad, for everything they have given me, and to the original resurgents, my Aunt Laureen and Uncle Thomas in Ganienkeh, for keeping the fire burning and showing us all the way.

Will this land of mine remember me?
— Eduardo Galeano

CONTENTS

FOREWORD: THE BATTLE TO DECOLONIZE OURSELVES INSIDE AND OUT

By Dr. Pamela Palmater

Dr. Taiaiake Alfred is a Mohawk thinker, writer, and scholar whose lifelong work challenges Canada's colonial past and present and confronts the brutal truths of colonization, forced assimilation, and the many genocidal laws, policies, and practices enacted by the Canadian state against our sovereign Nations. Some of his most controversial but essential work has been identifying the many ways in which colonial ideologies, imposed on us for generations, have seeped into our own thinking. His work calls on us to identify, acknowledge, and remediate the intergenerational harms of colonization to ourselves, our families, and our Nations through a process of decolonization. I've relied extensively on his ideas and philosophies in my educational journey as a Mi'kmaw academic. Taiaiake's latest book, *It's All about the Land,* builds upon his previous contributions by bringing together a curated collection of some of his most powerful lectures and interviews, with an Afterword that acknowledges his own struggles with shedding colonial ways of thinking and behaving.

The continuation of Taiaiake's work in challenging the unjust status quo is important for both Indigenous and non-Indigenous students and scholars. Today, the academic experience for many Indigenous Peoples in universities and colleges is an empowering educational journey where we develop or improve our skills in research, writing, and critical thinking. In the more enlightened institutions, we have also learned more about our own collective histories and present-day realities across our Nations. This has not been the case for us until relatively recently. Post-secondary education historically was, and in many institutions still is, isolating, stressful, triggering, and even harmful. Our collective histories have largely been taught within a colonial, Eurocentric world view, which ingrained "education" with anti-Indigenous racism and misogyny, and often not based on fact. For countless generations, universities and colleges have been dominated by white male scholars who have effectively erased Indigenous histories and downplayed current Indigenous realities. Even when there was Indigenous content in courses or programs, it was often imbued with racist stereotypes that not only hurt Indigenous students but also miseducated non-Indigenous students. While things are changing, we cannot overlook the substantial impacts on Canadian society and social norms, of generations of anti-Indigenous racism, misogyny, dispossession, oppression, and attempts to justify or normalize violence. This speaks to why Taiaiake's work has been so important.

I am an L'nu woman, a citizen of the Mi'kmaw Nation, and member of Ugpi'ganjig (Eel River Bar First Nation) in unceded Mi'kma'ki. My large extended family has intermarried with Indigenous Peoples from the Wolastoqey (Maliseet) Nation, and so I have had the benefit of the traditional Indigenous knowledges, values, and world views of two Nations. The lessons I learned from my family – especially my politically active siblings – are invaluable. The education I received from them would turn out to be invaluable as I grew into as adult. I have since tried to live my life by their strong sense of responsibility to protect our people, advocate against injustices, and rebuild our Nation based on our traditional values. They never gave up or lost hope – they continued to live, assert, and defend our sovereignty every single day, inspiring the next generation to carry on the struggle. Today, this is referred to as Indigenous resistance and Indigenous Resurgence.

I learned from a young age that part of this collective work includes being mindful. That means listen first and take the time needed to consider everything that has been said. At the same time, my brothers and sisters taught me how to think critically and not be afraid to challenge anything that doesn't feel right or might present a threat to ourselves or our Nations. It is not about being right – it is about speaking our truth from our hearts with sincerity. This can be a challenge because of the intergenerational trauma experienced by our Nations due to centuries of genocidal practices by settler governments, and the ways in which governments still use divide-and-conquer techniques. While I was largely protected by my family and relations when I was young, my experience in post-secondary education was dramatically different.

The barriers for Indigenous students, staff, and faculty at universities and colleges – past and present – have been numerous and significant, such that some Indigenous students quit and/or Indigenous faculty leave or are effectively forced out of their institutions. On a personal level, there were many empowering parts of my education, but I also experienced many of the same challenges – including deep-seated racism in both the educational content and interpersonal treatment. I was fortunate to have been grounded in traditional Mi'kmaw knowledge and education before entering the formal education system. As a single mother with two small baby boys, my ability to navigate racist and sometimes hostile institutions and complete my post-secondary education is due to the love, support, and encouragement of my large, extended family. That said, it became very clear that my Mi'kmaw world view didn't fit well within the Eurocentric academic world.

My experiences in university education – especially my graduate studies – would have been even more isolating without the benefit of the critical analysis, insights, and reflections of powerful Indigenous scholars like Dr. Taiaiake Alfred. His writings and speeches spoke directly to my lived experiences. He challenged the colonial status quo and argued that there was a way out of this unjust and oppressive relationship between the state and Indigenous Peoples. His solution seemed simple – decolonize ourselves – but this call to look within ourselves, our families and our Nations, made the path forward personal and uncomfortable. Decolonization is easier when it is facing outward to challenge the state's unjust actions. Decolonization becomes more difficult when we must turn inward to kick the colonizer out of our own heads. This is a lifelong journey of personal reflection and accountability. Taiaiake made me realize that I had my own personal work to do alongside of my advocacy work.

I first heard of Taiaiake during my legal doctoral studies focused on the impacts of the Indian Act on First Nation identities, legal rights, and their specific Nations. This is one area where colonization and colonial laws and policies have been forced on our families for generations, impacting our ways of looking at one another and our own sense of identity. When I had to consider the impact of Indian registration (status) on band membership (membership in First Nation communities), I came across his first book, *Heeding the Voices of our Ancestors: Kahnawake Mohawk Politics and the Rise of Native Nationalism* (1995). This book really spoke to me, as he wrote about the struggle of reasserting our sovereignty over our own citizenship and the ways in which racist ideologies of blood quantum have interfered with that. His insights about this political struggle within the Mohawks resonated with the same issue within the Mi'kmaq. His book, which took a critical look at how we may have internalized colonial ideas about race, was foundational in my doctoral studies.

His later books, *Wasáse: Indigenous Pathways of Action and Freedom* (2005) and *Peace, Power, Righteousness: An Indigenous Manifesto* (1999; reissued 2009) have also been part of my scholarship and teaching. His commitment and love for our Nations and the warriors that defend us inspired me to action. It also inspired me to meet him and take part in some of the educational work he did. Since then, we have supported each other's academic and grassroots advocacy work. Taiaiake and I have been called to provide critical analysis on Indigenous issues in Indigenous media and mainstream media and ended up attending similar events focused on Indigenous resistance and Resurgence. I also had the good fortune to attend a special Gathering of Warriors he held at his university to educate and empower young students. He has always been open to sharing advice and was a guest on my *Warrior Life* podcast talking about his work. I was honored to see that discussion included in this new book, "Rebuilding the Fire: In Conversation with Pam Palmater."

Part of our working relationship included sharing advice and guidance on our work and advocacy and providing critical feedback on our academic work from an Indigenous perspective. The harder part came from our friendship as grassroots advocates and friends. As friends, we committed to always be honest with one another and try to keep each other accountable. As with any friendship, we had some very tough conversations. As I went along in my own journey of decolonization, I came to understand the ways in which sexism have been normalized. I always understood discrimination, exclusion, and the harms that result from it, but I started to see how men being held to account for this reacted by denying or downplaying it or offering apologies that were more insulting than sincere. As I came to understand these dynamics, the way in which I saw my brothers, uncles, and nephews also changed. We have all been impacted by colonization, but that can never be an excuse to hurt people with our words or actions – whether intentional or not. I came to learn that harm is not about intention: it is about effect of words or actions.

This resulted in some challenging conversations between Taiaiake and I. There were times when I shared with him my concerns about the words he used in his speeches and how they might be hurtful and exclusionary. At the time, he did not see them this way. This made some of our conversations even more difficult. We both engaged in these conversations with respect but did not always agree. However, that never stopped us from continuing these conversations and from me trying to explain how these words hurt people – even those that never told him it hurt them emotionally. As sometimes happens when we haven't learned the lessons we need to, life intervened and Taiaiake was suddenly faced with the human impacts of his words, an experience he addresses in the Afterword to this book. We still have challenging conversations, but they are now more informed by our mistakes and lessons learned.

It is Taiaiake's call to face the uncomfortable truths of colonization and the impacts it has had on our Nations, families, and individuals that makes his work stand out. As his work is such a challenge to the current unjust status quo, it has been both embraced and rejected. This is a clear sign that he is on to something. We need to confront the ongoing genocide committed by settler governments, industries, and some segments of society but also look at how we as individuals have adopted Eurocentric traits and values and harmed others in so doing. That was the hardest part for me – to identify the colonizer in my head, acknowledge my own problematic ideas or actions, and then find ways to reroot myself in the wisdom of my Nation. The last thing we want to do is perpetuate harm against one another in our Indigenous resistance. Taiaiake reminds us that we must do more than decolonize: we must put as much energy into Resurgence – taking back our power – and revitalizing our cultures, traditions, laws, and value systems. This is much harder than it seems, but we are guided by his lifelong work to help guide us in the direction.

In this book, *It's All about the Land,* Taiaiake takes this work from the theoretical to the personal, speaking to his own journey of self-discovery. He speaks openly about the pain he has caused others by the sexist words he used in his position as professor – qualities that are not part of Mohawk values nor any other Indigenous Nation. He shares how he had to listen to those he had hurt, learn from his mentors about how his actions hurt people, acknowledge his harmful actions, and hold himself to account. That is a hard, humbling journey, and it is not for me to say whether he has been successful. Accountability means different things to different people depending on the hurt inflicted. The fact that he included this conflict in this new book means that other people can learn from his mistakes.

Taiaiake's mission has been about asserting, living, and defending our sovereignty, lands, and Peoples. His call to action does not align with Canada's reconciliation policies that downplay our sovereignty, our right to self-determination, and our ability to govern our own lands and resources. His life's work is laser-focused on our righteous battle to confront historic and ongoing colonization, genocide, forced assimilation, violence, and control of our Peoples. He directly challenges Canada's solutions to the so-called Indian problem through forced assimilation, institutionalization, control, and the destruction of our lands and waters in the quest for wealth. He counters this policy agenda by offering his own solution to the "Canada problem": Indigenous resistance to ongoing colonization, the revitalization of our cultures and languages, and the resurgence of our

Nations – a radical path forward when compared to the government's agenda that demands we integrate into Canadian society.

This book builds upon Taiaiake's previous books in a way that speaks to hard truths and personal accountability for the harm we cause others when we have not addressed our own internalized, colonized ways of thinking. Whether it is personal harms we inflict on others or the ways in which Indigenous leaders make decisions that hurt our people, it is his consistent call to decolonize and resurge that has been foundational in Indigenous scholarship. This book reminds me of the internal work we still need to do and to always remain resurgent. *It's All about the Land* shines a light on the tense relationship between the colonizer and the colonized and the battle Indigenous Peoples wage to decolonize ourselves inside and out.

Pamela Palmater, Mi'kmaw Nation
Ugpi'ganjig (Eel River Bar First Nation)
October 18, 2022

INTRODUCTION

by Ann Rogers

Onkwehónweh, the Original People of this continent, experience colonialism in different ways, in different communities and Nations, and meet it with different responses. Many, worn down through the generations by poverty, dispossession, and racism and punished in countless ways simply for being Indigenous in a colonial state, choose to accept the government's offer of reconciliation and live under the hegemony of a state that promises to be more benevolent, a choice based on reasoning that is understandable. Some make their arguments in colonizer courtrooms, painstakingly proving time and time again that even by its own legal magical thinking, Canada is committing great crimes against them. Still others resist more directly. They build tiny houses and healing centers in the path of so-called progress, reoccupying and defending the ancestral space that is their life. They fish and catch lobster out of season, reclaiming the primacy of their knowledge and ways by refusing to operate in colonial time. They blockade railways, logging roads, bridges, and ports; hold round dances in shopping malls; and pick up hunting rifles. Whatever the response, it is clear that the problem they confront is Canada itself.

"Every state is founded on force," said Trotsky.[1] While Indigenous readers live the truth of this, many non-Indigenous ones still flinch at the idea of Canada as a contemporary settler state that has never hesitated to use violence against its ongoing "Indian problem." Much of what Canada wants and needs is incompatible with Indigenous political, social, economic, and cultural orders that are based on living on the Earth and with each other in a good way. Onkwehónweh who assert such ideas stand in the way of Canada's wholesale, guilt-free occupation of Turtle Island. Canadian moves to innocence – through the recognition, funding, and celebration of Indigenous rights, governance, languages, cultures, arts, traditions, ceremonies – are ultimately limited by the state's existential commitment to keeping the structures of white power and extractive capitalism intact and functioning smoothly. And so Onkwehónweh can be consulted on and consent to, but not veto, decisions that affect them; they have constitutional rights that can be overridden by "national" interests; they are offered compensation and slices of the economic pie, but they cannot have their lands, waters, and Nations back. As long as Canada asserts ultimate control over their lives and lands, they are not free.

As the premier contemporary scholar of Indigenous strategies of resistance to the problem of Canadian colonialism, Gerald Taiaiake Alfred has analyzed and critiqued the options on offer and actively advanced a radical agenda for decolonial struggle and emancipation – an agenda that has put him in direct opposition to the colonial state. This volume collects interviews and talks Taiaiake has given since 2003, a small selection of a sprawling oeuvre that includes hundreds of speeches, op-eds, and journal articles that explores the sources of his concerns and the ways they can be creatively confronted. This introduction provides some biographical and historical notes to help place his work in its wider political and scholarly contexts.

Kahnawà:ke Roots

On paper, the Indian Act governs Indigenous existence in Canada, but in practice Taiaiake lives in and has always answered to the stronger social reality of the Kanién'kehaka/Mohawk People, in particular the self-governing community at Kahnawà:ke – Indian Reserve #14 on the colonizers' map. The Great Law of the Rotinonhsón:ni that still shapes its political culture was constituted centuries before the arrival of the first settlers in Mohawk territory in the seventeenth century. Consequently, the Mohawks of Kahnawà:ke have a long experience of adapting to and resisting colonialism, walking an independent political line while managing the tensions of tradition and modernity. Internally, traditionalist Longhouse supporters dispute with the band council administration of the Mohawk Council of Kahnawà:ke (MCK), factions clash, and there is cooperation with and defiance of the Canadian state, but the test is always what is the good choice, the best choice, for the Kahnawa'kehró:non, the people of Kahnawà:ke.

In Kanién'keha/Mohawk the name Taiaiake means "crossing over." As Akwesasne Mohawk Elder Ernest

Benedict told him, "You're doing what your name means. You're going back and forth between our world and the white people's world. That's the role that you were born to do. And you're doing a good job of explaining our philosophies and our ideas, and you're challenging the white people to respect them and to understand them. So keep doing what you're doing."[2] University was never just a career path: Taiaiake was given a responsibility to carry Indigenous experience and wisdom into the world of the colonizer with the intent – as of all revolutionaries – of changing it. That vision is to get beyond colonialism to a world where Onkwehónweh are again able to live freely, unconstrained by the settler state. While Taiaiake has taken this vision forward on many fronts, as a scholar his contribution is most deeply felt in establishing the intellectual grounds for an emancipatory movement known as the Indigenous Resurgence. The key difference between this and reconciliation is that it does not ask Indigenous Peoples to reconcile themselves to living a colonized existence under an occupying power. To Indigenous Peoples, reconciliation offers a comfortable material existence as Canadian citizens; Indigenous Resurgence imagines pathways to liberation from colonization and the freedom to live truly Indigenous lives.

Tour of Duty

Signing up to fight on the side of American imperialism was the surprising first stop on Taiaiake's journey. After high school he joined the US Marines. By eighteen he was an infantryman, and by twenty he was leading a platoon in Honduras. It was the era of Ronald Reagan's Central

American dirty wars, and Honduras served as both a training ground and launch site for proxy US forces fighting left-wing resistance governments and movements in neighboring El Salvador and Nicaragua. Serving in Honduras raised his consciousness of his own identity vis-à-vis the imperial war machine: "I saw war happening, and both sides were Natives, you know, little brown people with guns fighting other brown people. And everybody looked Indian to me. And here I was, I was Native in this occupying force. And it didn't compute in my head at the time. It's like, what's going on here? I don't understand it. There are supposed to be good guys and bad guys, yet everybody's a Native."[3] His three years immersed in the hypermasculine, white supremacist culture of the US Marines left negative and positive marks:

> I did very well in the Marine Corps.... I was leading men in the field at 20 years old in Central America. For me, that was a big accomplishment. But then these other questions started hitting me. "Do I want to keep doing this? Is this right what we're doing?" I've processed through a lot of the traumas of that experience, and the ideas that I carried from it about the utility of aggression and certain hard-core attitudes. I left those behind as not being useful as a daily practice. But I have kept that idea of being ready to stand up and do what's necessary, whatever the consequences. I think that that is very consistent ... with Indigenous teachings on warriorhood.[4]

At twenty-one Taiaiake was back in Kahnawà:ke, working variously as a smoke shop security guard, a bank teller, and gas pump attendant at a service station, and taking night courses. Eventually he enrolled at Concordia University in Montreal:

"I wanted to learn the history of US foreign policy, and I wanted to learn the history of militarism. I wanted to learn the history of all these wars going on in the world.... That's what drew me to college."[5] Success as an undergrad led him to graduate school: he took up a place in the Department of Government at Cornell University and also began working for the Mohawk Council of Kahnawà:ke as an aide to Grand Chief Joe Tokwiro Thornton and Chief Billy Two Rivers. Taiaiake was a year into his master's program when the long-brewing Mohawk Uprising/Oka Crisis erupted in 1990.

Standing as Mohawks

While Mohawks had been disputing colonial usurpation of their lands since 1680, in the summer of 1990 a land-defense action at Kanesatake/Oka turned violent when Quebec police moved in hard; the seventy-eight-day stand-off that ensued pitted 4,000 Canadian soldiers, along with federal and provincial police forces, against Mohawk communities that came out to support Kanesatake. Kahnawà:ke, located outside of Montreal, blockaded the Mercier Bridge, cutting off Montreal from some of its suburbs. This sparked angry protests among the non-Native communities – a Mohawk effigy was burned – and Kahnawà:ke in turn was blockaded by police, leading to shortages of food and medicine. At one point Taiaiake "biked out to the front line with my cousin Ron with a bat in my hands, ready to do battle."[6] How to respond to the crisis opened up fissures in the community along a spectrum that stretched from Longhouse traditionalists through Warrior Society militants to the elected

Mohawk Council. Working for the Mohawk Council of Kahnawà:ke, Taiaiake felt both despair over how internal factional politics "pitted Mohawks against each other"[7] and also pride in "the stand we took as Mohawks together to protect ourselves and our families and our land, the unity of purpose we demonstrated … in spite of the differences of opinion."[8] He became passionately interested in what underlay the Mohawk identity, what made the Mohawks a Nation.

While most Canadians remember the 1990 conflict as a summer of Indigenous discontent, it had lasting repercussions. "Living under the burden of a siege that lasted for two years, occupied by an armoured battalion of Canadian Forces troops, and still facing the constant threats of harassment by the Sûreté du Québec as well as constant assaults by racist Québécois," Taiaiake published his first academic article, "From Bad to Worse," which explored how factional politics were able to dominate the community's political culture by occupying the vacuum left by the confusion around Mohawk identity caused by colonialism. Reflecting on the article decades later, he wrote that the issues he identified became "the anchor point for the trace of my trajectory as a thinker and writer, of the development of my own oeuvre and political identity as an intellectual and activist."[9] He participated in the federal government's Royal Commission on Aboriginal Peoples (RCAP), which led him deeper into the politics of his community and also connected him with Onkwehónweh from across Turtle Island. It was here that an Elder from Old Crow in the Yukon named Rosalee Tizya instilled the message that became his guiding mantra: it's all about the land.

Grounded Scholarship

These early experiences influenced Taiaiake's approach to scholarship in ways that were instantly recognized as breaking new intellectual ground. The impact of his first book, *Heeding the Voices of Our Ancestors: Kahnawà:ke Mohawk Politics and the Rise of Native Nationalism* (1995), was immediate. While superficially a deep dive into a narrow PhD topic – the internal politics of an Indian reserve – the book stood out because of the way it grounded the study of Native politics in Native perspectives. Taiaiake's research approach combined Western theorizing with probing interviews conducted among overlapping generations of Kahnawà:ke people with lived experience of practicing politics under colonialism. This became the hallmark of his methodology: "The way I do work is to sit and talk and listen to people and listen to stories and try to integrate the perspectives of the Onkwehónweh, the Original People, the Indigenous people with what I was learning in university in terms of theory and people's ideas from other parts of the world."[10]

This work was never undertaken simply to fulfill academic requirements (he is, we think, the first Native on Turtle Island to receive a PhD in political science) but to provide the intellectual foundations for an activist agenda of decolonization and emancipation. This purpose, an early scholarly articulation of the ideology/movement now known as Indigenous Resurgence, was made clear in the book's preface: "to explain the resurgence of a set of goals and strategies embedded within the political culture of a Native community leading to the assertion of a radical form of Native sovereignty, as opposed to a process of political change leading to further integration with Canada or the United States."[11]

Taiaiake's second book, *Peace Power Righteousness: An Indigenous Manifesto* (1999), was more universally *Indigenous*, drawing on conversations with Onkwehónweh voices from different Nations and walks of life. Unapologetically political, it was indeed a manifesto, calling out bad leaders for making bad decisions as they attempted to work around, through, and with colonial power structures in Canada. It ruffled feathers and created enemies, as it was bound to – in its pages Kanién'kehaka anthropologist Audra Simpson pointed out that one of the reasons for poor leadership was that "Indians won't criticize other Indians."[12] But his method, which used critical reasoning to upend Eurocentric conceptions of nations, states, and sovereignty, was also intellectually generous – the measure of the worth of an idea is whether it works, an estimation that is made based on ongoing discussion and praxis.

Taiaiake has always been willing to say what he feels needs saying, and the book endures long after its immediate notoriety because of the rootedness of its critiques. The conversational form used throughout the book reflects the Rotinonhsón:ni tradition of governing by a consensus that is achieved through dialogue. In contrast to modern Western political rhetoric that has become increasingly unhinged from the delivery of actual political goods, in this governance model the rightness of a course of action is determined by living its consequences – the *truth* of that. Accountability to the community is at the center of the process: "the common will is determined through patient listening to all points of view. Leadership takes the form of guidance and persuasion.... [Individual] needs should be balanced with those of the community, and the entire debate must be carried out on the firm ground of agreed-upon values and principles."[13] Truth exists in a dynamic form that is framed by traditional values and evolves according to the experiences of living it. The good endures, the bad is discarded, and the future is remade through this fusion of experience, reason, and creative collective problem solving.

Peace Power Righteousness also foresaw danger in reconciling with the settler state. "The kind of justice that Indigenous people seek in their relations with the state has to do with restoring a regime of respect," he wrote. "This idea stands in clear contrast to the statist notion still rooted in the classical notion of sovereignty, which, in the name of equity, may direct more material resources to Indigenous people, but which preserves the state's superior position relative to them and to Earth."[14]

Peace Power Righteousness was reissued in 2009, a market-proven testament to the durability of the arguments the thirty-two-year-old Taiaiake made in his fearless manifesto. By then both the political landscape and his thinking had taken great leaps forward.

Strategies of Resurgence

For revolution to succeed, a new organization of social reality has to be imagined, and then it has to be organized on the ground. The vision of the Indigenous Resurgence is to take ever-evolving Indigenous cosmologies into the future, bringing about the possibility of living in ways and according to values that would be recognizable to the Ancestors –

Ancestors that constantly adapted in order to thrive. Indigenous Resurgence is born in actions and discourses among the grassroots in Native communities committed to this vision. It goes beyond recreating and performing fragments of things past, and in this it differs from much of the Indigenous Renaissance that falls under the rubric of reconciliation. While the revival of languages, ceremonies, foods, medicines, arts, governance structures, economic activities, and so on are all positive developments, they are insufficient if they happen in isolation as scattered examples of Indigenous beliefs and practices. Indigenous Resurgence is holistic: it holds that for people to live authentically Indigenous lives, it's all about the land – territories the Onkwehónweh never voluntarily ceded that are currently under Canadian occupation and control. Because it refuses Canadian claims to sovereignty (to use a Eurocentric framing of the status quo) the Indigenous Resurgence vision of decolonization poses an existential threat to the legitimacy of the Canadian state.

In his third book, *Wasáse: Indigenous Pathways of Action and Freedom* (2005), Taiaiake's research had led him to the conclusion that if decolonization is going to happen it must start with personal decolonization, the dissolving of mentalities and practices that give shape to colonial behaviors. This looped back to the primacy of addressing ongoing deculturation caused by being disconnected from the land. The central tenet of Onkwehónweh philosophies is that one cannot live Indigenously without connection to the lands and waters of the Ancestors, and the terms of that relationship cannot be controlled by the Canadian state, so a reconciliation that asks Indigenous people to reconcile themselves to white authority over their lands is a fatal compromise. From his growing platform within the colonial institution of the Western university Taiaiake began to concretely implement this vision, imagining and organizing a movement of mutual nurturing, sharing, and support of Onkwehón:weh actions that would build strong Indigenous Nations.

By the time *Wasáse* came out, Taiaiake was ensconced at the University of Victoria and a globally renowned scholar. He had joined UVic in 1996 where he founded and directed the Indigenous Governance (IGOV) program until stepping down as director in 2015 and resigning from UVic in 2019 amid a storm of controversy. The academic program he developed and implemented used decolonial methods to uproot colonial mentalities at the personal level: they were uncompromising, discomforting, and transformational and attracted students from all over the world. The first generation of scholarship associated with the Indigenous Resurgence movement came out of this anti-colonial research and teaching stronghold, including work by Jeff Corntassel, Glen Coulthard, and a former teaching associate in the program, Leanne Betasamosake Simpson, who later wrote: "[P]ostsecondary education provides few useful skill sets to those of us who want to fundamentally change the relationship between the Canadian state and Indigenous Peoples, because that requires a sustained, collective, strategic long-term movement, a movement the Canadian state has a vested interest in preventing, destroying, and dividing."[15] When Taiaiake resigned in 2019, only 1.3 per cent of tenured university faculty identified as Indigenous, according to Universities Canada: Canadian universities remain thoroughly colonial institutions.

The Indigenous "Threat"

Wasáse was a call to action, intended to spark "a spiritual revolution, a culturally rooted social movement that transforms the whole of society and a political action that seeks to remake the entire landscape of power and relationships to reflect truly a liberated post-imperial vision."[16] This put Taiaiake on a collision course with a Canadian state trying to sell reconciliation as decolonization. From the outset he had braided together radical scholarship, a revolutionary political agenda, and direct experience of defending land and people from the violence – whether actual or threatened, kinetic or systemic – of the Canadian state. As such, he had long been on the government's radar. The shadow of Oka stalked him in the corridors of his first university appointment in Montreal at Concordia in 1994, with visits from agents from the Canadian Security and Intelligence Service (CSIS) who tried to convince him that as a professor on the government payroll, he should become an informant on whatever was "going on" in Kahnawà:ke: "There could be implications if I don't cooperate with them. If I have information I'm withholding, that's a problem. When I asked him if he was threatening me, he was like, 'Oh, no, no, no, no, no, it's just my job. We don't do that kind of thing. We're not in the business of enforcement. This is not the RCMP.'"[17]

The Canadian state has always been willing to use force against grassroots expressions of Indigenous Nationhood. Even as the RCAP was underway as a conciliatory move to avoid another Oka, Indigenous lands reoccupations were being met with violence. In 1995 there were major actions at

Ts'peten/Gustafsen Lake in British Columbia, where 77,000 rounds of ammunition were fired at Ts'peten Defenders holding ground for the right to hold their Sun Dance ceremonies, and at Aazhoodena/Ipperwash-Stoney Point in Ontario, where Ontario Premier Mike Harris infamously ordered the police to "get the fucking Indians out of the park." They tried, killing unarmed land defender Dudley George in the process.

The RCMP itself has a history of mounting smear campaigns against Indigenous land defenders, characterizing them as thugs, criminals, and, following the 9/11 attacks on the United States, as terrorists. New anti-terrorism laws gave CSIS and the RCMP greater powers to protect the country from Al-Qaeda, but they criminalized political thought more generally, allowing the security services to draw a straight line between voicing ideas about Indigenous Nationhood and threats to Canadian national security. Taiaiake's scholarship investigated revolutionary efforts to upset the colonial status quo with seriousness and transparency, and those investigations included discussions of militant action. He analyzed Indigenous epistemologies for sources of strength and white power structures for points of weakness. He was high profile, holding a Canada Research Chair at UVic and winning a National Aboriginal Achievement Award. And he was now finding that academic freedom had hard limits.

Wasáse was not just a book, it was also the ur-text of an intellectual and political movement to build new kinds of social relations across Turtle Island that would "unify the people and motivate them to become strong and self-reliant, and to act against the injustices bringing pain and darkness into their lives," including "the Settler's greed and hypocrisy, the government's violence and lies, and our own leaders' fraud and corruption."[18] While nonviolent in its approach, the movement held space for the possibility that defensive actions against colonialism were justifiable – as in Oka in 1990 where the Mohawk Warrior Society had played a leading role. In May 2005 Taiaiake and his student Lana Lowe coauthored a report on Warrior Societies as part of the Ipperwash Inquiry, noting that they could only be understood "in the context of the larger struggle of Indigenous Peoples to survive as Nations of people with their lands, cultures, communities intact."[19]

Based mainly in British Columbia, Taiaiake and the Wasáse movement were associated with the West Coast Warrior Society, a group that had emerged from direct actions such as mounting a roadblock to protect traditional salmon camps on the Fraser River and traveling to protect an Indigenous fishery at Esgenoôpetitj/Burnt Church in New Brunswick. Linking the Warrior groups was Mi'kmaw warrior James Sakej Ward, a leader in the East Coast Warrior Society and a graduate of the IGOV program. Taiaiake interviewed Sakej in 2002 and published the discussion of Sakej's ambition to build a militarized movement in *Wasáse*, noting it "represents the most radical pathway to Indigenous freedom."[20]

Using their new anti-terrorism powers, the RCMP began targeting the West Coast Warriors to discredit them and drive sympathizers away. In September 2002 an entire neighborhood in Port Alberni on Vancouver Island was evacuated as the RCMP raided the home of a West Coast Warrior commander, looking for a nonexistent weapons stockpile in a specious "anti-terrorism" operation. Families and associates were threatened with having their children taken away by child welfare services. The RCMP overreach in this case was so egregious that the British Columbia Civil Liberties Association wrote it up in its 2005 submission to the Canadian government on the abuse of national security powers.[21]

But for the Warriors, worse was to come. In June 2005 the police mounted a massive "anti-terrorist" operation one afternoon on the Burrard Street Bridge in Vancouver, a location that could not have been more public. Three men – Sakej; the late David Dennis, who was the leader of the West Coast Warriors; and a member of the Alert Bay First Nation – were the targets of a full-scale national security takedown complete with officers in tactical military gear carrying assault rifles and submachine guns and wrangling police dogs. The alleged crime concerned the transport of hunting rifles to an Indigenous traditional training program at the Tsawataineuk (Kingcome Inlet) First Nation: all the necessary RCMP criminal record checks and accompanying paperwork were in order. There were so many anomalies in the way the men were taken by the police that, in an era of illegal rendition, they feared they were being sent to a security service black site. Instead, within a few hours they were released without charge, but their rifles and ammunition, cell phones, computers, and notebooks were confiscated. They were also definitively framed in the public imagination as terrorists. Behind the scenes, the RCMP and CSIS once again threatened Warrior members and associates with jail and child removal. In the face of this pressure, the West Coast Warrior Society voluntarily disbanded in August

2005. Taiaiake, Wasáse members and fellow travelers, and even students in the IGOV program and their friends and families were also being harassed by security services looking for informers and so the Wasáse movement also decided to stand down. New ways would have to be found to creatively confront the colonial state and assert Indigenous Nationhood.

Taiaiake began pouring energy into the wide range of academic and community projects that are chronicled in this book. In addition to sounding alarm bells over the government's unfolding reconciliation agenda, he worked in Indigenous communities on the environmental impacts of extractive capitalism, where he saw firsthand how the inability to carry out traditional practices on lands and waters contaminated by industrial activity was causing ongoing crises due to cultural loss. He also continued to work on his own personal decolonization, where he found a new set of conflicts.

Gender Trouble

For feminists, a traditional starting point is to ask a seemingly simple question: "Where are the women?" For Indigenous people, that question is a tragically literal one. Pushing for answers from the government, early in the 2000s Onkwehónweh across Canada coalesced around a Native women–led social and political movement now nationally familiar as MMIWG (Missing and Murdered Indigenous Women and Girls).

Given the colonial context, we need to ask another question: "Where are the men?" Lurking behind the MMIWG epidemic is the even larger, and still unaddressed, question of missing and murdered Indigenous men and boys.[22] In 2015 the Canadian government's Minister of Aboriginal Affairs repeated false RCMP claims that Indigenous men were responsible for 70 per cent of the murders of Indigenous women.[23] This statistic went viral when the National Inquiry's Final Report on MMIWG was released in 2019, feeding mainstream society's belief that Indigenous men were inherently violent criminals and thugs – and this happened in spite of the fact that the report itself specifically addressed inaccuracy of the RCMP's numbers.[24]

It was in this context that Taiaiake turned his attention to gender issues. Indigenous feminism had begun to make itself felt in the academy in the early 2000s, but theorizing about Indigenous masculinity had scarcely begun when, consistent with his approach of drawing on his own lived experience, he began to explore Indigenous masculinity and the frames and stereotypes Indigenous men were forced into by white society. He used his usual methodologies of engaging in conversations across diverse sets of people and looking at the academic discourses, which were scant: unlike feminism, the field of men's studies was unfashionable, unpopular, and grossly underdeveloped. From such shaky foundations, the study of *Indigenous* masculinity had to also consider the harmful effects of colonization and begin the work of rejuvenating Onkwehónweh knowledges to repair them. In spite of the pitfalls and complexities, and encouraged to start the conversation, Taiaiake began his inquiry: "What is the relationship between families, between men and women, between humans and the land? And what are the ways that our ideas, and rationalizations, and justifications, and senses, and ethics, and beliefs, and practices in those relationships, what are the ways they have been shaped by colonization, capitalism, patriarchy, and heteropatriarchy?"[25] This research, as always, was carried out in the public eye and in the classroom with a view to provoking discussion. As a leader, he felt he had a responsibility to use his privilege to open up spaces for hard conversations with the idea that everyone would learn from them, and he thought he knew what lay ahead: "As Indigenous studies goes, it's a very contentious, challenging environment to be talking about this," he said. Even so, the character and extent of the pushback caught him off guard. As a beginner in the fraught field of gender studies, he struggled and grew defensive in the face of a feminist backlash: "[T]his whole language and framing of it ... some of you in your whole intellectual career and adult life have been familiar using it, experiencing it, feeling it, but the reality is, for a lot of us of a certain age, and generation, and intellectually, and physically, chronologically in our lives, it's a relatively new vocabulary, a relatively new set of ideas challenging established norms and ways of being." He was quickly schooled into seeing himself differently. His efforts were interpreted as pulling attention away from the concerns of Indigenous feminism and diverting them into a misguided line of study that would perpetrate the very "heteropatriarchal" attributes he was struggling to dismantle. Fighting for so many years from an anti-colonial position, he had failed to recognize that he was now seen as a powerful man operating successfully within a white patriarchal colonizer institution who was reproducing many of those same traits.

The barrage of criticism was intense, but it did lead him on to firmer ground. By 2018 Taiaiake had pivoted from his initial approach to gender studies, abandoning the book on Indigenous masculinity he had been working on: "I started reading out passages and thinking about it in this context of this awareness that I have now, and it all seemed so hollow, so shallow.... I'm so glad that I didn't publish it, I'd have to buy up all the copies and burn them."

The university environment was also changing in response to demands for more trauma-informed pedagogies and supports for equity, inclusion, and diversity. In this new atmosphere the decolonial methods that had been the hallmark of the IGOV program were now leading to complaints. There were "assessments" and "reviews," and finally the university decided to suspend enrollment into a program that, although it was "too good to fail," was found to be "not sufficiently attuned to diverse worldviews and lived experiences," with "difficult classroom dynamics caused by a sense of entitlements, competition and unpredictability."[26]

Taiaiake resigned his position at UVic, seeming to have lost the battle, but he saw it all as part of a wider war: "You start to realize, especially as an Indigenous man ... that you are the problem. It's a difficult thing for men to acknowledge ... how we have been made into not only subjects but agents of colonization. That, to me, means we're getting down to the deep levels of colonization and how it works."

Stepping down, he told the media: "[T]here's a big culture change going on and people's ideas about masculinity are obviously changing really fast, and those of us that are in leadership positions are under the microscope, and there's room for growth among all of us, and I'm not different from anyone else.... [W]e've got to be open to honest criticisms about attitudes and ideas and methods.... I'm open to people looking at myself and the things that I say and do in a critical way, and I take that to heart and use it to build a better method and a better way of doing things."[27] He returned to Kahnawà:ke for a reset.

Fires Were Started

When Taiaiake gave up his position in the colonial academy, he left the intellectual landscape profoundly changed. Across Turtle Island IGOV alumni have moved into positions of influence as scholars and activists, and people continue to draw energy and wisdom from Indigenous Resurgence. Looking back at how CSIS managed to crush the Wasáse movement, he said: "It's funny now that I think about all the students that were contacted and harassed and identified by CSIS are all people that are solid and good. And are still, I would say, reliable advocates for Indigenous Peoples, all these years later."[28]

Onkwehónweh persist in the struggle against colonialism, creating sites of resistance across Turtle Island and evolving tactics to challenge white power structures that are met with harsh responses. In the winter of 2012–13 Taiaiake was involved in strategizing the Idle No More movement that arose across Canada to protect lands and waters from new federal legislation that removed environmental protections: the protesters used "non-threatening" flash mobs and round dances to raise awareness; it was investigated as a threat to Canadian national security. In the winter of 2020 the #ShutDownCanada movement brought road and railway transport across Northern Turtle Island to a halt, a formidable flex of collective grassroots Indigenous strength in support of Wet'suwet'en and Gitxsan land defenders in northern British Columbia. CSIS looked into laying terrorism charges against them, and also against the "1492 Landback Lane" occupation in Caledonia, Ontario, by Haudenosaunee activists. The Wet'suwet'en resistance to resource development on their traditional lands continues to face excessive militarized Canadian policing and dirty tactics, as well as endless and expensive legal battles in settler courts. CSIS has classified Indigenous activists and allies as "ideologically motivated violent extremists," who could pose national security threats, according to recently declassified documents.[29] When Indigenous Peoples resurge, the colonial state moves in hard against them.

Following Taiaiake's departure from the University of Victoria, the Indigenous Governance Program was suspended and has since been reinvented as a program designed to promote reconciliation and healing rather than political change. Nevertheless, his courageous demonstration of the revolutionary potential of education, where hard truths are confronted and values are not compromised, did not leave with him. Taiaiake's contribution to Indigenous thought and action cannot be overestimated: his perspective, rooted in contemporary and ancestral voices of the Kanien'kehaka, cross-pollinated with lessons drawn from decolonizers from Mao to the Black Panther Party, and refined and redrawn through personal reflection and struggle, is an enduring example of how education can create radical transformation in society. From his position within the colonizer's knowledge economy and grounded in the strength of the Mohawk Nation, he has developed a powerful critique of white power structures and demonstrated the potential for carrying out radical agendas from within them, never wavering in his open defiance of colonial injustice:

> I've taken it as my mission to understand, to keep pushing, digging deeper and challenging myself to be more of a Mohawk and to understand more what it means to be a Mohawk in a true sense, to cut through all those layers of our contemporary reality, decolonization and all this stuff, and get down to the root and then as best as I can, at whatever stage I'm at on that journey, represent that in who I am. And then share that with other Indigenous people and then bring that reality to the non-Indigenous world and challenge them to decolonize by respecting us for who we are. That's always been driven by my feeling of the responsibility I have because of the name that I carry.[30]

The clarity, purpose, and seriousness of the critique Taiaiake Alfred advances against the Canadian state and its reconciliation agenda demands attention, debate, and hard reflection. His vision of Indigenous Resurgence will continue to inspire Onkwehónweh and non-Natives who want to build relationships based on truth, equality, and respect. In his crossings between Kahnawà:ke and the colonizers' world, Taiaiake has created new paths that both Native and non-Native can follow, paths that can lead us all to a decolonized future.

This is Indian Land, Kahnawà:ke, 1974

We grew up in the midst of Red Power rising.

WASÁSE REDUX

Adapted from a conversation with Allan Gregg on his TVOntario show *In Conversation* for an episode titled "Taiaiake Alfred on his Indigenous Manifesto," which aired in June 2005.

When my book *Wasáse* came out in 2005, I made every effort and took up any opportunity to create space on the political landscape for militant Indigenism and Indigenous Nationhood principles. Ironically, it was a Conservative Party political strategist who gave me the opportunity to reach to a wider audience and talk about the concept of Indigenous Resurgence. It was the first time I had to defend what I had written in *Wasáse* and explain my vision of the future for Indigenous Peoples in relation to Canada. My main goal in this interaction was to get Canadians to understand how pathways toward justice that are rooted in Indigenous values and principles are very different from the futures promoted by the Canadian government and Indigenous elites, what I was then calling "Aboriginalism," which is now known as reconciliation.

ALLAN GREGG: *Taiaiake Alfred, the controversial Native scholar, claims that Aboriginal leaders have sold out by trying to advance Native interests within what he calls Canada's colonial system. He's one of the world's leading theorists on the lasting effects of colonization on Indigenous Peoples. Alfred is a professor at the University of Victoria.*

Taiaiake, most of us, if we see a Native leader who successfully negotiates land claims, is able to get Aboriginal law applied and self-government within their jurisdiction, we think they are a big success. You've come at it completely from the other way. You say that the direction they're going is all wrong. Tell me about that.

TAIAIAKE ALFRED: Well, I think that the starting point is that we have to understand that there are two competing agendas in First Nations politics today. One is the agenda of the Canadian government, which is the agenda, in essence, of Canadian society and is based on the visions of Canadians for what a just relationship is between Native Peoples and non-Native peoples. And that's essentially a vision that was developed in the 1960s and '70s by Pierre Trudeau and the Liberal Party, which is basically a kind of assimilation, an integration into Canadian society based on social justice principles. It suggests that what we need to do is look at Aboriginal Peoples as full members of Canadian society and eliminate any of the barriers to advancement, to put it in positive terms. In negative terms, it means to eliminate any of the advantages they have in terms of reserve tax exemptions and so forth and make them full and participant members of Canadian society. That's the main agenda of the Canadian government. And the Canadian government has done a very good job in the previous ten or fifteen years – actually since the Constitution was repatriated in 1982 – in drawing in a cadre of leaders and creating champions for this vision among Native institutions and among Native communities. And actually almost all of the high-profile Native leaders that you see in Canada from the Assembly of First Nations to the big Native communities, to the major organizations, even in the arts, you see have been kind of cultivated.

AG: *And they bought into this basic notion of what the goals are.*

TA: Exactly. And I believe most of them are quite sincere in this. They believe that the best answer to colonialism, to the colonial problem and its lingering effects, is this vision.

AG: *And why are they wrong?*

TA: There's two reasons. One is because it's inauthentic. The authentic vision of the Indigenous Peoples is not based on that assimilative model. The vision of the Native people and what separates the leadership from the people in this regard is the fact that Native people themselves on the whole believe in treaties and a respectful relationship between Nations, as opposed to an integrated vision of what it is to be part of this relationship. And so you have a divergence between the leadership and what they're representing, and the reality in the communities in terms of the culture, and what the grassroots people believe is the future, in terms of a vision for a relationship. The second reason that it's wrong, and I believe why it's failing, is that it is not responding to the central concerns and the central problems within those communities. And these problems are not money problems, they're not problems of jurisdiction. They're problems of the psychological effects and the cultural destruction that went on through this colonial process.

AG: *I want to talk about that at some length, but I'm interested first in the tactics. I mean, you say that the Native leadership who plays this game is leading itself down a disastrous path. How so? What are the negative consequences of sitting down, trying to negotiate land claims, self-government, and more control over band activity?*

TA: I think the first problem is that we're negotiating from a position of weakness politically and culturally. We're coming to a negotiating table from a position of having no organizational legitimacy in our communities. All of the organizations in our communities that represent us are in positions where every band council Chief, the Assembly of First Nations, and so forth are employees of the state; they're employees of the department of Indian Affairs or the ministry of state responsible for First Nations. There's no legitimacy in the minds of the people that these leaders are representing them in a true sense of the word. And so we have a real problem of legitimacy. In terms of the vision that's being put forward, the consequence is that the further we get toward success in that vision in terms of meeting the standard of social justice, the elevation of the standard of living in material terms in Native communities, and so on, the further away we get from the root of the problem, which is this kind of psychological anger, psychological discord, all of the pain in the community which comes from losing one's culture, from not having respect for one's way of life, and for having a definition and an identity which is different than the one that's being institutionalized in the society. And so you have this permanent state of alienation. And when you have this permanent state of alienation, these attempts to assuage it with material goods or to convince the government to give them to you, they're never going to get at the root of the problem: an anger and frustration over not having your culture and your values reflected in the systems of government and the way that the society's organizing. That's why we have so many social and psychological problems in these communities that are not being addressed. As we move closer toward the standard of social justice in Canada, the ironic thing is all of those problems are elevating.

AG: *But let's use a concrete example to kind of make that point. We all heard the story of what happened at Davis Inlet.[1] Terrible, terrible social problems. The government relocates 700 Innu, the entire band, injects 70 million dollars into a new community and the same problems of alcoholism, despair, and suicide re-emerge. Why did that not work?*

TA: It didn't work because it's putting the cart before the horse. The big institutional solutions will not work because the people in our communities are not prepared to handle self-government at this point. They're not prepared to handle the idea of governing and making decisions for themselves because, number one, it's not a form of government that is reflective of their culture and their values. It's not an Indigenous form of government. It's essentially an imposition of a Western form of government, so it's inauthentic. Number two, the psychological issues and the issue of what you might call deculturation of these people has not been fixed. You have a situation where people are colonized. You can look at the situation as analogous to – and I know Canadians don't really like to talk about it in these terms – to the way that Africa was so-called decolonized. In effect, what do you have left once the imperialist goes back to Europe? You have societies that are reflective of all the worst aspects of that colonial relationship and the way power is used and the way corruption has infused the society.

AG: *Well, in fact this is the major ideological or theoretical framework for your analysis: that Canada's Indigenous people suffer from a post-colonial mentality. Talk to me about that.*

TA: If you look at the relationship between our Peoples, the fundamental problem is that Native Peoples have been illegally dispossessed from their lands. Treaties have not been honored. Relationships of oppression have been created in all different facets in this society. We have to address those things before we can have reconciliation. We can address those things in a soft way and try to assuage the guilt of white society and create a salve for the pain that this has caused for the Indigenous Peoples. But as we're seeing through Davis Inlet, and now with our brothers and sisters in the United States with Red Lake, we're seeing examples like this where it's a constantly boiling turmoil.[2]

AG: *You're an interesting case in point. You're a respected scholar at University of Victoria in British Columbia. You're a former US Marine. You've come off the Kahnawà:ke Mohawk* *territory in Quebec. Tell me about your own evolution, especially in terms of your thinking.*

TA: It's a good question. I often think about that in terms of where I come from. A community like Kahnawà:ke, in most people's minds, people think of Kahnawà:ke and the Mohawk Nation and Oka 1990. Most people look at Mohawks as a very assertive, militant group of people who are outspoken in terms of Native rights and their own Nationhood. People often don't recognize that the Oka conflict was the result of twenty to thirty years of activism and the rebuilding of a culture. I was born in 1964, and at that time our community was 99 per cent Catholic and heavily controlled by Indian Affairs and the RCMP. A lot of people don't realize that before the 1970s, no three Native people could gather together without the RCMP present, and it was illegal to gather for the purposes of organizing or for any kind of meeting. In the 1960s, when I was born, it wasn't a modified form of colonialism, it *was* colonialism. I lived through our community shaking that off. It took me a long time to reconnect back to the traditional heritage of our community. I went in a roundabout way. I was trained by Jesuits. I went to a Jesuit high school, Loyola High School in Montreal. I went into the US Marine Corps. I went to an Ivy League university. I had the big three – religion, military, and liberal arts training.

AG: *You should have ended up on Bay Street.*

TA: I should be a millionaire now on Bay Street, but I'm not. The answer to your question is, I looked at other ways of succeeding. I looked at other ways of decolonizing. My first experience was defining a warrior in the common sense of the word, in a militaristic way. If I was an Indigenous activist who believed in that, I'd say, "Well, let's have an armed revolution. There's only a small number of us, but we can do a lot of damage." And you can spin all kinds of revolutionary theories about the possible effects of armed rebellion. In my mind it hasn't worked. My experience in the Marine Corps and reading military history and other histories has shown that there's always a connection between the means and the ends. If you want to have a peaceful coexistence with your neighbor, which we do – I have to remind people that Native Peoples are struggling for nothing but peaceful coexistence and sharing – if we want that, we can't use violence.

AG: *In fact, you say that the key to reclaiming a sense of autonomy, of understanding what the true meaning of being an Indigenous person is, in essence, is spiritual. What does that mean, and what does that look like?*

TA: What we want to do is return to what in our language is the real word for a warrior. There is no direct equivalent, but the word that closely approximates it is *rotiskenhrakete*, a Mohawk word that means "they carry the burden." In the 1800s and the 1700s and 1600s, if you came across a Mohawk war party and you asked them who they were or what they were, they would say rotiskenhrakete, I'm carrying the burden of my heritage. I'm carrying the burden of the mandate that's been given to me by the women. And they would be carrying that out. Sometimes that meant fighting in a physical sense. Sometimes that meant fighting through diplomacy. Sometimes that meant just doing ceremonies, spirituality, gaining the strength and integrity inside of yourself to be an authentic Onkwehònweh person. And so when I talk about the spiritual revolution or the need for a spiritual core to this, that's what I'm talking about. We need to recreate ourselves as people who are spiritually grounded and strong in order to withstand all of those forces of assimilation but also to represent and to embody the best values of an Indigenous culture and to recreate something new. I always took inspiration from Gandhi. For me, the most impressive thing about what he did wasn't strategic or tactical, it was that he took a stand against imperialism, and he took a stand against traditionalism. What he did was say, "We have to take this imperialism. We have to take this modern society, and this old society, and we have to create something new out of it that's appropriate to us today." And I think that's really the solution. There's no model. It's not like what the Royal Commission on Aboriginal Peoples [RCAP] tried to do, which is to say, what are the three models of government that are going to resolve the colonial problem? I worked on the RCAP myself, so I'm not disparaging the whole thing. I know people honestly tried to come up with a solution, but it shows how primitive our thinking was back then. It was, "Let's have three models. Natives can pick one of these models and then the government will fund it. And then the colonial problem will be over."

AG: *There are many who say one of the nicest things about Canada, the greatest thing about Canada, the most salient feature of Canada, is our multiculturalism, where people can be Italian Canadians, Sikh Canadians. Why not Aboriginal Canadians?*

TA: Well, in fact you're right, the vision of mainstream First Nations politicians is to have an ethnic category within Canada. And they believe in that vision, and they believe it is the most just vision in the world. And they celebrate they're Canadians. One of the major Inuit politicians up North, his slogan is "First Canadians and Canadians first." And I think that exemplifies this mentality. "What's wrong with that?" you're wondering. Truth is, assimilation leads to a divided identity that always has to be negotiated every day of someone's life. I want to be able to live free. I want to be able to live happy, and I want to be able to live fulfilled as a human being. And that means being able to live my culture and my values and associate myself in my own land with my own institutions and live a life as an Onkwehònweh person. That's no threat to Canada.

The only threat to Canada is in terms of the way that colonialism has structured the economic and political relationship. And I guess that's getting back to the root of the problem: all this cultural talk is interesting. But anybody who's in political power or sitting on the board of a corporation can recognize that what I'm saying is that it's a land problem. It's a resource problem. It's an economic and political problem. If all of what I'm saying comes to fruition, Native Peoples will have a lot more land in order to be self-sufficient so that they can live authentically and not have to take handouts from the government. They will have a lot more control over their land so that they can have their own true governments and not have to be dictated to by the Department of Indian Affairs. The more land the Indian gets, the less land there is for forest tenures or mining claims and all these sorts of things. When I say it's not a threat to Canada, I don't believe it's a threat to Canadians, but I believe it's a threat to the economic and political structure of the state of Canada right now because it's a situation that has been set up to promote an injustice. If Canadians can accept a notion of justice based on the treaties and fairness and so forth, then we can have a good relationship. Otherwise, that's where the contention comes in.

AG: *Now, how does official leadership of the Native community respond to your ideas? What kind of reaction do they have to you?*

TA: Well, it's not an easy situation for them to deal with because they can't dismiss me. And I think that's a responsibility that someone like me carries. I have the credentials and I have the experience both in the community and in federal and provincial politics and in Native politics such that no one can say, "Oh, he's just a dreamer," or "He's just a critic," or "He's ignorant, he doesn't know what he's talking about." I mean, if I'm better educated and more experienced than them, there's no way for them to do that. And so it's kind of a dicey situation. And when I write books like *Wasáse* and when I give talks like this, who is going to stand up and take me head-on, when that means identifying yourself as the corrupt co-opted leader who's going to have to defend that agenda? It's a tough political position. Right now I find they're giving me a wide berth.

AG: *Well, by your own admission, your views are held in the minority within the Native community. There are others who embrace the same basic philosophical tenets. What are they doing different? How are they living their lives? What's happening in their communities that's different from mainstream Native society today?*

TA: To give an example, the one that's freshest in my mind is yesterday I was over in Six Nations. Anyone can go to Six Nations and look at what's the "model community."

AG: *Yeah, here it is. It's got self-government. Its leaders are known. Their former band Chief is on the Canada Health Council. This seems like good news for most people.*

TA: It's clean, it's well-organized, nice buildings and everything like that, but that's the one agenda. The other agenda is that there's a growing crisis among the youth. There's increasing levels of violence. There's increasing levels of family violence, drug use, a booming cigarette trade, gun culture, gang culture emerging in that community. And then you have people responding to that – this is the alternative. People trying to take the traditional structures, take the traditional societies, the elements from our traditional culture in terms of philosophies and the way of working together, and to reintegrate youth into that. To restore the respect that the youth have for our own traditional way of governing in terms of how it involves people in their own lives. It's a direct form of democracy. And what it does is it respects the need for every individual to be involved in decisions that affect their lives. That's an ideal in every culture, but our culture has a way of doing it. And it's been proven over generations and generations as a very effective way of maintaining community. And so we have these people, the specific example that you're looking for. Last night I was invited to speak over there by the New Orators Group, a new youth group headed by former school counselors, and what they're doing is trying to re-instill an image of what it is to be a Mohawk or a Seneca or an Oneida or Cayuga in that community, based on the values and the image and the characteristics of what it was to be a Mohawk or a Cayuga or a Oneida in that era when we were still strong people. And so they're re-instilling dignity, they're re-instilling pride, and they're re-instilling the vision of oneself which is authentic, as opposed to one which is trying to fit into a mainstream society, which for all intents and purposes will never accept Native Peoples at the same level. They'll accept them in, but there's always going to be this kind of remnant prejudice against them. And we have to acknowledge that in society there's racism.

AG: *I was going to ask there too, because so much of this regeneration relates to a sense of communitarianism, that you get a lot of your strength from the fellow members of your community. Given the tremendous number of Indigenous people now who live off reserve in the urban centers, what can they do?*

TA: I'd say that's the biggest challenge that we're facing. As a preface to that answer, I've committed myself to working in urban situations in Vancouver, Victoria, Edmonton, working with people to try to get a handle on exactly that question. How can I be Onkwehònweh living in a situation where I have no real social interaction with my home community, no real cultural connection?

AG: *Reinforcement too.*

TA: Yeah, reinforcement. And so we need to create relationships between those people in the city and those home communities. And that brings up a second-level problem. The home communities are problematic in a lot of cases in terms of the culture, the politics, and so forth. And then also we need to create a situation where these people have the means of reconnecting physically, culturally, and socially. And so a big part of the agenda that I'm working on is creating the strength within these urban communities to try to get younger people oriented toward that objective of reconnection and then working with the home communities themselves and opening themselves up to people coming back in for cultural learning and social interaction and working political alliances between people in the city and people in the home community. It's kind of a reflection of my own background. I come from a reserve, I grew up on a reserve. I lived there till I was thirty-two, aside from stints in the Marines and so forth. And so I believe in those communities. For all the problems that we're talking about, they are the last strongholds of an Indigenous existence. We have to protect them, and we have to heal them, and we have to make them strong again; that's one agenda. The other agenda is that we have to make them the strongholds of an existence for those people who are not living in those communities. My vision is not bounded by the reserve system or the Indian Act. It looks at them not as reserves but as strongholds of Indigenous culture. And if we can heal those communities, they can be the kind of accountability mechanism. They can be the support centers for an Indigenous existence which gets spread out all over this country. I'm working on both sides of that equation, trying to get the youth oriented, but also working with Elders and groups in communities to try to recreate the tools that accomplish this objective, using ceremony, using rituals, and just using new networks. One of the things that I've tried to start doing this with is a website. This is mainly for those technologically savvy, younger people in our communities who think this way, but maybe find themselves as the only person in their reserve thinking this way and needing some sort of connection, some sort of vetting mechanism for their ideas and some sort of validation for what they're doing.

AG: *I wanted to ask you about the young people, because I mean, one of the statistics we know is verifiable is that more and more of Canada's Indigenous young people are going to university, they're getting good educations. Are they going to embrace this more traditional notion? Are they going to go back to warrior culture when they're getting law degrees and becoming doctors?*

TA: I think you see a lot of the energy around what I'm talking about emanating from university environments, which is kind of ironic given the history of education being used as an assimilation tool. The problem that I see is that the universities today, aside from a small number of programs and individual faculty members and staff working in various institutions, are still oriented toward that kind of halfway solution. It's generating pride in being a Native person. It's giving them skills and capacity to be self-sufficient and so forth and that's all great, but it's still not the kind of agenda that I'm talking about. It's still not an Indigenous agenda.

AG: *It's toward what end.*

TA: Yeah, it's like the Aboriginalist versus the Indigenous agenda. Aboriginalism versus Onkwehònweh. And that's where I see the challenge of people like me – there's professors, there's faculty, there's Elders who can work within these institutions to make it something where people can have a choice. And we're not talking about brainwashing, we're just saying, "Hey, this is your true culture. This is what's offered to you. You make your choice." And whether you're a lawyer, a doctor, a political scientist or a social worker, in every day of your life in every way, you can make the choice to support that Indigenous truth, or you can make the choice to support the vision of the colonizer.

AG: *You're enough of a realist to know that the stuff you're advocating isn't going to come to pass quickly.*

TA: Not quickly, no.

AG: *What's your purpose here? What is the message that you're trying to send to members of your own community and the larger Canadian community?*

TA: My message and my purpose, I've had to reflect on this a lot. And a lot of Elders have spoken once they've heard me talk. It's been years now since I've been trying to promote a message like this, it's a wake-up call to inspire the next generation of Indigenous leaders. The present generation of Indigenous leaders, I don't know how much they can be changed. Once you get to be what, forty or something, it's hard to change your ideas. I think the best we can do is contain that agenda. Really what I'm talking about is the next generation of Indigenous leaders and their agenda. What is the agenda of the next generation of Native leaders? I think it should be based on a successful regeneration of the culture. And I think it should be a political and legal and economic program to force Canada into a reconciliation with reality, with the reality of our existence. And that means a political agenda akin to, you mentioned earlier politics of contention, so akin to a social and political movement like the Black civil rights movement. In my job, I get to talk to young people of all different races. I'm a university professor and I see white people, Chinese people, Black people, and so forth. And you know what? A lot of things I'm talking about are same concerns that these young people have. They have an ethical framework for living their lives that is out of sync with the one that's governing this country. And so I see a great potential for alliances between the Indigenous movement as I'm describing it and environmental movements, human rights movements, and so forth. And so a big part of what we're trying to do is create a new generation of leaders in this society, not necessarily Indigenous leaders, a new generation of leaders that are going to transform first, the cultural assumptions that go into governance, and then after that, the institutions, because as you know well, trying to change the institutions before you have a kind of consensus on what should happen with the laws and so forth is futile. It's basically an attack on the legitimacy of the current system.

Heeding the Voices, Geneva, Switzerland, 1999

A warrior says what is in the people's hearts.

FROM NOBLE SAVAGE TO RIGHTEOUS WARRIOR

Adapted from a keynote address at the Global Encounters Initiative Symposium hosted by the University of British Columbia at the Museum of Anthropology in Vancouver on March 6, 2010.

Although most of my public speaking has centered on Indigenous political philosophy, governance, and political movements, in this speech I focused on the issue of identity and, specifically, the reclamation of Indigenous truths, in the way we think about ourselves as Indigenous Peoples of this land. To explain my concept of a truth warrior, which was the focus of much attention and critique at the time, I focused on the importance of art in representing the kind of people we were, are, and could be, and what we should be fighting for in all realms, as opposed to the racist ideas of Indians and inauthentic images of us that were created to serve colonial intentions but that still held/hold sway over our bodies and minds. The points in this speech, I think, presage the debates around cultural appropriation, performativity, and false representation that have become central to the current discourse around Indigenous identity.

What I want to offer you are some thoughts and reflections on what contestations on the notion of Indigeneity are playing out in Canada, in North America, today. It's been present in the minds of many people in the last couple of weeks, as it's been manifesting in these displays of Indigeneity during the 2010 Winter Olympics and Paralympics here in Vancouver. There's an active effort on the part of Indigenous people on so many levels to move away from the notion of Indigeneity, of being Native, that has been constructed in the whole colonial process up until today. As an individual person, as an educator, as a parent, I'm really concerned, more than I was before in a theoretical sense, about what's going on in the minds of Indigenous people and how is the country, how are the institutions, how are non-Native people responding to our efforts to redefine what it is to be Native?

This is more of a creative exploration of the idea of what it is to be Indigenous. I always like to preface my remarks to give people an indication where I'm at on these questions. I've been in academia for quite a while, and I've been thinking about these things, and I've been active in the Native community in terms of activism, politics, and so forth, since the mid-1980s, and I've gone through certain phases. At one point, I was really concerned with Indigeneity in terms of a political movement – I'm not so much concerned with it these days because of what that political movement has become – but also in terms of thinking about colonization and decolonization in a deeper way. It's moved me away from considerations of politics and economics and economic analysis and policy engagement and so forth to really looking at the effects of the colonial process on the individual: the transformation of our psychology, our personality, and on a really intimate level, in the way we relate to each other on a family level, on a human level, the way we relate to our environment, and the way that we really think of ourselves.

Of course, I am not unique or the first one to think about this. While most of our preoccupation as Onkwehónweh has been in the process element of focusing on gaining access to institutional power and reconstituting our governments in a formulistic sense, for generations now the literatures on colonization and decolonization from other parts of the world have focused on this more personal level as a central element in defining what colonization and decolonization is. The ones that have had the most influence on me are Frantz Fanon's analysis of the colonial mind and Albert Memmi's work.[1] My own work in the last few years has really been an effort to kind of translate those understandings of colonization and decolonization to the context that we live in here. There have been very few Indigenous intellectuals in the realm of political studies that have adopted this kind of approach in looking at what colonization and decolonization is and how they impact the reconstruction of Indigeneity. So while this is a new direction for me, it's an older direction in other parts of the world.

I am a Native person, I'm engaged, I'm participating, like everyone else, as an actor as well as an observer in this collective movement on the part of Indigenous Peoples. We are becoming aware in an emotional sense, in an experiential sense, of where those other pathways to decolonization, those political or economic conceptions of decolonization, are leading us and the kinds of dissatisfactions we have.

I wouldn't go so far as to say emptiness, because, of course, they're constituted in something, but the dissatisfaction that we have as people, as communities, as families, as a movement as a whole, with the results. This is becoming more of a factor in people's consideration of what they want to do with their time, what they want to think about, what they want to do, the kind of things they want to devote themselves to. My own trajectory has gone from being a person really seriously involved in the political and the economic side of things to a person considering these psychological and cultural dimensions. And I think that my own understanding of what colonization/decolonization is has been deepened by that different type of engagement. So I'd like to share some reflections and thoughts on that.

Recovering Stolen Identity

The central task of anyone who's engaged in a decolonizing effort is to recover the identity and the sense of what it is to be an Indigenous person that was stolen and remade for purposes other than that which assisted us in living a good life. There are all kinds of analysis that go through the history of the specific interactions here in North America that resulted in us thinking of ourselves in the 1950s and 1960s in terms that had barely any connection to that authentic existence of our Ancestors. We collectively as Indigenous people were almost wholly remade in the eyes of the Canadian and American public but tragically, I would say, in our own eyes as well. I think about my own experience, in my own community, going to look at ceremonies, going to participate in Native-type events when I was a child, and this wasn't that long ago, it was in the 1960s and 1970s, when I was a little child. The imagery that comes back to me when I think about these types of engagements, very little of it had to do with any type of historically accurate representation of Iroquoian Peoples or Mohawk Peoples. A lot of it was reflective of a process of trying to emulate the image of a Native as it was constructed by the larger society. And what means did that larger society use to reconstruct, to construct, an image of the Native? Well, art, literature, movies, television, and so forth. And so from the time I was a child I have been, and I think everybody of my generation has been, bombarded by images of what it is to be a Native that served someone else's purpose. But they left us with a huge gap in our own understanding of ourselves in our own souls. This is largely responsible for many of the psychological and social pathologies and the problems in our communities that are fundamentally related to our lack of a sense of purpose and understanding of who we are as a people.

These are not just interesting questions on an artistic level or a cultural critique level; these are serious questions for Indigenous people. The work that's being done in terms of people coming to understand themselves better through representations, whether it's through objects or art or literature and so forth, is crucially important. I used to think it was all about politics, all about money. I used to think at one point – and I haven't really disabused myself of this completely – that it was all about contention and fighting to gain our land back. It's all of those things, of course. But if we disregard these contestations over the representation of ourselves and the understanding of ourselves, then I think we're spinning our wheels on those other aspects.

That's where the title of this talk, "From Noble Savage to Righteous Warrior," comes from. My use of the term "Righteous Warrior" comes from an Iroquoian teaching, and it's not so much righteous in the meaning of upright behavior; it's more akin to a sense of carrying yourself with a sense of justice and rightness.

As I mentioned earlier, Fanon has been greatly influential and helpful to me in understanding and unpacking and helping me become critically engaged with all of the ongoing efforts on the part of Native people in these communities to remake these images and to remake an identity and to develop one that's meaningful for our people. And when I use the word authenticity, that's really what I mean. Hopefully people are not responding to the word authenticity as a sort of essentialist dismissal of anything that doesn't reflect a kind of museum-like image of a Native, that's not at all what I mean. When I say authentic, what I mean is that it's rooted in our culture, that there's a true link to the community, and that it has a real meaning for our people in helping them make good choices to live a good life according to our teachings.

I bring in Fanon because I love to talk about Fanon. He talks about the artist, the writer, literature, and intellectuals, going through certain phases and coming out of their colonized mentality and colonized existence and recreating themselves in the decolonizing process. In trying to think through these things, I've always been fascinated by the three phases that he outlines. These are not obviously chronological phases. In any movement, in any country, among any people and even within any individual, it's not like a chronological movement from one to the other. These are things that gradually progress and hopefully people come to the third phase realizing how they all kind of play off against each other at all times: people are different and communities are different and things happen at different paces at different times.

The White Way

When people get involved in a decolonizing movement, for Fanon, the first phase is emulation: the first thing they want to do is prove that they're just as good as their colonizer. He outlines brilliantly the psychological aspects of that, from basic attitudes toward oneself – he even gets into sexual preferences and these kinds of things – but the emulative phase, I think, is something that every individual who awakens to the fact that they're colonized begins with. I'm talking for all of us; we're all kind of emulative to begin with. If you think about what I just referred to when I was a child, I recall going to an event which was supposed to be our Mohawk cultural days and seeing people dressed in firemen's outfits, people dressed in suits like I am today. People were actually trying to activate their sense of self and to act on their sense of self in ways that were very, very reflective of what the outside society saw as success, as validating a useful and honored purpose in life. It could be occupations, it could be the way you dressed or carried yourself, or most tragically in almost all Native communities, it could be speaking the English language. How many people who are Indigenous can recall their grandparents telling them, "No, don't talk the Native language. You talk English if you want to succeed." That seems bizarre to a younger person today who's being taught about the culture. But when we were growing up, that was the most common sentiment – if you wanted to impede your child and force that child to live in poverty, to live a marginalized existence, the best way to do that would be to teach them their language and to make them emulate the Ancestors rather than white society. That's just an anecdote that illustrates the larger process of what this Indigenous movement went through. What was it to be successful, what was the good way? Well, it was the white way, whether it was Christianity or liberal thinking or following the social mores or choosing a marriage partner, it was very, very clear that whatever else went on in that relationship, the good choice, the successful person, chose the thing that could really hold them in esteem from the point of view of white society.

The Return of the Native

Fanon outlines how people move through that on an individual level and on a collective level oftentimes, and as so happens in life and in nature, things go to the opposite extreme – and that's Nativism. You know, that part when we realize we're not white and what we need to do is to really emphasize that in an extreme way, and to take up as much as possible the position that Natives are Native and everything needs to be Native, and dismiss everything white, and really build up and try to restore in every different way that element in you which is Native? And that means just taking it, even if you don't relate to it, even if it's not true to your family history, even if it's not true to your community, taking something that was not white and making that part of who you were. And so, similarly, here's another anecdote about me growing up, this one from the Nativist phase in our community a few years later, when I was in my teens in the late 1970s. I was seeing people at that same kind of community gathering, but now they were wearing Plains Indian headdresses, bone chokers, riding horses – riding in the community parade on a horse and a Plains Indian headdress in a Mohawk community. That's Nativism. That's the cultural representation of what it is to be Native. On a political level, on a larger cultural level, there are all kinds of manifestations of this, with Red Power and the American Indian Movement and so forth.

The most interesting part of this process, though, is the one that we're finding ourselves coming into now, as we come through this process of decolonization, and the shift from emulation to Nativism. After experiencing both of those, people who are thoughtful in engaging with this are coming to realize that the useful and meaningful position is one that doesn't dismiss our reality, which is constituted in large part by our engagement with white society and European society but which also doesn't give over to the fact that this is who we are. And so it's really trying to find a way to be in this modern colonial reality but not of it. How do we maintain ourselves as Onkwehónweh, as true people, as Iroquois Peoples or whatever other Nation we're from, and still be cognizant of the realities of this society and not be kind of a caricature of ourselves, dismissing everything that doesn't reflect our idealistic notions of Iroquoian culture? This is the struggle that we're facing right now. And you see it representing itself and being played out all over the place.

If you have seen the Border Zones exhibit here at the museum, you'll see the work of Marianne Nicolson, which I was very honored to comment on and to write a companion piece for.[2] My reaction to her work was right along the lines of what we're talking about here. Marianne and I sat down for a couple of hours and talked about it, something we hadn't had a chance to do before, and amazingly, I think we find ourselves at the same place. I am able to articulate it through words and she is able to articulate it, I think, through the art that she does. It was about taking tradition, about taking who we are, and regenerating it so that we maintain our connection to our ancestral values and philosophies but at the same time, not bowing down to tradition. And so for her, the question of boundaries was one that was constantly on her mind, one that she was constantly trying to negotiate and to figure out, and it's the same thing with me.

For Marianne, it's how much do you show? I think that's what her piece is about: Where and for who is art done? Is it done as a display in the emulative phase to say, I can be an artist too? I have technique. I can do things. I can make grandiose works of art. Or is it just for us? Should it be behind the curtain? Should it be just in the Longhouse, should it be hidden? Should there be all kinds of borders in terms of who can access this knowledge? And we've gone back and forth, and in fact, there are people in both of those camps, so to speak, working in our communities today as writers, as artists, as political actors, and so forth. But I said that Marianne and I are kind of at the same place because we both agree we haven't got it figured out. It's something that bothers us. It's something that is a preoccupation. And I guess where we agree is that we both really need to focus on that and get people thinking about that as the next phase of our movement, in terms of not allowing people to take the two easy ways. You know, the two easy ways are the Noble Savage and the Righteous Warrior. Okay, we want to engage with both of those.

Playing the Good Indian

The Noble Savage is a creation of the European mind. In the old days, it was meant to create an enemy that could be easily destroyed or marginalized or explained away as a thing of the past so that the European society could validate its existence in this territory. I think there's still a bit of that going on, or a lot of it, in the sense that the Noble Savage is still present in Canadian and North American culture. A slightly different take on it now, though, is that the Noble Savage is no longer being pushed away or marginalized or killed off. The Noble Savage is being embraced as a brother and sister so that there can be a connection and legitimation of European colonial society in this land. So people have realized that yes, we do need to have a legitimate connection to this territory, there needs to be an inheritance, there needs to be a line of succession, so to speak.

That's where the Noble Savage comes in, the Good Indian. The Good Indian says to settler society, "Yes, you do have a place here, yes. All you need to do is listen to me, buy my art, invite me to the Olympics to perform, all these kinds of things. And I will sit behind you and smile while the Prime Minister and the Premier take all the glory and say, 'This is Canada.' And Michael J. Fox can get up and say, 'Everybody in the world, this is your home too.'" That's the Noble

Savage. That's the Good Indian. So, not to be too harsh on my friends and relatives because of course I have relatives who participated in the opening ceremony and so forth. But we have to think about it in a serious way.

What's happening is the Noble Savage is alive and well and serving a different purpose today. Look at the work of John Ralston Saul. In his most recent book, he is critical of right-wing conservative dismissals of Aboriginal culture as backwards – he is embracing us.[3] But where does he end up? His argument is that we are a Métis society, that we always have been, and that we've been in denial. But what is he really saying? He asked me what I thought about it, and I said, "You know what? I think you're saying that you have a right to be here and that you have a rightful ownership of this land. If you are a Métis society, what's Métis? Half European, half Indigenous. Your Indigenous half obviously is completely legitimate and everything that you're claiming and doing here is legitimate." So there's a huge problem in the way that the notion of a Native reflects the Noble Savage. We've tried in various ways through art and literature to get away from it, but it is the main and most attractive image of the Indian for mainstream society.

The alternative image, the image of the Righteous Warrior, has always been a very, very difficult thing for non-Native society to get a hold of and to understand and to accept. To think about it in a very contemporary way, at the opening Olympic ceremonies the four host Nation Chiefs were late.[4] Why were they late? Because they were being protested by Indigenous warriors, female and male, blocking the caravan that was leading to the ceremony. It led to a totally unfortunate reiteration of a bad stereotype – the Natives were late and the whole Olympic ceremony had to had to wait for twenty minutes. But at least the Governor General was late with them. Although that's another stereotype, you know – it was hard to win on that night. But everything turned out all right in the end, everybody got there.

But think about the playing off of types: the Noble Savage, the Good Indian, and the Bad Indian. Think about the way the media responds, the general public, your friends, to the two types of redefinition of what it is to be a Native person played out on the ground, on this fulcrum of the Olympics. The iconic symbol of the Righteous Warrior, the Warrior Flag, is something that I'm proud to say came from a person in my own town: the red flag with the Indian head, and the sun, the beams of the sun coming out – that was originally a flag for the Warrior Society in Kahnawà:ke but has since taken on a completely different meaning.[5] It symbolizes, I think, their reaction to not only the Noble Savage but also a sense of Indigenous revolution in a cultural sense, in a political sense, in every way. That flag is waved around at protests and as assertions of people who are acting on a sense of Indigeneity, which is, I think, reflective of not Nativism, which would be easy to dismiss. They are actually trying to activate a sense of what it is to be Indigenous that means something for their people, and not simply satisfying the expectations of the larger society.

And on the other side of the coin – and this is me kind of provocatively making a little bit of fun of them – are the Chiefs of the four host Nations, in terms of their posture. I don't mean to disrespect them, but I mean to say that what kind of signal does it send when they display their regalia for the purposes of legitimating a relationship when that is not the kind of clothing they wear every day, it is not something they have as part of their everyday life? Whereas the people who were outside in the street waving the flag were dressed the way they do all the time, they are actually living out an authentic Indigeneity that they live every day, which is their commitment, that is something that they do that is not instrumental to a political objective or anything, but it's truly who they are. So not to dismiss the utility of what was done by the four host Nations, but it is performative.

Who and What Is Indigenous Art For?

To get back to what Marianne and I agreed on, the thing that bugs her most about Native art today is the performative aspect of it, and how so little is channeled back into educating our youth in terms of who they are. So little of it is actually done for Native youth and Native communities. So much of it is done for the market.

Of course, the instant response in people's minds is, "Well, we've got to live somehow. You have a job at the university! You know, people need to make a living." That's obviously true. But people have to think about the usefulness and the uses of the work that they're doing. If they call themselves Indigenous artists, Indigenous writers, Indigenous professors, activists, and so forth, what is the end result? What is the effect of the energy that they're putting into their work and into the environments where they produce that work? Marianne's piece, I think, is a commentary on where the actual utility of Indigenous traditions lie. You look at it, and it goes against the instinct of the person coming to see

Native art because you can't see it. When you come to see Native art, you're looking for really beautiful and technically brilliant displays of craftsmanship, impressive, usually Kwakiutl and Haida designs, Coast Salish designs. You expect to see all that, but on Marianne's piece you get a blank on the outside. On the inside is where everything is. On the bottom you see the pictures of the faces of those people from the Ancestors. I think her message is that artistic production, artistic work, literary work is for those people inside. People can come and look, but they better have a respectful posture when they're looking at it. It's not something that is there just for the taking.

And in fact, if you're useful to anybody, it should be to those Ancestors and those younger people who have to reconnect to those Ancestors in order to survive. Not to prosper – but to survive. That's how crucial it is this time. Look at the suicide rates. Look at all of the problems in our communities. And art matters. Literature matters. Philosophy matters. All these things matter because we're not doing them for us anymore, we're doing them, in large part, for other people. And we're living with the results because our communities are becoming decultured, to use a phrase from Blackfoot philosopher Leroy Little Bear. What do you have in a decultured environment, where there are other stressors, economic stressors, health stressors, and so on? You get a disaster, a social disaster, and in fact, that's what's happening in our communities. So there's a very compelling need to really look at these questions in a serious way. And whether you're an artist or writer, a professor, an intellectual of any sort, a political actor of any sort, whatever you may be, we really have to consider the necessity of channeling back into the question of what is it to be an Onkwehónweh today in our society and giving the younger generation of people something meaningful to work with. We're not going to solve their problems by the work that we do as intellectuals. But I think what we can do is give them the tools. Right now the tools they have to work with are very poor.

A Cultural Rock to Stand On

The cultural foundation – I use this metaphor a lot, because it was one that was given to me – the cultural foundation that our Ancestors stood on to confront the challenges that they faced was huge. Their language, their culture, their knowledge of history, their ceremonial engagement, their social connections, their spirituality, this was a huge rock that they stood on so they could successfully engage in a lot of different challenges at the same time and maintain themselves. Over time we've seen that cultural foundation whittled away through the bleeding away of energy, of people, through the direct attacks on our culture and our communities, to this point we're at now. I had a graduate student who came to me this week, who comes from a First Nation, who said, "You talk about that big rock foundation, but I feel like I'm carrying around a little pebble. What can I do, carrying around this little pebble? What right do I have to even say anything?" The question of art and culture is so crucial, and so much more important than the kinds of negotiations we're having, making political agreements and trying to get funding and so forth.

The central fact about all this, as Fanon alludes to, as every writer who's written from a decolonizing perspective, and those of us that have lived and thought seriously about decolonization, is that it's a very personal and difficult challenge to face. It's much easier to say, oh, it's all about money. "I'm Clarence Louie and all it takes to decolonize is us starting businesses. Hey, all you Natives, pull your socks up and get to work on time."[6] Those are the things that come out of that perspective. Really, is that what decolonization is? What about the promises that are made in treaty negotiations about how once we have our own form of government, things will fall into place? If you look at the people that have signed and implemented treaties and begun living in those arrangements, it's not solving anything. Problems are getting worse.

I focus on this because it's the example that works. Part of my own understanding is experiential, but part of it is also visiting and working with people that have really successfully maintained their Indigeneity and not only maintained it but made it larger and shared it with others so that people can actually come to a sense of Indigeneity that allows them to be in this world without having to suffer that big, gaping hole in their soul. And that has always been through cultural resurgence. A classic example is the work that was done by anthropologist Adrian Tanner in northern Quebec among the Cree. In the eastern part of Canada there are communities that were very recently affected by industrial development in the 1970s, and previous to that they had been living a relatively traditional nomadic existence on the land, right up until the 1960s and '70s when they began to settle in one place and became sedentary. The central lesson was that through the consistent maintenance of a connection to that traditional lifestyle through cyclical camps, through art, through ceremony, through spirituality, those people who engaged in that culture were able to maintain themselves because that became the normalcy, and the messed up existence of the Indian reserve became the thing that was bizarre. Right now we have the opposite. In most Native communities today, what's normal is very, very sad. What's normal is lateral violence, sexual abuse, drug and alcohol abuse, all kinds of very mean and destructive things that become the norm in the community. Even in these other pathways that are laid out for success, what's the norm? Materialism? All these sorts of things are laid out, and it's not satisfying.

The pathway of cultural regeneration, moving toward the sense of being Indigenous that is a resurrection of an older way of being Indigenous but in a conscious engagement with the larger society, normalizes that person and gives them a sense of self which is honorable. It is something that actually teaches people how to be on the land, how to treat each other with respect, all the values that are universal and reflected in Indigenous teachings. Even if it's only for a part of the year, even if it's only for a part of someone's life, that becomes the normalcy, and it shields them with armor, psychologically, emotionally, and culturally so that they can then do battle with the reality of their lives on the reserves and in the cities. So when I talk about from Noble Savage to Righteous Warrior, that's really what I'm talking about. And I think that my own experience, and that of our students, and collectively, I think people are coming to realize this. So all of us that are teachers, writers, students, and activists, I think we really need to think about the pathway to decolonization in these terms, because our survival depends on it. Not because it's a good thing to do, but our survival depends on it. We're at a crucial stage in our history. There won't be any Indigenous Nations around here to speak of two or three generations from now if we don't move in this direction.

Hanging Moose Meat, Witset First Nation, 2001

For Natives, being a hunter means carrying a sacred obligation to family, to self, and to Nature.

THE PSYCHIC LANDSCAPE OF CONTEMPORARY COLONIALISM

Adapted from a lecture delivered at the University of Ottawa on November 9, 2011.

My goal in this speech was to share the deeper understanding of Indigenous Resurgence that I gained from my commitment to putting my ideas into practice in real community settings. In 2004 I started working for the Mohawks of Akwesasne in their struggle to hold major corporations accountable for their contamination of the natural environment. I was responsible for documenting the adverse impacts of contamination on Mohawk culture and working with the community to develop an approach to cultural restoration in the wake of environmental clean ups. Through this experience, I came to realize that the cure for the colonial disease is the restoration of land-based cultural practices and reconnecting the generations of our people to their homeland in cultural, spiritual, and physical ways. This is the learning I was excited about at the time, and it was the message I wanted to share with the young people who came to my talk that night looking to me for an antidote to Aboriginalism.

I'm very glad to be here; it's a real homecoming for me. A lot of what I've learned about the things that I write and speak about came from the experience that I had here in Ottawa, and with some of the people in this room. I want to acknowledge my teachers and friends and students in the room here and give a nod to the multigenerational aspect of learning and teaching.

I'm going to talk to you about the psychic landscape of contemporary colonialism. What I mean by the psychic aspect is how we think about and understand what the struggle is that our people are facing. How do we think about and process how it affects us as people, and how do we channel that into a program of political and cultural action? Over the years this has come to be the main thing that I grapple with in trying to put forward something new for the people to consider and perhaps use to survive and build up our strength again. And today, since many of us here know each other already, how can I say something that would be innovative, that wouldn't bore you, and yet still get to the heart of the matter, the key issues that we're facing right now?

I refer to it in psychic terms because I think that a big part of this is our understanding of who we are, my understanding of who *I* am. I think this reflects the transformations Indigenous communities have undergone in their political culture and to a certain extent the culture in general. There's people in the room that have been involved much longer than me, but ever since I got involved in politics in the mid-1980s, there have been two or three major transformations on that big question: What is the problem, and what are we doing about it? What is colonization, and what is decolonization?

Today I'm going to trace my own intellectual and to a certain extent personal development through the process of decolonizing and discuss how my books are artifacts of that process. The lesson that I was taught as a young person coming into this environment, working with some really dedicated people who were involved for years in struggles in our communities and who were doing really good work in the academy, was that scholarship reflects a lived experience: it's working through a living reality and contributing whatever insights and knowledge come out of that. I've always taken that to heart, and it's come to define my approach. I don't write about anything that I haven't experienced or lived myself. I'm not saying that in any way to project arrogance, I'm saying that because I honestly believe that is the true pathway to wisdom. You need self-knowledge in order to recognize your position in relation to colonialism and to find ways that you can transcend it and remake yourself in order to be something that reflects the best values of the Ancestors that are our reference as to what is a good way of life.

The Crown and the Nation

The first book that I wrote, *Heeding the Voices of Our Ancestors* (1995), was based on my PhD dissertation, which was the most intense period of learning for me intellectually: I was trying to come to grips with the question of what was Kahnawà:ke living? What was my community living? Why were we the way we were, subject to the colonial power of people who had no right to be imposing power on us? Why did we lose all our land? Why were our people behaving toward each other in the way that they were? And so that was my instinct, getting into this academic project. The understanding that I had at that point reflected my own level of knowledge: self-knowledge, and knowledge of the larger context of colonization and Indigenous realities in Canada. Of course over time I have developed deeper levels of knowledge both about myself and about those larger realities.

So I'll start there: I'll take people back to what was colonization, what was the Indian problem from the Canadian perspective, and what was our problem from our perspective. It was basically a problem of governance. People thought that the problem we were facing was that we were governed by others. This is not something we've entirely transcended. It's certainly true that others govern us, that the imposition of laws, the imposition of land regimes, the imposition of the band council system and all this sort of stuff is wrong. But at that time, the work that I did here in Ottawa was related to the drive to free ourselves from the most direct forms of colonization and control in our communities and over ourselves. It's come to be known as self-government: defining ourselves in different ways and developing the capacity to govern ourselves. I always remember Andrew Delisle Sr., who's still around Kahnawà:ke, still vital and contributing, who has been on the scene since the 1960s.[1] I remember him telling me in the 1980s when I first approached him for knowledge about what the problem was and what we should be doing about it. By this time, we had a band council, we had elections, we basically ran our own community the way that we wanted to run it. He said,

> Think about where we are now. It wasn't that long ago, probably only ten to fifteen years ago, when three of us couldn't get together without a priest or an Indian agent or an RCMP officer in the room. If three of us tried to gather, the RCMP would come and break it up. That's why bingo became so popular. We did it in the basement of the church, under the sponsorship of the church, and we all got together and we all did our politics, we strategized as how to fight the government – all under the cover of the priest!

He made me think about how far we had come in such a short period of time. The wider context of that era was the repatriation of the Constitution in 1982, which led to the idea of a Canada that was opening up to the possibility of a relationship with First Nations that was not colonial. If you think about those two things – the recent freedom of Indigenous Peoples to actually govern themselves and the legal possibilities that the Constitution presented for redefining the relationship on something other than hard colonialism – in theory at least, these things structured that phase of our political movement.

And so colonization became defined institutionally. Elders, teachers, political activists told me, what we need to do is fight hard to define and use section 35 of the Constitution – which hadn't been defined in courts or in policy at that point – as the bridge between the Canadian society, the Crown, and our Nations.[2] The Crown and the Nation. Whether you were Cree, Anishinaabe, West Coast, Dene, whatever, those were the terms that were used when talking about the issue – the Crown and the Nation. Most importantly, the Nation. When the Dene were fighting the Mackenzie Pipeline in the 1970s it was the Dene Nation.[3] The

National Indian Brotherhood became the AFN, the Assembly of First Nations. That sense of Nationhood, of Nation, of autonomy and an existence that had been suppressed by colonization by Canadian society became very strong. There was an effort to break free and build a new relationship based on the principles that are reflected in our treaty visions. In our Haudenosaunee conception, it was the Two-Row Wampum, and I understand other Indigenous Peoples have similar concepts.[4]

That was the project at the time: the thrust of Indigenous action reflected that dynamic of the need to govern ourselves. It was institutionally defined. Over time there were varying degrees of success, there were communities that developed the ability to govern themselves, that convinced the Canadian government to hand over some power. First Nations actually began to govern ourselves: to make decisions, to move toward the conception of Nationhood that had been the one that was guiding our Ancestors and our people throughout the long period of colonization. Colonization and decolonization was thought of as simply a matter of structural reform: regaining control over institutions, over law and policymaking mechanisms, the levers of government, the managerial aspects, the capacities of delivering services, even the legal and constitutional aspects of Nationhood. That was self-government.

When I wrote my first book, that was my level of understanding. I would say now that it was kind of a limited understanding because when you look at colonization/decolonization strictly in institutional or structural terms, you're forgetting significant parts of the experience of what colonization is and what it did to our people. I think people became concerned with that aspect because they began to see that self-government was not delivering decolonization. When you think about things in terms of the life of your people, the lived experience, the health status, the ability for people to relate in a happy, healthy way, to be productive, to live their own laws on their land, to live out their culture, to have a culture that's resurgent in their community and informing the world view for the next generation, self-government was doing nothing for that, it was doing nothing. And people who are thinking about that began to think that decolonization can't just be about structural reform. It has to have other aspects to it.

While this may seem obvious in retrospect, it's only through reflecting on those experiences that it became clear. People who are involved in political projects can get totally involved in them because in order to be successful, you have to be all in. So when people get obsessed with taking back power, they begin to structure their personality, their understandings of the world and the way they relate to others, all for the purpose of getting that power. People that knew me in the early 1990s here in Ottawa, you probably knew a different kind of person because, as any person who is hoping to be successful, I was the same way. I was totally oriented toward doing what was necessary: structuring my personality, my way of being, my skill set, my capacities to engage with that opponent in order to gain the victory. I struggled, and I think that our communities came to reflect that. The types of leaders that we have in our community coming out of that era, the type of politics that we have among ourselves, the cultures that emerged, reflect the fact that when you engage in that kind of struggle, you become like your enemy. The people that were dissatisfied with that began to think about it as a negative thing. If our goal was to have a better life as Onkwehónweh and pass it on to the next generation, we were not succeeding.

Selling Us Out

In the early 1990s people began questioning the whole self-government project. For me personally, the next level or different type of understanding I came to came from that, and also through my experience with the Royal Commission on Aboriginal Peoples. I came to Ottawa for self-government negotiations in the '80s, and for a long period of time in the early and mid-'90s for the Royal Commission. I'm sure there's people in this room that had some affiliation and did some work there – actually, I'd be surprised that anyone who was politically active or could read or write and was Native at the time *wasn't* involved. That's how wide the net they threw was to try to co-opt us all! My second book, *Peace, Power, Righteousness* (1999), reflected this experience. It was fairly critical, reflecting my conception of where we were at that point. I think it's consistent with what a lot of the people in our communities at the time were thinking – questioning where we were going.

In hindsight, the instinct we had was that we need to repeat the whole thing, not just self-government. Colonization is also a cultural process, an economic process, a spiritual process. Colonization is all of this. And the Royal Commission was an attempt to gather all of that knowledge, put it in a box, put it under the table, and move forward. That's what Royal Commissions do. We didn't know that at the time. We hoped that it would create another opportunity to engage with Canadian society. Just like after 1982, when the Constitution seemed to be an opportunity to redefine and engage with Canadian society, so too was Royal Commission. In the context of Nationhood, it became this massive enterprise of laying out knowledge, laying out the reality for our Peoples, thinking through it and coming up with a different sense of what Canada could be and what kind of relationship we could have with Canada. My second book came out of that expansion of my understanding of ways to be Native. I was exposed to different perspectives from other Native people all over the world, and I also deepened my understanding through the interactions I had with teachers from my own Nation about what it is to be a person, what my responsibilities were, and what the dangers were of engaging in politics in the way that we were. People were bluntly saying, "What good is taking back power if all you're going to do is act like a White Man with that power? I get confused when I look at this guy: he knows the talk, he comes from the same place as me, but yet he's doing the same thing to me as the Indian agent."

There had to be a substantive change, and that's what we were hoping for. There was a move toward a cultural resurgence, although there's not a strict chronology, these things overlap and blend into each other. But in the Haudenosaunee communities in the late '80s and early '90s there was a very strong push and a widening of the scope of what traditionalism was. It became the defining feature of our movement, and many people were involved with it. It became the alternative to the assimilation process, to the band council, the alternative psychic place to Catholicism and to all of the other identities that had been put on us by the colonizer. Traditionalism and a critique of the established order in our communities became a very big issue.

My book reflects this. It was a response to the frustrations of those in the community who were committed to the vision that our Ancestors had in fighting colonization. Our Ancestors were fighting for the right to live on their land, according to their laws, worshiping their gods, and to pass that on to the next generations without being impinged on and without restriction. People who were still committed to this found that the self-government project was very limited and unacceptable. *Peace Power Righteousness* is basically a long essay that criticizes our leaders who were co-opted and selling out. I wanted it to reflect these frustrations, but it wasn't a rant. It was grounded in the way of our being that has come to us as our heritage, through our ceremonies, through our teaching, through our songs, through the oral histories, and through the established consensus in the community as to what is a good way of life.

As a younger person at that time, to stand up and say, "No! You're taking us down the wrong path; and many of you are doing it for the wrong reasons; and a minority of you are corrupt; and I want everybody to know that," it was an intimidating thing to do. I needed the back-up of our tradition, our knowledge, everything that our culture could afford me. I didn't feel comfortable as an individual with the level of experience and knowledge that I had at that time to just say, "I'm frustrated with you all, stop selling us out." I had to have more power behind me. So the structure of the book drew on the condolence ceremony, which hadn't been done in our community. There was no real direct experience with it, at least on my part, and I was worried about getting it right, I grappled with the ethics around using it. But in the end I was satisfied that it was the appropriate wisdom and knowledge to use to stand up and bring forward a critique to those leaders who were taking our people into the future. These are powerful people, both politically and personally. To criticize them isn't to deny the fact that they're very skilled, that a lot of them have integrity, that they believe in what they're doing, that they have long years of experience and commitment to the struggle, and that they are convinced that they are right. But I drew on the wisdom of Elders and others, and I believe that the critique still stands. There's people who read this book today and say, "Oh, he's saying exactly what's going on in my community, he's talking about my Chief." Or people will say, "You're talking about me. I had to put that book down five times because I was so angry and frustrated because you were actually talking about me." And well, I'm good with that because I was talking about me too: this book came from a personal journey.

The answer to these criticisms coming out of our communities was, to put it succinctly, traditionalism: the effort to restore the ancient ways of governance, the ancient cultural way, the ancient ways of relating to each other, the community that we understood was the community of our ancestry. So there were Longhouse movements and the revival of traditional cultures all across the land. But to cut a long story short, people became frustrated with that endeavor as well. I think instincts bring you and drive you forward in a movement. But when you're living in it, you get to see that it's not that simple. In hindsight, the traditionalist endeavor was based on people, based on women, men, kids, and Elders, these were the people that were doing the ceremonies, running the Longhouse, engaged in language revitalization. And over time people came to see that it wasn't simply enough to say, get the Indian Act off our back, bring back the Longhouse, let's all move in there, let's all do our thing and then we'll all be Onkwehónweh again. I think that I'm not giving away any secrets here to our non-Native brothers and sisters, but the practice of traditionalism and the ceremonial culture is also ridden with problems. There's great power and strength, and don't misunderstand me, I still believe it is the foundation of our culture and our society. I am totally committed to its revitalization and survival. But there's abuse, there's neglect, there's co-optation, manipulation, there's monetization – people began to see that it's not that simple. All of this is founded on people. And people began to question: "Who is that person running that ceremony? Why is he doing these things? Where did he come from? What is the effect? What am I getting out of it? What's happening from here?" All questions that naturally will occur as people begin to relate on that basis and use that culture as the way of living their lives.

So decolonization was even more complex. It wasn't simply capacity building, self-government. It wasn't the revitalization and revival of traditional culture. And here's where the younger generation really came in, evaluating these things from their perspective: self-government, community governance, band governance, on the one hand, and traditional culture and practices, on the other. They wanted to know, "How is it helping me be become more Indigenous? How is it helping me move through the world as an Indigenous person? How is it helping me carry out my responsibility in the culture for my Ancestors?" A lot of people found it wanting. They found it didn't have the transformative power that they knew deep inside was at the core of their own decolonization.

My experience reflected that, and I began to look for answers in ways and in places other than those that had been established as the decolonizing sites. I began to just talk to people in the community who were experiencing the sense of frustration, again, at how their lives were still not together. They didn't feel together. They didn't feel like they had decolonized. They may be participating in the Longhouse, learning a language, experiencing a community resurgence in terms of power. In Kahnawà:ke you've got self-government, big funding, very strong political identity, language revitalization, and all that. But there was still a gap in many people's souls, psyches, bodies, whatever you want to call it. This process of decolonization was not complete.

And so I took up the responsibility of starting to think about it again, a kind of luxury I have as a professor whose job is to read and think and talk to people and really engage on these problems full time. But it wasn't as straightforward as the previous phases: in the first phase I could count on Chiefs and the Elders who were involved in the self-government struggle to inform and advise me and give me the context. With the second phase I could go to the Longhouse Elders and traditional Chiefs. But this time, the question was, "Well, who do we go to now?" Those are only part of the answer. And that was the real struggle: to find people and to develop relationships in terms of learning and teaching to address the question of "How do we get at this basic problem of the psyche?"

Fighting False Notions of Indigeneity

I came to an understanding of this phase through reading some important works on colonization/decolonization, and I was deeply influenced by Frantz Fanon, to the extent that the Indigenous governance program that I run is basically founded on the process that he describes in *Black Skin, White Masks*. Fanon argued you have to understand your psychic closeness to the colonizer. You have to understand yourself, your obsessions, and your desires in order to be decolonized. And then you have to channel that into a political project that makes sense in terms of a break from the power of the colonizer to define who you are and what your future is.

If you think about where we are right now, where has the movement led us so far? I think we get to the psychic landscape of contemporary colonialism. Where has self-government taken us? How many leaders are operating on a basis of autonomous Nationhood in contention with the Canadian state? There are very few, if any, leaders on the national or provincial scene who are advocating goals and structuring their actions consistent with that struggle for the revitalization of our Nations. In our Haudenosaunee communities the Two-Row Wampum is the guiding premise, and while there is a rhetorical deference paid to it, looking at our politics, I don't know how many people are really acting in a way that's consistent with it.

And so in *Wasáse*, my third book, I critique Aboriginal politics. The idea of being an Aboriginal in Canada to me seems like a betrayal of the heritage of struggle that our Ancestors put into our survival. In the '80s and '90s, the whole notion of "Aboriginal" was defined in terms of the jurisprudence and policy on section 35 that came out of the Department of Justice, the Department of Indian Affairs, and various other ministries and adjudicated by Canadian courts. Aboriginal politics today is really about being consistent with the false notions and instrumentalist notions of Indigeneity that are created by judges, lawyers, consultants, and Indigenous and non-Indigenous academics in order to facilitate the removal of our people from the land.

Removing us from our land has been the project from the beginning. People didn't come here 500 years ago to be friends. They came to escape their own lives in other parts of the world and to exploit. When they found that we were on the land and in the way to the extent we didn't cooperate, they devised means, governmental, military, medical, and otherwise, to remove us from the land. Nothing's changed. It's still that. Apply that dynamic I've described to Denedeh or up north or in Northern BC or anywhere where the Native opposes the development of the land for exploitative purposes: that Native is defined out of existence or pushed out of existence. For us to defer to this notion of Aboriginal and try to structure ourselves and conceptualize our processes and goals accordingly is the end game of colonization.

The political survival of Canada depends on us accepting this Aboriginalism, defined in Canadian terms of citizenship, where we all get some share of what's going on, but our rights and needs are balanced against those of the larger population. For us, the only way to survive is either to move out of the way or face destruction, or redefine ourselves so that we don't have a psychic conflict between who we think we are and what we do. A lot of people are caught in this dynamic. Being an Aboriginal today is really a crazy complicated hypocrisy. This Aboriginal is not who we are as Onkwehónweh, Dene, Saanich. This Aboriginal is defined in terms that are coming down from Canadian courts and Canadian policy, the media, popular culture, CanLit, all of these things, and they help to define us in ways which create a sense of ourselves as inauthentic. By authenticity all I mean is coming from ourselves: these other things, they're impositions.

It's a crazy complicated thing to resolve on a personal level. On one hand, the reason I am being focused on and I have the attention of this society is because I'm part of a First Nation. I am an Indigenous person. I was here first. We have a long heritage. We have a culture. But at the same time, I'm a Canadian, an Aboriginal Canadian, and Canadians defer to democratic institutions within the society. Canadians are citizens that have an ethnic heritage that is respected, and in no way, no how do Aboriginal Canadians have a right to trump the rights of other Canadians. The jurisprudence in the Supreme Court is very clear: it's about balancing the overwhelming need of the Canadian society to continue to progress against the remnant Aboriginal rights that are a "burden" on Crown title, in the language of Aboriginal title law. I don't think this is something that we can square.

That's the argument I make in *Wasáse*. The reason we have this big gap in our souls, that we feel empty, that we feel like a bunch of hypocrites is because we've accepted another person's definition of ourselves, and we're living out someone else's notion of what it is to be an Indigenous person in our land. When we're think about our struggle now, it has nothing to do with taking back land, reimposing our laws in our communities and the maintenance of an identity for our people that is rooted in our area, our language, our world. If we are true to our own original visions, the teachings that come through the ceremonies and through our Ancestors, if we know our own history, look at the way our Ancestors talked and acted, we wouldn't be doing any of this politically or culturally. *Wasáse* is an attempt to draw very clear lines between the pathways that have integrity from Indigenous perspectives and the pathways that are Aboriginalist co-optations oriented toward the assimilation and the eventual destruction of our people.

Wasáse works through a lot of different perspectives and with very, very clear guidance from people that I spoke with about their insights and experiences. The conclusion I reached is that this Aboriginal framework leads to the notion of reconciliation as surrender. It basically defines us as victims of progress, people who are unable to keep up, who need help, people who need to be brought up to speed and into the mainstream, people who need to be taught how to live in this world. In societies all over the world people become integrated and over time generationally lose the original sense of themselves. I guess the argument can be made that that is natural and even good. That's progress, people coming from the forest into the city. My point in *Wasáse* is, if you accept that, you might as well just be a Canadian, you might as well join the project. You might as well just stop talking about the idea of Mohawk Nation, Cree Nation, because this approach is the dissolution of any independent basis for existence in this land. If you're going to do this, don't call yourself a First Nations activist. Don't call yourself an Indigenous person – the Indigenous person only exists in the context of the heritage and elements of an Indigenous identity that were handed down to us by our Ancestors, one or two or three generations removed. These things are very clear in every Nation, in every part of the country. You don't have to make an extensive effort to dig up or uncover what those teachings are, what those defining features of what it is to be an Indigenous person are. All you need to do is talk to an Elder or participate in some ceremonies or participate in community life as it's oriented toward cultural practice on the land and these things become very, very evident. If you then go and try to relate it to the existence that you have in law, politics, economics, and academia, you will see a great disjuncture.

Disconnection from the Land: Learning from Akwesasne

The real struggle we face right now is, How do we continue to confront colonization? If we understand all of this, what do we do? What's next? The answer that has come to me has come through the work that I've done in Akwesasne over the last seven years. Akwesasne is a Mohawk community on the St. Lawrence with a long history of activism and leadership in the Indigenous world. The community asked me to think through the effects of the loss of their connection to the natural environment, and it brought me to an understanding of what colonization is at the core. Not that the journey of knowledge has ended for me in any way, but I'm starting to get at a core understanding in my own life. I think that in dialogue with the people that I've worked with in Akwesasne and having written and talked about it in other communities, I'm starting to really get at the heart of what colonization did: it separated us from our land. When we say we're dispossessed, that's a legal term and we understand what it means. But what does it mean to us in terms of the way we live our life, the way we experience our life? I didn't really understand that well enough intellectually to be able to process it, to talk about it, until I worked in Akwesasne on this question of what has been the effect.

In Akwesasne it's a very specific problem: the effect of industrial contamination, mainly PCBs, in the river and on the land. What has been the effect culturally on the people there? I came to realize that the disconnection from the land has had the most profound effect on our people in terms of our ability to sustain ourselves psychically, culturally, and physically as Indigenous Peoples. The health effects are very obvious. People talk about the traditional diet and its replacement with junk food and a sedentary lifestyle, and the loss or forgetting or inaccessibility of a lifestyle that maintained our bodies in a healthy way. But culturally, the loss of the land also meant the loss of actual collective activity on the land, which meant the loss of the transmission of knowledge. The land is the way our people taught and learned, where the way to understanding our world view, our relationship to other elements of creation, and our language were transmitted. You stop doing that and you sit in front of the TV and it can't happen. My job was very depressing, I basically traced the decline of the Mohawk Nation in Akwesasne over time. As we went along I learned some positive things, but I also learned a lot of negative things. The most important part for me was the psychological effect of being disconnected from your land because all of this – the health effects, the language loss, the loss of kinship relationship, the transmission of knowledge – had the effect of creating a deep sense of alienation in the people that breeds a sense of distrust in each other, in oneself, in the future.

I think you see where I'm going with this: the most profound effect the dispossession of Native Peoples through colonization has is the creation of the sense of alienation. This in turn creates the context for most of the social ills and psychological ills that play out in our communities. Attempting to address this with economic or political structural changes, or in any way other than finding a way to reconnect the people to the sources of their existence and their power, is futile. In Akwesasne, it's not to say that all of a sudden with that realization everything changed and everybody's happy and healthy and 100 per cent Mohawk again. But I think at the heart of it, understanding this on an individual and collective basis is key to addressing colonization.

I'm not saying that in order to be truly Native and to live a Native life today you have to wear buckskin and feathers and beads. What I'm saying is, your Ancestors, would they recognize you? If you're ever going to survive as an Indigenous person in an overwhelmingly colonial society and maintain yourself into the future and transmit something of what it means to be a Mohawk or a Cree or an Algonquin, you have to have a sense of yourself that comes from that place. This is what our normal needs to be – not this crazy life that most of us live either in the city or on a reserve somewhere. If that's the normal, then what are we giving as a legacy to our kids? At best it's mainstream middle-class capitalist consumer values – but in Mohawk. The central point I've come to in all this intellectual work, all this political work, all of this journeying and trying to find teachers is that the answer has always been the same as at the Royal Commission: it's about the land. It's all about the land. You need to understand, at a deeper level, that we need to get our land back, and have a relationship with the land.

When it comes down to it, we don't have a strong relationship with our land anymore. I think that our existence, our sense of Indigeneity, our politics reflects this. My preoccupation is our survival. People who are involved in all these other aspects, they think they're doing a good thing; they're committed to this program. But think about it in these terms: If success is the ability for me to live as a Mohawk in my territory and to go about in the world with a Mohawk world view, with a sense of connection to my Ancestors, to the spirit world, and to carry myself in a way that honors our Ancestors, well, I can't get that from the outside. That has to come from my culture, and my culture is land-based. If the criteria for success lie beyond the individual, to have a community that fosters this in its youth and teaches it to its children multi-generationally, and to give the next generations the opportunity to be more Native than we are in all of these different ways, that's successful.

We're coming from a very colonized existence. Every single one of us. And the criteria for success shouldn't be us having more money in exchange for being even less Native. We're already starting from an extremely precarious position. I'm arguing for a criteria of success where my four-year-old and the kids coming forward can honestly have the opportunity, if they so choose, to live on their land, to live up to their teachings, to believe in themselves and to see themselves and relate to others as Onkwehónweh. To me, that's what we should be shooting for. Not any other criteria defined in legal terms, economic terms, or cultural or intellectual terms coming from someone else whose society has always been and remains oriented toward the removal of us from any authentic sense of ourselves on the land.

My analysis is that most of our understanding of colonization and decolonization still comes from other people. So I would say to our Indigenous leaders, what are you doing to advance the ability of our younger generations to live an authentic Onkwehónweh life? What are you sacrificing in order to achieve it? We remain oriented toward satisfying the demands, imperatives, and preferences of others, as opposed to the profound need in our communities for a reorientation away from those understandings and toward giving hope and chance and opportunity to future generations to live as Onkwehónweh on their own terms.

Aronhiénte, Wet'suwet'en Yintah, 2013

My son standing in the place where his ancient roots enter the earth.

PRACTICAL DECOLONIZATION

Adapted from a talk at Queen's University,
in Kingston, Ontario, on April 9, 2012.

In this talk, I wanted to make a concise statement on what decolonization meant to me in personal terms. By this point, I had written and taught and spoken about decolonization as a political and social theory for two decades. I felt that it was important to shift my focus away from systems and historic processes toward understanding colonization as the process of disconnecting us from our homelands and in doing so obliterating the ancestral vision of ourselves and replacing it with falsehoods manufactured to serve Settler society's interest and desires which we are forced to adopt or unwittingly choose to live out in our self-conceptions and the ways we relate to our families, communities, and the land. Decolonization, as I had come to understand it, is a form of spiritual rebellion that is practiced, lived, and felt on a bodily level, in each and every one of us.

I want to expand the notion of decolonization to include decolonizing in a very personal sense – healing yourself through very specific ways and practices. I'm talking about teaching people how to be Indigenous on the land.

Colonization has broken the spirit of Indigenous people. In many cases, colonization keeps people in a state of anomie, alienation, frustration, anxiety; they are caught between two worlds, a big hole in their soul. The only way to restore them, to make them full and whole again, is to put them back into connection with the land. It's not only the connection to the land that is achieved in the physical sense. Their health is re-established because they begin to eat healthier foods, traditional foods. They become more physical beings, they act more, there's a physical component, a restoration of the body.

When I'm talking about decolonization, this is really what I'm talking about. If you want to learn how to take a perch from the St. Lawrence, and how to do it properly, and you're taught in Mohawk, and you spend twelve hours a day doing that with other Mohawk, talking about perch and grass and water, instead of at the mall, or watching TV, or doing whatever, you're inherently becoming more cultured. Your community is becoming more unified. You're becoming closer and you are restoring the very thing that colonization took away, which was your unity, your connection to the land, your connection to the planet, and your understanding of yourself.

Besides that, simply by virtue of the amount of time and energy spent doing all this, you're insulating yourself from the negative influences that are out there on the outside that affect all of us, and particularly affect Native people who lack the cultural means to balance and understand themselves in this outside life unless they completely surrender to it. Assimilation is still a possibility in this society, although you do pay a spiritual price for that.

It's been a long journey from understanding decolonization as hating the White Man, hating the Indian Act, which I still do. Nothing personal against any white people here, the White Man is a metaphor for white power as it's been put on top of us, and yes I hate that. And I hate the idea that one society, one group of people think they have the one right way and everything else has to accommodate. That's what reconciliation is, that's what Indian policy is. That's what mainstream society's view of Native society still is, really: "You guys were left behind. You guys are somewhat backwards. You guys, I don't know what's wrong with you but you're not keeping up with progress." That's the general sense of things, and I still hate that. But I'm not obsessing about it because I have kids now, and I know that the kids need to learn how to be Native; they don't need to hear me hating on the White Man all the time. They get small doses of it. Just to keep them motivated. They are Mohawks after all, so I've got to keep them motivated. But I also want them to spend most of their time as young men learning how to be young Indigenous men in terms of their responsibility.

What's my responsibility? To wait for the eventual collapse of Western civilization? I don't think so. Wait for the resolution of land claims? That's just as likely. Considering all of these options, the real option for me is expressing ourselves in terms of the dedicated commitment to loving our mother the Earth and teaching our children their responsibilities. It's that simple. Before, it seemed so complicated for me, but now it's so simple. If my kids can be more Indigenous than I am, then to me that is decolonization.

I've still got all those other things I hate, all those things I fight, and I totally support other people that have different commitments, but I think that this is an element of decolonization that hasn't really been talked about. It was assumed that people would heal by doing those other things, but that hasn't been the case. And so what this does is kind of expands the notion of decolonization to include these very specific practices and very specific ways: decolonization in a very personal sense and then channeling that.

Here's the political element. A lot of people might say, "That's a beautiful thing you got going. You know you're teaching Native kids how to fish, and you're bringing them to youth camps," and things like that. Great, let them see it that way. But teaching people how to be Indigenous on the land is not an end in itself. It's radical because what you want is strong generations of Mohawks willing to defend that right. What you'll find, I believe, is that when kids grow up that way – when they grow up speaking the language and understanding it, the ceremony, they are being taught how to be a true Onkwehónweh. And when they are that person, they're not going to let anyone take that away again. They're not going to let anything happen to that environment. And they're certainly not going to let another St. Lawrence Seaway come through and wreck it all.

Kaniatarowanenneh, Kanien'ke, 2017

I never feel so alive as when I am in the power flow of our great river.

WARRIOR SCHOLARSHIP

Adapted from an interview at the University of Victoria as part of doctoral research by Veronica Tawhai, a scholar from Aotearoa/New Zealand, on March 18, 2013.

Higher education is thought of by many as a pathway to empower our people with the knowledge, tools, and networks to become change agents in the struggle to liberate our Nations from colonial dominion. But it has not been that long since the days when our Elders were, instead of encouraging us to get educated, warning us of the dangers of immersing ourselves in non-Indigenous ways of knowing and submitting to the deculturing authority and assimilative intentions of the white people who control the business of higher education in North America. I felt this tension for all of the years I was involved in academia, both as a student and as a professor. In this conversation, I attempted to reason through, in Indigenous terms, a justification for being in academia. I argued for seeing education as a battlefield, which is what I believed to be the only way for an Indigenous person to see and operate within educational institutions – these pillars of colonial infrastructure – without being co-opted into becoming part of the business of colonization themselves.

VERONICA TAWHAI: *What is it that drew you to education? Why is it that, of all the things you could have done, you chose to be an educator?*

TAIAIAKE ALFRED: I could give you two answers and they are both true. One is that it presented itself to me as an option for a career that I didn't expect or even have that much knowledge of. When I did my bachelor's degree, and even to a certain extent up to my master's, I was expecting to do them as a terminal process. I was in the military when I was younger, and I was pretty taken by that. The only commonality between that and what I do now is that it was action-oriented, and I always loved doing stuff rather than talking about it. I was in the US Marines, and I figured if I went to university I could get a degree and be an officer, not just a grunt, and I could be in intelligence or – I don't know, I had some crazy plans. When you're nineteen years old, you don't always have the most consolidated vision of your whole life and the best political sense. Then as I went through university what's supposed to happen happened. My eyes got opened. I started to realize more about myself and where I came from. It triggered a lot of thoughts and instincts that I had suppressed. Because you grow up in this colonized reality, and you may believe that you're part of a Nation, that your people have the right to their homeland, but it's kind of suppressed because you're like, "That's never going to happen." Then I started to study these things – political strategies and visions for revolution – I was like, "Oh, okay, maybe this can happen. Maybe I should be using this education to figure out a way to get our damn land back, or how to revive our Nation." Of course this had been going on in our community, but I was more taken with the "big things" happening in the world, I wanted to be involved in the "real action" as I thought of it at the time. But now I was like, "Hey, I've got this going on right in my own community. In fact, my community and the people in it are leading in this area. They are leading thinkers and have been, and our people have been at the forefront of this idea of anti-imperialism. There's a lot happening that I can get involved in."

I did my bachelor's degree in East Asian history, and I didn't know really that there were opportunities, but I did pretty good and my professor at the time said, "Oh you should go to graduate school." I had to go down to the library and actually look up what "graduate school" was and look up master's degrees. I knew that professors had advanced degrees, but I had never really looked into it. Then once I looked into it and talked to my supervisor, I thought I would give it a try. I chose a combined master's–PhD because I thought if I didn't like it, or if they failed me, I could still get a master's. I still had it in my mind at the time that I might do something besides Native politics. In the meantime, halfway through my bachelor's degree I started working in the political life of our community. In our tribal government I was the assistant to the Chief and the communications guy – I wrote letters, press releases, followed him around taking notes, and I would get to be part of these big strategy sessions they had for land claims negotiations. So I got a political education that way. Within the first two weeks of grad school I pretty much had decided that I was going to be working in my community and contributing that way. So my whole graduate school was oriented toward that.

I realized from my own experience that education could be transformational. All of this happened to me in higher education. I learned more about being Mohawk, I became more connected to my community, I did all this stuff by going to university. I realized it's got to be a good thing, at least for some of us. Then when I started teaching when I was twenty-seven, I started to see how you could shape people's minds, take Native people and give them proper advice and expose them to a vision. Then with the non-Native students you can correct any misconceptions they have, turn them inside out and let them flail around intellectually and psychologically for a while, and then pick up the pieces and make them into, hopefully, settler allies. Again, a pragmatic vision. I wasn't attracted to the idea of sitting alone in a room doing scholarly research. It was about finding ways to use this environment to get our land back: that was always the main question. Over the years people have said, "Why are you here, why are you doing this? Why are you committed to education?" It's because I see it as a battleground.

What I'm telling you is the way I came to realize it over time. But I realized too I had a foundational perspective on education to begin with, because I had a military background and came from a radical community that was involved in politics and political battles all the time. I always saw information or the "propaganda war" as very important. Communications and information and education to me, I always recognized their importance, although it took time for me to come to realize that that was my strength. Once I did realize it, I pursued it fully. I didn't realize it on my own, it took time, and people saying, "Oh, you're good at doing that" or "You should be the one." By the time I finished my PhD, people in my community were always calling on me to say, "Okay, you need to be the one to speak to the media, write the letter, write the policy," and it turned out that was my strength: being able to argue and communicate. It's a combination of intellectual skills and training and then just personality. You have to enjoy it, and you have to have a certain knack for knowing your audience. I was never much of a big fist fighter but arguing, I enjoyed that a lot. So that's how I got into it.

Over time I realized the power of it. I experience it through our students, seeing how they get transformed and how their lives change. That's the big attraction for me, the engagement with Native students, to decolonize them and to see it happen in their life. It's a pretty good job too in practical terms, a good stable base from which you can operate if you want to maintain your political activism and your community activism. Often people suffer because they don't have income; their lives can be a mess because of that. I've got this stable job, I've got tenure, I can say what I want. I can get involved in a lot of things. It's pretty hard for them to take this all away from me, so I might as well use it to its full extent. I've come to appreciate being in that position.

Here in Canada, people have seen what some of us slightly older ones have done, and they get into that right off the bat, without having the solid foundation. They've got to realize that they're in the university. Some people think I'm totally radical. Well, I am, but I'm also very appreciative of the reality of the situation and respectful of the authority structures that exist in this society. Not accepting or legitimizing them, but accepting them as a reality that we need to operate through. So I'm never compromised in my political activities or statements, but at the same time I've always done what's absolutely necessary in order to guarantee me that voice. A lot of people just do the political activism and expect that because they're a Native in a university they're going be somewhat protected, which is not the case. It never has been and is certainly not now, because there are a lot of Native people who want your job. There's a lot of Native, younger scholars coming up and there's competition. Every job we have, it used to be one Native applying for it and a whole bunch of white people. Now it's all Natives. You really have to be good at what you do. I think that the people who stand out in previous generations as the most outspoken ones were the ones that knew this from the beginning.

What do you need to have to be protected in a university? You need to have a CV, and a publication record and a teaching record, and you need to do all of the things that regular professors do but more, because that "more" is your shield. If you just do the minimum you're fair game for anyone. If you do more and you beat them at their own game, the level of respect rises, but also they have to fight through a lot more in order to get you. If you're winning awards and publishing more than they are, how are they going to say that you're not doing your fair share? Which is usually the tactic they take. They don't come right at you. They'll be like, "Oh, ah, maybe you should ease up on your political activism because you're not really producing or contributing as much as you should." I can say, "I have three books. How many do you have?" That's the kind of attitude I think you need to have, but you can only have that attitude if you can back it up. I put a lot of work into publishing in the earlier part of my career in order to have that foundation. Once you get tenure you can say "Okay, now you can all kiss my *** basically, now I'm going to do what I need to do." That's a lesson. A lot of people know that, but a lot of people don't. You get too many people thinking that they can just be activists in the university without doing the other part of it, and it's not just doing the minimum; it's doing more than the average white guy.

VT: *What is it that you want from your students? What is your vision for those students?*

TA: What I want from them is a 110 per cent effort first off, in order to go through this process that we're laying out in front of them and guiding them through: to know themselves better as a colonized person and to understand what decolonization is, what transformation is, based on Indigenous political teachings, and then, number one, to be capable of being useful in the Native community; and then be committed to actually going out there and doing it. I want them to have the key set of teachings they need to be transformational leaders in our Native community. Said simply, that's the goal.

But it takes a lot of effort and suffering on their part in order to get there. So the openness to that is in the first instance what we demand of them, and then it's our job to lead them through this training program in order to create a person that is capable of helping, in a serious way, Native communities transform themselves and then again, get their land back.

VT: *What do you mean by "suffer"? Do you mean stay up, studying all night?*

TA: Yes, well that's part of it, but I think about it more in terms of suffering psychologically and spiritually. I think everybody comes in to a program like this on a base level, even if they're humble people, thinking that they're smart and they've got it figured out. They just want some guidance and help. When they realize that they are part of the problem and that their behaviors and their attitudes are actually the very thing that they're claiming to be critical of, it causes a psychological fracturing and an inability to function. They're judging themselves as they go through this process and they recognize themselves, but they don't yet have an alternative way of being. It's always that process of being open and stripping away, and then recognizing how colonized they are. Then there's a lag period where we give them opportunities to replace their bad ideas with the good ideas, and it's in that period there, usually in the middle of the semester, where they suffer. They haven't yet grasped onto a new idea that they can then transform in their own mind and then through their practice in their newly decolonizing personality. It's in the period when they know they're wrong but they don't yet have the answer that everything seems kind of bleak. They're like, "I thought that I was decolonized, but I realized that I'm still colonized, and if I thought I was decolonized before maybe that will happen again." There's all kinds of crazy questions. We're here to hold them together and to keep forcing them to continue thinking through this so that they'll find the answer that feels right to them and then they'll build on that. It happens [snaps fingers] like that. I always tell students when they come in, "Here's a line graph of your emotional state. For the next three months it's going to go whiiiish-boom, and then it'll come back again." And it always happens. When they work through the material that we present them with – it's all the standards, like anti/decolonizing literature plus our Indigenous critiques – they get excited at first because then they start to get all this information and these new perspectives. Then it starts to hit home that they and/or their communities are so colonized that it seems beyond hope. Boom. But then they start to get the Indigenous teachings and philosophies, and they get really excited again about taking in these new ideas and it starts to pick up again. So it is personal suffering.

There is also the workload in our Indigenous Governance program. We put them through pretty heavy reading and writing, and beyond that we also make them go into the community and take part in all these political things. For some of them the first three months must seem like a whirlwind. In the second half of the first year we start asking them to put together a strategic vision for action, to critique other peoples' visions and then to put together their own based on what we're doing. Then I involve them all the time in things that I'm doing, and things that our larger network is doing, and it's a lot of stress on people. We're also judgmental about their bodily choices in terms of what they eat and their activity level, and then inevitably it comes up in terms of – for a lot of them – their marriage situation and things like that. All of these things happen in a really compressed time period, and so I see a lot of suffering. But most of them come through it, most of them do. The only ones that don't really make it through the program are those that are not willing to be honest about themselves and not really willing to be honest about how much help they need or what kind of help they need. Anybody that's honest and open, they might suffer, but they'll get the help because we have a big network of people – Elders, healers, teachers, friends, and colleagues – all kinds of people that could help. But we have failures every year because people just stay closed. They don't want to admit it: they don't want to look beyond their very practical vision of job training, "I'm here to get a certificate in order to get a better job in the Government" kind of thing. Those kinds of people just fail. They usually last a week or two and that's it. So we get some students like that. You just know after a few weeks as you get to know them that it's just not connecting.

Then the challenge that we take on, my colleague and I, mostly me because I'm the bad guy, he's the nice guy. I tend to take on the role of provoking or causing crisis because that's what it comes down to. It's like we have got to find a way to engage with these students. If they're going to cruise through here thinking that it's all fun and games and take the easy route, and if they're not willing to open themselves up and engage with people for transformational purposes, let's do it the hard way then. Let's put them in situations that are going to result in some kind of a crisis for them where they're going to have to open up or other people are going to force them to. Those situations tend to be a bit dicier in managing, but we don't let anyone just cruise through. Everybody has issues that need to be resolved, that's our philosophy, and so that's my job to find out what that issue is for each person and then to poke at it a little bit.

VT: *Honestly that is so amazing, that's what I want.*

TA: It's usually me deciding that the student needs to be placed in an uncomfortable situation that they can't handle. For example, it could be a white student who is brilliant academically and is a little bit arrogant about it, and he's just cruising too easily through the academics. How would that student feel if he was to participate in a sweat lodge ceremony where he knows nothing and his knowledge counts for nothing? How would he react in that situation? Or, how would the student who thinks that they're such a great communicator feel when I call on them unexpectedly to be a spokesperson for a certain cause or to take my place at a talk somewhere? Or what if someone's brilliant and has all the culture but is out of shape? And we say, "Now we're going to hike up the mountain and yes, it's part of your requirement. It's part of our mentorship class, we're all going to hike up a mountain. Can you do it or not?" Then people break or they rise to the challenge, and when they rise to the challenge it's awesome. It's just like, "Hey, you didn't think you could do it, but you did it. Great." But lots of times they snap and they're just like, "That's it." There's the opening, and once the opening is there, as an educator that's where you come in: "Okay, alright, now I've got you." So you use that as the window to what they need to learn about themselves and maybe what they should be learning generally.

VT: *Can you give an example of how you engage them?*

TA: Basically I tell them what they don't want to hear, and it causes them a lot of grief. It causes them to react to me and then it causes an emotional breakthrough. Then it's like, "Okay, let's talk about this. Let's work through it," and it forces them to let go of this persona they were trying to put out there. It causes them to think, "Is Taiaiake right or is he just messing with me?" I am messing with them a little bit, but there is some truth to what I say.

I'm just giving you these as examples of how you have to personalize it. You look at the person. Think about where that person comes from, what are their strengths and weaknesses, and come up with an educational program for that person. Not like an educational program to which that person fits in. There's that, there's the structure to the program, but everyone that comes in, we're small enough to deal with everyone as an individual, and when I look at the class list at the beginning of the year I don't just say, "Hmm, student, bachelor's degree," I look at their age, their background, and community, all that stuff, to get a sense of where they're coming from and what's driving their need to be here, what they're probably bringing with them, their issues. Then I construct some sort of approach to them based on the individual, always willing to be corrected of course, because they may not be what you figure. But you do it for twenty years, you pretty much get a sense of what people are all about. After we've spent a week or two with them, we work out a strategy to work on that person as an individual.

You have to be willing to take the heat as an educator. It's easy to let them just go and do their work, but if you want to engage them on a personal level it takes a lot of extra work and it creates stress sometimes. But you have to be willing to do that. You also have to be willing to alienate them too and not feel as an educator you have to please everybody. You can't live by the course evaluation. If you live by the course evaluation then you wouldn't do any of this, right? You'd just say, "Oh, I'm going to do whatever makes the students happy." So you have to say, "Damn the course evaluation" and then just do what you need to do as an Indigenous educator. We always get good course evaluations anyway, aside from the one or two.

VT: *So what you're saying is that it is actually the breaking point that is the opportunity moment to teach?*

TA: To me it's all about pushing them to that breaking point. Some people think that sounds overly harsh or too much like the Marine Corps, but I think that any Indigenous method is predicated on that too. What is the ceremony about, the vision quest, other than reaching your breaking point and having a transformational change through new knowledge coming into your life, whether it's spiritual knowledge or material knowledge? To me this is taking Indigenous methods and putting them in practice in academia. But yeah, it is the breaking point. So if someone's awesome academically and they're really good in class, I'm going to keep pushing them until they can't keep up anymore. Then we'll see what happens. We'll see what they're made of and we'll see what they need. That happens all the time. Sometimes it's just something small, someone's perception of them, you know? Like you just say, "Sorry, you can't really relate to what we're talking about here, and I wouldn't really expect you to because you're Canadian and this is for Native people. So maybe you shouldn't talk for this class. Maybe you should just sit and listen." That drives some people crazy because it really affects their sense of entitlement and privilege, but also it's a judgment on them, like, "What? He thinks that I'm not capable?" And I'm saying, "No, you're not capable. You haven't shown me that you're capable." Or maybe we organize a radical politics event and for that reason we have to be assured that the people involved can handle it. Maybe I say, "Based on what I've seen, sorry, you two or three, I can't invite you to this because you haven't really demonstrated that you're committed to that. Your work seems to be more orientated toward governmental processes and stuff, maybe that's where you should be while this stuff is going on." That drives some people crazy, right? So they have to go through that, process the anger, and you get to see how they relate to being angry and whether they lose it or are still coherent, and then they have to rationalize if they want to participate or not. Then they have to engage with me, and I might say, "Well, it's good to hear what you're talking about, but you're not demonstrating that. We're not seeing that. You may say that you're radical, but you seem like a Government Indian to me." That's a crisis point for some people.

So yes, you can see how it's a bit manipulative. But I think it is all part of our responsibility. What is a vision quest? Sitting on a mountain for four days with no food; that's a manipulative act. You put young people through that, for what though? It's the intention, and it's with the confidence that it's going to lead to something transformational and good. I don't have any problem being labeled as being a manipulator because what else are we here for except to manipulate people's lives through our program in order to help them learn? I don't see this as any different than any kind of learning process that happened with our Ancestors. Our Ancestors were a lot tougher than people think, certainly the way it's talked about in academia today. That's what ceremony was all about: fasting, sitting through hot rocks, sweat lodge, running for how many hundreds of miles, tattooing, and all these kinds of things. That was suffering. You need to do these kinds of things and you need to suffer. Going through an academic program is not some sort of a vision quest, not the way they're normally conducted. There's very little suffering in today's world. It's too comfortable, and I think the results show. Comfort leads to mediocrity; suffering leads to excellence.

VT: *What is it that you then do? I know you said it differs for every person.*

TA: That's when the real mentorship happens, because then they're in a place of acknowledging with humility that they need to learn a different way of being, whether it's in a technical sense of practice on a certain skill set, or just a way of being as an Indigenous person or as a non-Indigenous person in solidarity with us. They have to model a new way off of you, so the relationship gets closer at that point where you start talking to them about "What do you feel you need? If you're in crisis right now, what would make you feel stronger? Like, is it more knowledge? Is it more confidence? Is it more support?" So whatever their needs are, it's our responsibility to meet them. We can't give them everything, but within our program we have the capacity and the ability to address them. So then I have to figure it out. Say this person is saying, "I'm at a loss for motivation because now I'm realizing that I'm white, I'm a colonizer, and I don't really see a place for me in this thing, and you're right, I can't understand." Then I say, "Okay, maybe you need to go into a community if you've never had that opportunity, and maybe you need to experience that environment in order to find a place for yourself. I can't tell you what your role's going to be, but maybe you need to go have an experience in a Native community or in a Native organization under the guidance of people that we know and trust that are part of our network, to help you figure that out for yourself." Or "Here's where you're missing some intellectual understanding, so maybe you need to do a different set of readings." Or "Maybe we just need to have some more conversations so that you can appreciate more what I was trying to say to you." That kind of thing. It just depends on the individual, but I guess the difference between exposing weakness and supporting the person is actually committing to do more work with that student, to take the extra step and say, "Okay, what can I give you now? There's an answer and there's a place for you in this struggle and you have to figure it out, but I'm going to help you. I'm not going to tell you, but I'm going to help you. Whatever you need, you tell me, and if you don't tell me anything, I'll tell you what you need. If you're just going to sit there and be this blob of crisis, then I'll start telling you stuff to do, but I'd prefer if you said with some self-reflection, 'I think this is what I want and need.'"

For example, we had the one non-Native who was great, but she couldn't speak in the second semester because of some spiritual-psychological paralysis she was in because she realized that her whole family and her whole existence was colonial and she couldn't really see any way out. So she just refused to speak. "Everything I say is colonial. I can't even rationalize me being here. I'm here now but I don't know why." What do you do with that? We said, "Well you have to trust us then. You got to this point because of our knowledge and experience, so now you're going to trust us to take you forward." I said, "Here's the first thing. I want you to talk to four or five other women who are like you – white, committed to work in this area, having gone through crisis, and now are doing productive things that we value in our program. I'm recommending them to you. I want you to go and not do this standard paper that the other students are writing; I want you to go and have a conversation with these five women and then write a paper on how you're going to be just like them and how you're going to join that group for the next white student that comes through so that I can send them to you. That's what I want you to do." Sometimes you need to go outside the rules and say "Forget about your paper on Paulo Freire, do this instead. Because that's what you need."

VT: *That's a great example of when your white student is going through the guilt thing. Do you have any insights into how our own people react? With our people I usually find intense anger.*

TA: We get that a lot too, usually in the men in our experience. There's angry women too, but they tend to deal with it differently, I find they tend to internalize it. The women get angry, but it tends to manifest itself in self-destructive behaviors, whereas the men tend to act out in these very obvious ways. Both are harmful. I'm not averse to anger. I think that anger is absolutely necessary and should be cultivated, and I think that we all need to be angry, but at the same time we need to really understand the proper place for it as a motivating force, not as something that you allow to control you. How we deal with it is by placing it on them and showing them that the way that they're processing their anger is very egotistical. Say a guy is walking around, angry at this, angry at that, causing a scene and yelling and going to Starbucks and causing a fight because it's so colonial and all this stuff, I'd just say, "Hey, it's not all about you. You don't think that everybody's angry? We're angry, I'm angry every day, I've been angry for a lot longer than you've been alive. Have some self-discipline, have some self-control, and be useful. What you're doing is being very egotistical. You're using your anger to get attention. Figure out a way to use it to be useful. If a situation arises where that kind of anger is necessary, hey man, call it up. If we're in a riot or a blockade or a big fight, you better be able to call up that anger if you want to survive and get in there and scrap. But walking around the university, sitting in Starbucks, come on. You're a tough guy and everybody knows that, but what are you proving? Everything you claim to be angry about, either all of us are suffering, or if it's particular to you, maybe you suffered some kind of abuse or mistreatment, or something was taken away from you and your family, hey, welcome to being Native. Figure out a way to use the anger as a weapon, not something that controls you."

That's how we deal with it. Basically we don't take anybody's bullshit. I grew up on a reserve and I know a lot of angry people, like anybody who grew up in a Native community. I experienced that my whole life, so I'm not about to sit here and waste my time with some guy acting out. So it's basically that, it's like "Come on man, get over yourself. You want to act out on your anger, go get drunk with your friends and get in a fight or something. But when you come here into this environment, you don't have any right to act that way." Similarly with the women, "You don't have a right to be aggressive or passive-aggressive in class, and judgmental and all that kind of stuff among your colleagues. You're not allowed to do that. This is an environment for learning and so if you have a problem with someone" – I literally said this recently – "go outside right now. If you two want to act all angry go outside and fight, I don't care, I'll watch from outside and see who wins. Then come back in class and figure out a way to work with each other."

It's about self-discipline, maturity. It's a lesson, it takes a while, but it's an absolute quality that you need in order to be involved in Indigenous politics in the long term. Otherwise you'll burn out or alienate people and you just won't be useful to the struggle. So I relate it to that. "You want to work in this business, you better figure out a way to control your anger, to keep it, but figure out a way to not let it color everything you say and do." If you can't manage your anger and use it in a disciplined way, it's not part of the way we do things and people have got to move on.

VT: *Do you consider any of this to be "citizenship education" or do you have any thoughts on citizenship?*

TA: No I've never thought of it in that way. In fact my reaction to just the word *citizen* is negative because to me, at least in a North American context, it's used as a kind of code word for "liberal citizenship," that is, belonging to a state. It has an anti-Indigenous tone to it. The idea of citizenship is interesting, but it's funnelled through the political community that's been created in this colonial situation, so it's almost impossible to talk about alternative concepts of citizenship. It always comes through an institutional lens – electoral, limited by constitution, civil rights – there's no conception of citizenship outside of that political, legal construction. We sometimes try to talk about citizenship in terms of "I'm a citizen of the Mohawk Nation," but even so I don't think that's right. I wrote something critical of the idea of using citizenship as the concept to talk about membership in a Native Nation because citizenship implies acceptance of the kind of political structures that's represented by states, not our own Indigenous political communities.[1] That's the extent to which I've engaged with it. The way that that concept is operationalized in North America as a technical concept, we use the word *citizenship* a lot because it was only recently that Natives were granted citizenship – including voting rights and things like that. So it's talked about in the context of "our full realization of our rights as citizens of this country." I think that's a pretty colonial statement. To me any discussion of citizenship is accepting of the idea of assimilation into the larger political community, and that's why I stay away from it.

Sasquatch Dance, Lekwungen Territory, 2018

To embody and dance such mysterious energy was a special honor.

CONSTITUTIONAL RECOGNITION AND COLONIAL DOUBLESPEAK

Adapted from an interview for ABC Radio National,
Melbourne, Australia, November 27, 2013.

I happened to be in Australia amid a national debate on whether or not to enshrine the inherent rights of the Aboriginal people of that continent into the constitution of the Australian state. At the same time, people there were weighing the political implications of treaty-making, as up to that point Australia had not entered into formal treaties or constitutionalized the rights of the Original Peoples of that land. Encouraged by the influential Aboriginal leader, and my friend, Marcia Langton, Australia's national broadcaster invited me to share my views about the lessons from the Canadian experience with legalizing and constitutionalizing the rights of Indigenous Peoples.

INTERVIEWER: *Prime Minister Tony Abbott was speaking earlier this year, promising to devote efforts to the recognition of Aboriginal and Torres Strait Islander Peoples in the Australian Constitution. It's just one voice in what's a pretty concerted campaign for constitutional recognition of Indigenous Australians. But our next guest would argue that constitutional recognition might not be all that it's cracked up to be. Taiaiake, that idea of constitutional recognition, to go back to the Canadian experience; this is something which occurred in Canada in 1982, and I think you'd argue that the results have been mixed.*

TA: Yes. The constitutional recognition exercise in Canada was one that represented a potential development of a decolonized and just relationship between the newcomers' society and the Original Peoples. The formulation of section 35 of the Canadian Constitution, which is the section that recognizes Indigenous rights, represented *either* a bridge to that future *or* an instrument for the Canadian government to reinforce its old colonial practices and ideas. And I think that's the important thing to consider in any kind of exercise like this: What is it that the government is trying to accomplish? Are they recognizing Indigenous Peoples on their own terms? Are they trying to foist another false identity and false sense of Aboriginality on the Original Peoples?

INTERVIEWER: *Or are they making a recognition that perhaps serves the interests, in a funny way, of the colonial population rather than the First Peoples population? A soothing of guilt, perhaps?*

TA: Exactly. And I think that's probably driving a lot of people's celebration of constitutional recognition, because they're assuming that it's not going to fundamentally challenge the basis of the relationship.

INTERVIEWER: *Is that a matter of the detail of that constitutional amendment or the precise words used? I mean, what in the Canadian experience was offered in that recognition?*

TA: I think it was both. The meaning of the actual technical wording of the amendment has been playing out in the Canadian context in the courts and in politics ever since 1982. There's the phrasing of it: "the existing aboriginal and treaty rights ... are hereby recognized and affirmed." The question is, What is existing, and what is recognition? That's been open for the courts to interpret, amid, of course, advocacy on both sides by Aboriginal Peoples and by the Canadian government that wants to keep things pretty much reflective of the status quo. And so the courts are left to determine the meaning of those terms. So that's one aspect of it.

The other is the more fundamental question about the basic intent. Is there sincerity on the part of the government to really redress the historical wrongs of colonialism and to have a just relationship? In Canada I think that the fact that this constitutional amendment was forced on the government by external political pressure from Great Britain and from internal political activity at the time, meant that they weren't sincerely committed to restoring – I use the word *restoring* – the original relationship: the treaty-based Nation-to-Nation relationship between Native Peoples and the Canadian state.

INTERVIEWER: *In this country the conversation around a constitutional recognition has sort of overwhelmed an earlier* *conversation around a treaty between Australian Indigenous Peoples and Australian white peoples. And I think you would argue that that treaty would be a beginning point, before a constitutional recognition.*

TA: I think so, in the way that people understand treaty as a fundamental agreement that is solemnized and recognizes the fundamental equality of the two parties to the agreement. It creates a commitment on the part of the two parties to recognize both the independence of each other and the interdependency of each other on the land. That's what we mean by treaty in the Canadian context. Unfortunately even this has fallen victim to kind of a colonial doublespeak in the sense that we have a treaty process in Canada, but it's not leading to anything like the relationship I just described. In fact, even the word *treaty* has come to mean something of a process by which Canadian First Nations surrender their underlying Aboriginal title in exchange for some kind of enhanced status beyond a municipality in the Canadian governmental system.

INTERVIEWER: *You just can't trust the colonizers.*

TA: You said it!

INTERVIEWER: *Taiaiake, you're in Australia for the Narrm Oration for the University of Melbourne Institute for Indigenous Development, speaking of colonial powers and trust. Your talk is about the Resurgence against contemporary colonialism – tell us about this idea.*

TA: Contemporary colonialism is a way of thinking about the ongoing practices that continue to harm Aboriginal Peoples and continue to replicate the things that we identify with the historical process of colonization. If you boil it right down, Native Peoples were subjected to the process of colonization in terms of losing their land, losing connection to the land, having their communities disrupted, their ability to continue their culture was not something that they could do anymore. Colonization is usually thought of by settler people as something that happened in times of their ancestors. I think that both in Australia and in Canada there are ongoing processes which continued to disconnect people from land, which continued to disrupt Native families, which continue to undermine the ability of Native people to have healthy lives and to strengthen their communities by doing their cultural practices on their land. If something is doing that – it's colonial. It's not historical; it's not people with felt hats and muskets coming to take land away in some distant colonial era. In fact, we are all the colonizers because we inhabit a country that prevents Indigenous people from being Indigenous.

INTERVIEWER: *That's the great disconnection surely in this whole conversation between First Peoples and colonial peoples. In this country it's dismissed as having a black armband view of history, that you don't assume the guilt of the acts of previous generations. What you're suggesting is that, of course, that endures and, of course, that fundamental relationship as enacted in colonial times is the absolute core of contemporary issues of disadvantage, dispossession, dislocation.*

TA: Yes. And I'm not a big fan of guilt as a political tool. I think what guilt does is it paralyzes people, and it alienates people. What I am a big fan of is people taking responsibility for their privilege and for the things that allow them to have the society that they have and enjoy.

And one of those responsibilities concerns the crimes that were committed in their name that allow them to have this prosperity. And so it's not pointing at someone saying "You are guilty." It's saying, "You need to take responsibility for making amends and fixing a fundamental wrong in your life, which is the fact that you, as a settler, have inherited stolen property; have a history that you're benefiting from in terms of the prosperity you have; that people were subjected to heinous crimes; and that we continue to institutionalize this in this society so you to continue to benefit." And that may sound like a guilt trip to a lot of people, but it's not really; if you think of it as a responsibility, that allows you to overcome it. If you accept that it's a responsibility, the next step is to say, "Well, what do I need to do to live up to that responsibility as a person of good conscience, as a person who believes in fundamental tenets of justice?" As opposed to just painting one side of the equation with a broad stroke of guilt.

INTERVIEWER: *And if it's guilt, it's a thing that can be changed by palliatives, like adjustments to a constitution, as opposed to any sort of concrete action. Where is this conversation at in Canada?*

TA: In Canada, what we're facing right now is a real turning point. I think what we have is a younger generation of people who are realizing what we're talking about and who are demanding not only from the Canadian government but from their own established leaders, a fundamental change in the relationship, and they're not willing to settle anymore for any of those palliatives. Let me say too that there are a lot of Native people, prominent Native people who believe that we shouldn't talk about colonization, that it's time to move on.

INTERVIEWER: *Those kinds of arguments exist here too.*

TA: Yeah. And so the younger people are saying, No, what we really need to do is address that fundamental basis of colonization. We need a relationship with the land that means something: we need the ability to continue to speak our languages, to relearn our languages, to conduct ourselves on our land as Indigenous people. That's decolonization: things that address that and allow us to do that, to allow our children to be more Indigenous than we are; that's decolonization. Never mind the political grandstanding over self-government, over treaties, over reconciliation, and all of these things. To the extent those big things help kids be more Indigenous and happier and healthier in their territory, great, but for the most part, what we've seen is that they're distractions. It's a politics of distraction versus this real move to have an Indigenous Resurgence movement in our communities so that our people can be stronger in the future.

We Are Warriors, Lheidli T'enneh Territory, 2019

We drum to call for the warrior spirit to motivate
our boys and men once again.

ON BEING AND BECOMING INDIGENOUS

Adapted from the Narrm Oration delivered at the University of Melbourne on November 28, 2013.

I was honored to deliver the Narrm Oration, an annual event in which influential Indigenous people from around the world are invited to present their vision of possible futures for Indigenous people in Australia. The thought that came to my mind as I took the stage was the transnational and perpetual nature of colonialism and how all Indigenous Peoples the world over share in the common experience of being dispossessed of their territories, subjugated physically and politically, and subjected to brainwashing about who they are and what the causes and solutions are to the problems they face as people, communities, and Nations. As I stood up to speak, I decided to hold up the *Kahswentha*, the Two-Row Wampum, I was carrying with me; share what I knew of its meaning; and talk about the principles that guide our struggle as Onkwehónweh in North America. I hoped that the people gathered on that territory would take something from it to further the struggle of the Aboriginal people of that continent to restore themselves to their rightful place as cultures and governments in their homelands.

I'm looking forward to the opportunity in the next little while to bring our minds together on one of the central questions facing not only Indigenous people, but all of us who live in countries with colonial histories and colonial presents: How do we transcend the relationships that have gone into forming the societies that we have inherited? How do we transcend the histories of racism, the histories of dispossession, and the histories that encompass injustice, as opposed to the just relationships that we all hope to have in the countries that we inhabit? In this sense, Canada is no different than Australia, and so I feel I have a connection and something to share with you all in terms of the experience that I've had personally, that my people of the Mohawk Nation have experienced, and that we are confronting today collectively as Indigenous Peoples. And, I'll also add, as non-Indigenous peoples.

If I gave this talk fourteen years ago, which is the last time I was in Melbourne, I wouldn't have added that last sentence. But that's something that's changed in Canada in the last couple of years. We've had a real transformation of the conception of the struggle. Previously we were in an era that defined the colonial situation as Us versus Them, as a problem that was a historical reality of an injustice that needed to be confronted but confronted by us as an Indigenous people. We were defined as the problem, "the Indian problem." The problems that our people are suffering – lack of clean drinking water, substandard housing, all of the social and psychological challenges that our people face – were seen to be a failure on the part of our people to adapt to the natural reality of the development of a modern society.

Fortunately, there's a silver lining to climate change. People are starting to question the entire basis of Western capitalism and societies that have developed industrial economies. There's a little bit of suspicion as to whether or not countries like Canada represent the apex of human civilization: there may be some trade-offs, and there may be some problems with the way that these societies have been constructed. One of the realizations that comes from thinking through history in a different way, and thinking through the problems that are besetting communities, is that people are beginning to recognize that they have some form of responsibility for transforming the fundamental institutions and relationships in so-called Canada that do not necessarily focus the effort on redefining Indigenous people or helping Indigenous people to overcome challenges in order to fit into that larger society. That's a fundamental shift. It's something of a psychic change, but it's also beginning to manifest in the way that politics is practiced, in the way that change is being constructed in Canada today.

Our Histories Have Not Ended

First of all, I'm going to back up and talk about the fundamental concept, which is my conception of colonization and the framework that we use for confronting all these issues in Canada.

Colonization, for most Canadians, is something historical. People think of colonization as a time in the past when their ancestors from Europe came and did things, both positive and negative, that resulted in the formation of the societies that we call Canada, the United States, the Latin American countries, Australia. People think about European peoples coming with a pioneering spirit and, with a lot of determination, getting a foothold on these continents. They put the hard work into developing these institutions and relationships and societies, which are now paying off in terms of the prosperity and the level of comfort that people enjoy in the situation that we live in today.

People think about colonization in the past, and it's true that it is a historic period and a historical phenomenon. From the 1500s on, people came from Europe to Canada and in effect dispossessed the Indigenous Peoples of their lands and imposed their own belief systems and ways of being. They came with the intent of imposing their own law and their own sovereignty. Those things happened. But the problem in using this framework for understanding and resolving issues today arises when people imagine that it is a strictly historical concept. People imagine that because we are now Indigenous Peoples in universities, speaking English, we're Christians or post-Christians for most of us, that we drive cars and live in single-family dwellings that resemble everyone else's, that colonization is in the past. This is a fundamental problem for those of us who are still living with the legacy of colonization in terms of the fact that our land was dispossessed, our belief systems and our cultures were disrupted, our families were dispersed, and all of the other things that people associate with that historic era.

If colonization is defined as the intent to take land away, to impose foreign laws and to disrupt culture, if that defines colonization in 1609, it still pretty much defines the relationship today. Colonization is not an historical reality; it's a contemporary political, social, cultural, and psychological framework for the relationship between Indigenous Peoples and non-Indigenous peoples in countries like Canada.

We're not in a post-colonial society; we're in a contemporary colonial society. For people who are part of the settler state it has become necessary to redefine themselves in terms which allow them to release their burden of colonial guilt, and so new words, new frameworks, new understandings are used to create legitimacy for their presence on the land, for the things that happened in relation to culture, for the kind of privileges that they claim in relation to Native Peoples and so forth. What is not acknowledged is that colonial processes are just as vital, just as ongoing, just as harmful, and just as present in the lives of the Indigenous population as they were in the 1600s. If you're going to conceptualize a resolution or conceptualize justice in any of these countries, this is the fundamental problem: these societies are built on an ongoing recolonization of Indigenous Peoples that allows non-Indigenous people to continue to enjoy their privileges and prosperity. Admittedly, some of us Indigenous people enjoy them as well. And so what is the fundamental problem of justice and injustice in these societies? It's not that the Natives have failed to keep up.

It's also not the problem that social justice posits: that we should be looking at Indigenous Peoples and trying to elevate them to the same status of material well-being. Of course, we should be doing that. Nobody wants to deny Indigenous people the right to take advantage of all the opportunities to create happiness and health and the like. But that's social justice. That's a conception that is laudable and something we should acknowledge as good in a society. But it's not enough: if we just focus on that, we're only looking at the symptoms. We're not looking at the fundamental problem, which is the land: our dispossession, its continual occupation and use, and the separation of Indigenous Peoples from the fundamental essence and basis of who we are. We have a massive engine generating social, cultural, and psychic discord that leads to more and more and more problems that need to be addressed by social institutions. And tragically, because of the increasing numbers of Indigenous Peoples in Canada, there is an exponential growth of these problems, and the institutions are finding themselves unable to keep up with the issues that Indigenous Peoples are living with because that engine is rolling. That engine is continuing to produce discord, harm, continuing to produce the psychological effects of dispossession.

I focus on the word dispossession because in all the work that I've done over the years, I've ranged in my interest and I've ranged in my experience from looking at this problem as a governmental problem, as a problem of a lack of understanding, or a lack of capacity in our communities and so forth. But I've never really felt like I've understood the problem in the sense that I could look inward, or that I could turn to my family, or I could turn to my community and have 100 per cent confidence that we are moving in the right direction, that we are talking about the right things that are going to lead us confidently to a resolution of this so that I could say to my children and the people in our community, "The future looks good for you guys. If we follow this path, if we do these things, if we fight these fights, if we get involved in these struggles, you will be able to have a happy, healthy, productive life in the future." I've never felt that capacity while I was working on land claims. I've never felt that while I was negotiating treaties, which I did for years. And I never felt confident until I got involved in working on reconnecting people to the land in our Mohawk communities.

Dispossession and Reconnection

If the fundamental objective of colonization was removing Indigenous people from the land so that other people can use it, either for settlement or for economic enterprise and so forth, we're fooling ourselves if we think that we can resolve the problem of colonization without addressing the fundamental need to put Indigenous people back on the land. It's not simply a matter of dealing with the effects of colonization: we have to recognize that the disconnection from the land is more than just economic deprivation or a political injustice. When Native people are disconnected from the land they cannot be Indigenous. They are prevented from living out the basic responsibilities of their Nation in terms of their original teachings, in terms of what it is to speak as an Indigenous person, what it is to be spiritually and culturally connected and to feel Onkwehónweh. Unless you are able to live out your culture and have the connection in your own homeland, to relate to that in a meaningful way, there's really no justice in the relationship at all. There's really no justice in that person's life.

In Canada a lot of effort, including a lot of my own effort, has gone into thinking about colonization and decolonization as political issues, as governance issues. And so it's something when you realize it's all about the land: in Mohawk we say, *khenorónhkwa ionkhi 'nisténha tsi iohontsá:te,* "love your mother, the Earth." That phrase talks about what your responsibility is to the Earth. When you realize that that is the thing that makes you Indigenous, having that intimate relationship, having that kind of connection, fulfilling your responsibility, taking the love, taking the knowledge that comes from the Earth, then settling a legal claim is really not important. It's something that maybe has some benefit to the extent it advances this relationship and allows you to continue to develop a deeper relationship with the land. But if it's simply a legal structure in order to have political control over territory, which your people then take advantage of in order to gain control over the company that's polluting the land, and your people and the younger generation continue to not have access to land to do ceremony and live out their culture on the land, what good is a legal settlement? What good is self-government? What good is a treaty that redefines the relationship if it doesn't actually give the character of your life something different than you had under colonization?

That fundamental thing is that we need to redefine ourselves and to reconstruct our lives in relation to our land and each other – that's where the concept of Indigenous Resurgence comes in. It's a resurgence of a true way of being in the world that is Indigenous. And it's really an answer to the question of what is the basic result of a colonial relationship. All of these other things happen, but in the end, the basic result is you have culturally confused people who are not living on their land, who don't know how to relate to each other in a happy, healthy way, even inside their own body. And you have a situation where those people are subject to control by other people who have agendas to take advantage of them. The individualizing concept of colonization is what led to this turn toward Resurgence, which is this: let's look at recreating the cultural strength, the cultural knowledge, the capacity to love and trust, family relationships, child-rearing, language, knowledge of traditional healing practices, all of these sort of things that give people the ability to stand with some confidence and some security in their own skin and not have to live with the constant anxiety and the anomie that comes from living out someone else's vision of what it is to be an Indigenous person.

In Canada, it's the great struggle that we're undergoing right now, to succeed in this vision of decolonization against the Canadian government's continual effort to impose false conceptions of what it is to be Indigenous on us. When it comes down to it, in Canada today the state is still manipulating identities and creating new conceptions of what it is to be Indigenous that are just as harmful, just as distracting, and just as strong an obstacle to Indigenous healing and re-strengthening as those old terms like *Indian, Redskin, savage,* and so forth were.

Sorry about the Past?

What about the idea of reconciliation? Sounds good. Everybody likes the idea of reconciliation as a concept, but as it's being developed and applied in Canada, it's a problem and, I would say, even a manifestation of contemporary colonialism. In Canada, reconciliation is a whole process and framework and academic paradigm that builds on the notion that the time has come to turn the page on history and become a better, more just society. The Prime Minister of Canada got up in 2008 in Parliament and read an apology. He said, "The treatment of children in Indian Residential Schools is a sad chapter in our *history*"; he said it was all a great mistake, it was entirely unacceptable, it was wrong to take those children from their families and to allow them to be abused in schools by the people who ran those schools.[1] Reconciling with the reality of residential schools and what they represented has become the sole focus of the whole reconciliation framework in Canada – but notice the conception that the Prime Minister laid out. Turn the page on that history. Those kids shouldn't have suffered, and we will make amends to them.

The reconciliation process in Canada is entirely focused on documenting, evaluating, monetizing the suffering of those individuals who went to residential school, paying them money and then moving on. When we talk about reconciliation in Canada, we're not talking about the multigenerational effects of that phase of history, the reality that my cousins don't speak Mohawk because their grandmother went to residential school. Is the harm of residential school just that their grandmother suffered abuse and was not allowed to speak her language and despised her Indianness and moved to Brooklyn and still calls herself Irish? Is that the harm? Of course that's harm to an individual, but it's a very narrow perspective. There's also harm to the grandchild who does not speak the Mohawk language, to the grandchild that lives in Brooklyn and not in Kahnawà:ke. These are multigenerational effects.

We must also recognize that residential schools weren't there just to harm kids. What was the actual intent of residential schools? The real intent of residential schools was to prevent Nations of people from connecting to the land, to remove children so that the next generation would not know the land, would not be present on the land, would not have the ability to take in the knowledge and the language to be able to defend that land, politically, culturally, and physically from the intentions of the people who wanted to come and use the land. That was the intent of residential school, and that's not being addressed at all. Instead, we get a redefinition of the colonial relationship, and this time it's called "reconciliation." It was one thing in one era, it's calling itself a different thing in a different era, but it's always doing the same thing: It's preventing Native people from being who they are.

When I first heard the term *reconciliation* I actually had to look the process up in a book. Basically, someone admits that they're doing something wrong, stops doing the thing that they're doing wrong, makes amends with the person who was harmed, and then a new relationship is formed where they move on together. That's reconciliation in a classic sense, and I think that anybody who comes at the concept in an objective sense would say, "Yes, because of what happened in Canada, we need to go through those steps." But in Canada, reconciliation is not that. It's Native Peoples reconciling to the fact of their own colonization. For Canada, reconciliation means "You Native people need to reconcile yourselves to the fact that you lost your land and you are never going to get that land back. Instead, you really need to understand what it takes to be a successful, productive consumer-citizen in this country we're calling Canada." I'm not saying those are entirely bad things: becoming a citizen, getting educated, doing the kind of things that you need in order to have some degree of economic power, success, freedom, autonomy, and so forth. But when that's the only option presented to you, and when it's forced on you, and when all the other options for maintaining the essential connection between you and the very thing that defines you and allows you to have a normal, healthy, happy existence, which is that connection to the land, is continually severed, and there's no hope of restoring it, it's an injustice. It's not reconciliation. It's recolonization. And people in Canada today are starting to recognize that this is what reconciliation is.

They're also starting to recognize that just about everything the Canadian government is putting in front of Native Peoples as a purported solution for colonization is a form of colonial doublespeak in the Orwellian sense of the way the state controls people. In Canada we have a developing awareness and resistance among young Indigenous people who are experiencing the futility and the failure of these other strategies and approaches. They've experienced self-government, and they don't like what they see. They see Chiefs making $200,000 a year when people on reserves are living in houses that are dilapidated and full of black mold, living in abject poverty, not having access to any kind of lifestyle that anybody would want. And yet they're proudly self-governing First Nations.

That's unacceptable. Younger generations of people in Native communities are starting to recognize that it's a significant problem that needs to be confronted. They're also starting to recognize what this whole doublespeak reconciliation-recolonization Canada is doing to them. They're starting to look deeper for more authentic senses of themselves, and starting to confront their own traditional institutions as well. They say, "No, it's not enough to put on this beaded vest, a deerskin velvet hide beaded by a Mohawk woman. You have to live it, you have to know what it means, and you have to represent what this thing is supposed to represent, or I'm not going to pay attention to you. I'm going to call you out." That's the younger generation's attitude toward both the colonial system and the traditional system.

The Winter of Idle No More

This was reflected in the Idle No More movement. I know some of you in Australia were in solidarity with it because I saw Idle No More Australia banners. People here were affected by the idea of this surge of energy on the part of younger people who were aware of the problems across the board and demanding an authentic representation of their voice in Native politics and in confrontation with the colonial reality and organizing in order to make sure that happened. Idle No More was a movement that started in November 2012, led by younger Native women, most of whom were trained academically as lawyers, a lot of students, artists, and so forth, who were saying it's time to stand up. People were using social media, organizing on the ground, all kinds of ways to develop the movement and to fundamentally advance one objective: to hold our Native leaders accountable, to make them represent what it was to be truly in confrontation with colonization, and not to allow themselves to be co-opted and cooperate with lesser agendas.

It was near Christmas, and people recognized that one of the most effective ways to bring out the idea that things are not all okay in Native communities and that things are not all okay in Canada was to go into a mall and do a round dance, or whatever culturally appropriate dance in whatever region you were, to disrupt the flow of commerce, to disrupt the normality of the average citizen, and to remind them that there's a lot of work that needs to be done. People did that. It all led up to a real heady time at the beginning of January 2013. The Government agreed to meet on January 11 with Native leaders.

I was part of the strategizing on this, and we all had this beautiful vision of a whole bunch of kookums, the Cree word for grandmothers, standing in a line outside the Parliament of Canada. We had a vision that it would be snowing and the winds would be howling and there'd be a group of kookums dressed in their traditional robes, and there'd be warriors drumming, and there'd be young women dancing. And the Chiefs would be walking into the Parliament. And then the kookums would say, "Don't go in there. Stand with us. Let's have a movement, let's reconnect to the land, let's demand the land back, let's bring this country to its knees. Let's do it. Stand with us. You have the power to actually affect these people. We're here telling you what to do. We're demanding that you do it." We had this vision that that's what would happen. And then these guys would walk out and be embraced by the grandmothers. And then we would have a struggle. And then the game would be on because it would be Us versus The Colonizer.

Our vision was that there would be white people standing there with us. There would be white people who recognize that Canada needs to be changed fundamentally, that it's not only a vision of Native people, that in fact, everyone who cares about justice, anyone who cares about Canada, who cares about the land should be concerned with the things that are being done on Native land in the name of Canadians – pollution, enterprises operating with no environmental regulation or concern, the de-listing of protections for streams and rivers, basic democratic principles being overridden to serve agendas of economic development with no concern for the impacts beyond profit. Our vision was that there would be white people who were concerned. And guess what? There were, marching with us. Not only white, all of the different ethnicities that make up Canadian society. It was a significant movement.

That beautiful vision, it vanished on January 11. I wish I could continue the story and say I'm here to report from the front. There's a great social and political struggle underway in Canada between people of good conscience, millions of white Canadians and all of the Native people who are standing in defense of the water, and of the land, and for democracy and justice, against people who have these outmoded ideas about what Canada is. But that's not what happened.

We got so far as to have the vision realized with the kookums. They were all standing there in Ottawa. It was snowing. It was an awesome spectacle, political theatre, but also a real political and social movement. The level of excitement was palpable; to see young people so excited about the possibility of change was incredible. But the thing that defines January 11 is not the success of that day, but the failure of it. The failure of it represented most clearly in a prominent Chief named Matthew Coon Come, whom I know and whom I'm naming because I used to work for him as a speechwriter when he was the head of the Assembly of First Nations, and who has other great qualities but who represented, unfortunately, the problem that we're facing. He's a fluent language speaker, he knows his land. He arrived not wearing Native clothing but wearing the suit and tie. He went right up to one of the grandmothers who was blocking the door of Parliament and said to her, "You better move out of the way. I got business to do in there." Drums beating, snow flying, people yelling, dancing. "You guys don't know how this country is run. If we don't take advantage of the little things that they got in there for us, then we'll never have anything." It's on YouTube, you can watch the conversation.[2] They told him, "You are not going in there. We are Cree women. We're telling you to stay away. If you're a Cree leader, you will not go in there." And he was just, "Pshaw. You don't know what you're talking about. Get out of my way," and actually physically busted his way through and went in. I mention him too because he was the one that had the courage to do it in public. He was the one that had the courage to stand there in front of all those hundreds of people and say, "This is my vision, and I'm going." The rest of the Chiefs went in the back door. They had their meeting with the Prime Minister, they came out again, and he gave them nothing, nothing. The whole intent of that meeting was to break the Idle No More movement. And when Matthew Coon Come went through that door, he did that.[3]

Natives being Natives, they're hilarious. Even in that moment of pain, the grandmother says, "I can't believe he just did that. I'm calling his mom. Give me my cell phone. I know his mom. I'm calling. You won't believe what your son just did."[4] You have to laugh, and it kind of broke the tension. Otherwise, I'm sure she would've collapsed and just fallen on the ground out of shame and frustration.

The kind of organization and the kind of instinct that went into Idle No More, it wasn't futile, it wasn't a waste. The problem with Idle No More was that it was directed toward holding people in the colonial system accountable. And they can't be held accountable to us because they are by definition accountable to the Minister of Indian Affairs and to that colonial system. Indian Act band councils are creations of the Indian Act. They derive their authority solely from the Canadian government and they are paid by the Canadian government. If we're going to construct a decolonial movement that has some hope of really working and changing things in Canada, it needs to be directed at the proper target. And I think the proper target is the powerful institutions of the Canadian government, on one hand, and also our own people.

We need to define for ourselves what this movement is: it should be a movement back to the land. I'm not meaning to seem like a complete romantic here, a total dreamer, saying, "Let's all turn away from the city and go live out on the territory." That's not even possible, unfortunately, because of the kind of environmental destruction, the loss of animals and so forth, in our territories. What I'm talking about is that we need to recover the ability to have a relationship with our land that can sustain us spiritually, culturally, and economically, in partnership with the society that came here and promised to do that from the beginning.

The Endurance of the Treaty

Tekani Teioha:te is the Two-Row Wampum, the Kahswentha in our language, the wampum belt. It's a very potent symbol in Canada and the United States where it is the oldest agreement continually in existence between Indigenous Nations and newcomer peoples. It represents in very stark and clear terms the vision of Native Peoples as they bring it to this struggle to redefine the relationship away from colonization to decolonization. And I'll just tell you about it. The Two-Row Wampum is a very simple principle. There's a belt that represents an acknowledgment of the fact that we share an existence: the metaphorical language is of a river, the river of time. We're traveling the river of time together. Right there, you have a concession on the part of the Native people to the new reality. A lot of people say the vision of the traditionalist is so radical it's impossible to conceptualize: "What is it that you want? You want us all to go back to Europe? You want to do this, that?" Well, no. Actually the foundation of the Indigenous perspective is of a peaceful coexistence, which was the very thing that allowed these societies to develop on Turtle Island in the first place. Canada and the United States were built on this commitment on the part of each party to honor our coexistence going down to the river of time. Three beads in between the two rows represent honesty, peace, and friendship. If you have friendship as your intent, if you are peaceful in your conduct, and if your words are honest, for all time the canoe of the Native person and the ship of the white person will travel together. Our autonomy and our interdependence will be respected, and we will have what the Kahswentha represents, which is peace, peace and prosperity together. If this belt is lived out this way, forever will we travel. At no point does it start to bend slightly to the point where in 2010 the existence of the canoe is now under the existence of the ship. That's an injustice. At no point does it become the One-Row Wampum, where the sovereignty of the Canadian state supersedes the sovereignty of the Mohawk Nation, for example. Very, very clear and very simple: respect for autonomy. Yet look at our interdependence and acknowledge that we rely on each other. If we're going to have happy, healthy, prosperity in our country, we need to live it by this Nation-to-Nation principle called the Two-Row Wampum. That's what Native people are fighting for.

This is the expression of it in Haudenosaunee culture. But I have the honor of teaching in British Columbia, a territory that's very far from my own. And I travel all over the place, like many of you do. I talk to Native people all over. And although the manifestation of it may be different in cultural terms, the principle is the same. People did not surrender when the white people came in. Contrary to what many people think, people were embraced in our area of the world, and they were given a seat. They were told, "You can share in what we have, and if you're going to do that, you have to abide by these principles." Unfortunately, our history in North America is that the European peoples abided by these principles until they didn't have to anymore, until the population demographic shifted, until the military balance shifted, until things were such that people could throw this on the ground and say, "Now we don't have the Two-Row Wampum, we have the Indian Act, what are you going to do about it?" That's the callousness with which history and the commitments that we had that went into the founding of the country called Canada were thrown away.

Back to the Future

So when we're talking about a new struggle for Indigenous Nationhood, we're talking about reconnecting back to this original belt, which is something that shouldn't be seen as so radical for our people whose Ancestors made commitments explicitly to this belt. It's not radical at all. It's actually a restoration and a resurgence of an original way of being, not just for Natives but for the settler society as well. The movement toward Indigenous Nationhood is taking the energy of Idle No More, the frustration of the younger generation of people, it's reforming it and developing a way of articulating it. We're calling it the Indigenous Resurgence, but it's a very old movement, it's the oldest movement on the continent because Indigenous Nationhood, it's the Two-Row Wampum. And everybody, as we say in Canada, would be a treaty person. We're all treaty people. Treaties are not just for Natives. You can't have a treaty with yourself. We made treaties with other people, and that means Canada and the nations of people who came afterward.

I'll leave you with the final thought, which has always been a commitment of our people. From our perspective, Indigenous philosophy and ideas are not just things that are going to save us from colonization. They are actually necessary to save the world from the impulses and the imperatives of the capitalist development that is happening without an ethical frame and without a set of principles that talks about sustainability and that puts limits on the idea of growth and exploitation. This has always been a part of the Tekani Teioha:te, how to live sustainably in an environment. Not to block out realities, not to deny that change happens and time is moving on, but to work through it together, to develop a relationship, not only with each other that is sustainable, but with the other Nations of animals and plants and the Earth so that you can have *Skennen*, which is peace, and that you can have a reality that we can be proud to pass on to all of our children, Native and non-Native in this country. *Niawen'kó:wa*. Those are my words for tonight. Thank you.

Decolonize, PKOLS, W̱SÁNEĆ Territory, 2019

Decolonization means reclaiming, renaming, and reoccupying our land.

RECONCILIATION AS RECOLONIZATION

Adapted from a public talk at Concordia University in Montreal, on September 20, 2016.

This public talk had special meaning for me because it was at the university I had long considered home – I attended high school on its campus, and it's where I did my bachelor's degree and had my first teaching position – and there were more than a few people from my home community of Kahnawà:ke in the audience. I had done an engagement at Montreal's Dawson College earlier that day that was attended by hundreds of teachers and students from high school and pre-university-level schools and had heard that people, even non-Indigenous people, were dissatisfied with reconciliation as they had come to understand it: that it seemed hollow and ineffectual given the seriousness of the crimes that had been committed against us. This prompted me to focus on dissecting and deconstructing reconciliation in this talk: to try to convey to people how the Christian roots of reconciliation shape the entire enterprise and in doing so not only limit its effectiveness as a pathway toward justice, but also in fact make colonialism an ongoing and entrenched reality for our people.

Today I want to look at reconciliation from the framework of the contrasting visions that the government and Canadian society have brought to the problem of colonization. I named this talk "Reconciliation as Recolonization" because it's really a choice that Canadians have to make. The choice is, is it reconciliation as healing? Is reconciliation just something to get past? Or is reconciliation intended to recolonize us and put a cap on it, saying that Native people have to accept what's been done to us?

The problem of colonization is really the issue that we're all dealing with. It's not a problem of Natives, I'll start off by saying that. It's not a problem of Natives failing to keep up with a great vision of a society that somehow left them behind. And it's not a problem of Native people having some sort of a deficiency or deficit in their culture or in their communities whereby they could not keep up with progress. All of the issues that we're dealing with in Native communities across Canada – lateral violence, poverty, all these kind of things – are related to the essential fact that our land was stolen. It may seem over-simplified to some people, but every Native in the room will say, "Yes, that's the central problem." That is the problem that we're dealing with because it has manifestations, and it's reflected in almost every aspect of Indigenous existence. The fact is that we are disconnected from our land.

When we talk about colonization and decolonization, often people think about it in terms of treaties that were not honored, residential schooling, people being left out of the economic development of the country, all kinds of things that went on in the history of this country. And those are all absolutely true. Those are things that happened. Those are things that shaped the relationship between Native and non-Native people. But I want to look at it at a more abstract level and have us understand and talk about and think about what impact that separation from the land has on an individual and a collectivity of people – Indigenous Nations and individual Native people. What is the root impact? It's an alienation, a separation, a disconnection. So colonization is really disconnection: disconnected from the land, disconnected from ourselves, and disconnected from our culture. It manifests as this alienation that we feel of being of being caught between two worlds, not able to be a true and authentic Onkwehón:weh.

This is the impact that we feel as Indigenous people, and it's all related to the central fact of the history of this country. It is not history of glorious occupation by people with a mission to civilize and all of these sorts of mythologies that we're all familiar with. It's a history of dispossession. I focus on that before I get into analyzing reconciliation because we really need to bring our minds together about what it is that we're dealing with: What is the problem? So I'll emphasize it again; if the problem in Canada is that Native people are suffering some sort of deficit in their standard of living, or some sort of problem related to being left behind, that leads to a whole bunch of solutions. That leads to a discussion. That leads to policy. That leads to a whole bunch of different things that take us toward a solution to that problem of a deficit, of a problem, the Indian problem. So Indians are the problem. That's one way of looking at it.

If the problem is that Natives had their land stolen and therefore can't live out their culture and can't ever have an existence which reflects their own values and their own teachings which reflect a sense of justice where they are able to take advantage of what is rightly theirs in their homeland and to live out that culture and to live out that existence in their homeland which they had never surrendered, that takes us on a whole different set of pathways leading to different types of solutions. So it's very important to not skip over the step of identifying the root problem. It's all about the land. It's absolutely necessary to continue to remind ourselves of the fact that it is all about the land. And I will credit someone in particular for that phrase.

In the 1990s the government wanted to study problems in the Canada–Indigenous relationship that had come into the spotlight with the Oka Crisis and some other conflicts, so they put together a Royal Commission on Aboriginal Peoples. The first thing the Commission decided to do was to come up with a concept of Canada that was amenable to people on both sides of the divide, between the Native and the non-Native, something people on both sides could buy into, could relate to, and could live with. I was a part of it, and I was a younger person coming at it. There were all kinds of possibilities and visions that could come forward with that frame. But there was one person there, an Elder from Old Crow in the Yukon named Rosalee Tizya, the idea came from her. She would remind all of us who were working in this Royal Commission, the younger people and the older people too, that it's good to envision all of these different things: you can talk all day about culture, you can talk about reconciliation, talk about self-government agreements, talk about money, talk about shared powers, all kinds of visions about how we're going to integrate into the parliamentary system or become a third-order government and all that. But for five years I heard her say it every time we had a meeting: It's all about the land. Don't forget that.

I always raise my hands to Rosalee Tizya because I think a lot of us are realizing that it is all about the land. That's what colonization was, that's what colonization is, and that's what decolonization has to be. It has to recognize that we are disconnected from the land and that we need to reconnect to our land. Without that at the core of any project, whether it's the Royal Commission, whether it's reconciliation, unless it deals with this core question of land, it achieves nothing and it allows the larger society off the hook. It lets non-Native people feel good about themselves, saying this country has done right by Native people.

Reconciliation without Land

If reconciliation is being offered without land, if, as Justice Murray Sinclair said, reconciliation is just all about us agreeing to be friends, then I disagree with him. He is a man I respect for his dedication and his work. But think about the meaning of that. We all agree to be friends. If he followed up and said, "If we all agree to be friends so that we can talk about getting the land back for Natives and having their homeland respected and their traditional governments respected and so forth," I would agree with it. But unfortunately today, the reconciliation framework is all about being friends. Reconciliation without land.

If you look at the Truth and Reconciliation Commission recommendations, the policies that are being developed, the general discourse, the ideas, the art, the music, all of the talk in the media, and academia, the kind of programs that are promoted, there's a lot of good things that go into reconciliation, a lot of things that none of us could argue with. Justice on individual terms, payment and restitution for harm suffered at residential school, who can argue with that? People suffered. There's all kinds of things about promoting more enlightened ideas about Native culture, integrating Native art into the larger society, and getting Native people to be considered as components of Canada and respected in that regard. Okay. Those are things that are good, they're inherently good. The question is whether or not it's enough. My answer is no, it's not enough. It's only enough if you think about Canada as a complete project and as a good country. If Canada is a good country, period, then the Natives are the problem because they don't realize how good a country it is: they can't find a place in a good country; therefore, we have to either educate those Natives, give them medicine, or further change them so that they come to realize what a great country Canada is and find their place within it. That way of thinking is only possible if you don't know your own history and if you don't value the fact that the central founding act of Canada was dispossession through fraud and abuse and the breaking of treaties.

Occupied Territory and Broken Treaties

The occupation of territory in this country by non-Native people is an illegal occupation. I can say that outright because there are treaties. There are treaties all over the place, and they should provide a legitimate basis for coexistence. In this area there was a legitimate basis for coexistence between the French, the English, and the Iroquois, the

Haudenosaunee, for instance. That was a state of affairs that existed for a period of time in this country, but it doesn't exist now. Even in areas that have treaties, they're not being honored and respected. Where there's a treaty and therefore the possibility of a legitimate Canadian existence on that territory – meaning, the original owners have transferred a degree of legitimacy to the people that have come, and they've solidified that in a contractual arrangement and it's been made sacred – even where that was the original state, it doesn't exist anymore because the treaty's not being respected. The treaty's broken; therefore, there's no legitimacy. That's my version of history.

Now, is it a problem of Natives not fitting in? Is it an Indian problem or is it a colonizer problem? To me it's a colonizer problem because Canadian society is founded by colonizers. People who don't want to be colonizers and who react with horror to the idea that they are colonizers are actually inheriting all the benefits of colonization and not doing much to challenge it. Some people might think this characterization is unfair: "Well, in the '90s you had the Royal Commission. We had this residential school apology, now we have the development of this reconciliation framework and we're just starting." Well yes, okay, the reconciliation framework is just starting, but that's letting people off real easy. People have known about all this for a long, long, long time, and it's only now that people are getting to the point of dealing with it in a kind of abstract way. To me, it's time to actually just be honest and be authentic and be real in looking at the relationship and to say, "Well what kind of country am I a part of?" And make some serious commitments to doing what's necessary in order to heal the founding crime of this country, which is the theft of land. I'll say it again.

I come at this current framework for reconciliation with a clear sense of what it needs to do in order to be something that I can validate. Native people obviously have different views, but I think you can go around the country and talk to people – and I know this for a fact because I do it – you can go to any country that's dealing with reconciliation and they'll all articulate that same vision about what's necessary in order for it to be a healing process, as opposed to a process which puts the cap on the damage that's been done in the past. I lay out the challenge for the non-Native people: non-Native people whether you're French, English, or part of a group of people who have come more recently to this area of the world, the challenge is to imagine yourself in a position of being honest about the history and doing something about it.

Our Ancestors Didn't Fight and Die for Canadian Citizenship

I was in Australia discussing reconciliation and a Native woman there phrased it in a way that I think is really powerful. She said, "Reconciliation is something I could support if it meant us reconciling with our ancestral vision as opposed to us reconciling with colonialism." You got it. People are being asked to reconcile themselves to colonialism, not reconcile themselves to their Ancestors. And she gave a very powerful intervention about how the harms of colonization are continually reproduced because we are being forced into this mode of reconciling with newcomers which every

Native knows in her heart is wrong because the land is not being returned. Deep down you feel like you're doing harm or injustice to your Ancestors, or at least ignoring them. You're not paying attention to what your ancestral vision is and what your Ancestors fought and died for. Our Ancestors didn't fight and die for Canadian citizenship. They didn't fight and die in wars against people who came to take their land and steal their kids and all that stuff. They didn't fight and die in order to be just like everybody else. They fought to be Mohawks and Cree and Dene. They fought for that and they suffered for that, and who are we to turn our back on that vision simply because it's a struggle that we have to face today in a different way than they did?

As an Indigenous person there's a challenge there. It's not easy to always be in a position of struggle. Our people in the last two or three generations know what it's like to be in a position of struggle and contention all the time. It takes a psychological toll, and it's draining, and it takes a toll on families and communities. It tears at the bonds of people. It's a difficult thing and people from other parts of the world that have been in these kinds of situations of political resistance know that. So it is a tough choice for Native people who access education, who access the benefits we have now in order to educate ourselves, to take the best of our own ancestral knowledge and to pair it up with training in universities and to become lawyers, doctors, professors, or advocates for their people. It's a choice that people make because part of this reconciliation framework says, "Let's all be friends now." Canadian society is opening its arms and explicitly saying, "Come, we're not going to block you out anymore." People forget that two, three generations ago

Natives couldn't go into certain bars or they couldn't go into certain places; their mobility was controlled. People were overtly racist. That doesn't exist in the same way now – in general in the society people are much more open. It's getting to the point now where people are talking about Indigenous culture as integral to being Canadian. Now people want Northwest Coast art, A Tribe called Red, all this kind of stuff, Canadians are embracing it. Society is not pushing Native people away, they're welcoming them – but on certain terms.

Making Model Citizens

There's an idea that's been around since the 1960s or 1970s of "the Good Indian." It's outdated now, but it captures the idea: the Good Indian is the one who meets the criteria of the larger society. It's a creation in the mind of non-Native society that says, "What we need are a group of people who give us legitimacy by acquiescing in colonization." I don't want to pick on anyone in the public sphere, but anyone who's familiar with this, you know you have your own Good Indians, people that serve that role some way. I'm not saying they're consciously choosing and aspiring to be the Good Indian; it's the fact that they've made the choice between resistance and acquiescence. What I'm arguing is that the Good Indian becomes the person that the wider society validates and honors and puts up as the image of what it is to be an Indigenous person because that person suits the needs of the larger society at that particular time.

What happens to the Bad Indians? They're the ones that, first of all, are not saying and doing the things that the larger society wants or needs them to do. They're not doing it to explicitly go against society; they're doing it because they're Onkwehónweh. They're being Indigenous. During the Oka conflict in 1990, it wasn't a matter of some Natives going crazy, to paraphrase Chris Rock; it was just some Natives going Native. It was Natives who lived up to the demands of their own community, who lived up to the requirements of that time in order to preserve themselves, and they did things in order to accomplish that. So the Good Indian serves the purpose, while the Bad Indian is the thing that needs to be continually suppressed and eliminated.

The politics of recognition is essentially the Good Indian/Bad Indian thing as expressed in legal and political realms in that the Canadian government will recognize certain aspects of Indigenous Nationhood and certain aspects of Indigenous governance and certain aspects of Indigenous rights and solidify them and put them into agreements and make that the concept of Aboriginals. So it's recognizing and it's picking and choosing certain aspects. So there's that. That's a greatly simplified version of it.

The reconciliation framework is something that tries to overwhelm the ideas of resistance, overwhelm the idea of land-based culture, overwhelm the idea that you can be a separate but distinct Nation; it wants to overwhelm all these kinds of things in favor of the amenable vision of Indigeneity. Reconciliation asks us to accept the idea of the Aboriginal, as the official government terminology goes, and to forget the idea of a land-based, culturally connected Onkwehónweh that even today remains a fundamental obstacle to the Canada project.

Denying Reality

We were the fundamental obstacle from the beginning. When people came from Europe the first thing they encountered was the fact that their Bible was wrong. First, this place wasn't supposed to exist, and secondly, the teachings that had developed in that society out of the biblical perspective didn't make any sense. There were people here who had civilizations, cultures, languages, there were flourishing societies here, and that didn't make any sense. And the choice they faced at the time was, they could either say, "No we were wrong. Let's have a relationship, let's find out what this new world is really like, let's find our place in it, and let's build a relationship there." Or they could deny the reality that was in front of them and stick to their teachings. And unfortunately, the historical choice made by the Europeans at that time – at least the ones that made the decisions – was that they were going to deny the reality and live with their European ideas. So the idea that there was no civilization here is something that undergirds all Canadian law – *terra nullius*: an empty land. How does Canadian society account for the fact that there were flourishing societies with laws, governments, for thousands and thousands of years and yet Europeans who have only been here for a couple hundred years have legitimate ownership of everything and the British and French own the whole continent? How is that? There's no logic to that unless you believe in one of two things: inherent European cultural superiority, also known as white racism, or *terra nullius*, which allows you to say that there weren't really "people" here. Sure there were some people but they were moving around so much that they weren't really attached to land; there wasn't really any law here, so it just doesn't factor into our legal reasoning. It's a legal fiction that's at the heart and at the root of Canadian law, and that's still the case today.

Why was this put forward? It was put forward because the Europeans who came here needed to access and use the land. The Native story and the relationship between Natives and non-Natives and the image of the Native and everything I'm talking about flows from this reasoning. The Europeans made treaties when they needed to, as long as they could get what they wanted from the land. When those treaties stopped being mechanisms that allowed them to access the land, they broke them and violently moved the people away from the land. They wrote us out of law, and they attempted to write us out of history.

That's the Indian Act of 1876, although the processes began earlier; the Indian Act consolidated earlier laws. A lot of people don't realize that if you read the Indian Act, there's no mention of Native Nations, there's no mention of anything but the fact that the Canadian Parliament created a thing called Indians, and they numbered those Indians, and created little Indian reserves and numbered them. That is, in Canadian law, the only existence for all of my Onkwehónweh sisters and brothers. Canadian law doesn't recognize anything. It's been modified somewhat but in ways that are so limited in their application that I'm not even going to talk about it. As a practical thing, it hasn't altered the relationship at all between Native people and the government of Canada.

So this is how we stand in Canada today. We have *terra nullius* where Canadian government, institutions, and law are based on a legal fiction – also known as a lie – that says there was no law and there were no people in this land; therefore, our law is the one that stands and there was no such thing as Native Nationhood; there were these people that we call Indians, they only exist by our own creation, and we can give and take it away, just like we can give and take away lands. Why does all this exist? Because Canada then and now needs access to the territory. So the Good Indian is an Indigenous person that by act of acquiescence or by explicit treaty or by their own posture in relation to this enterprise allows it to happen and validates it. So treaty-making, self-government, art, music, literature, people's personalities, it's all intertwined in the sense of the Aboriginal person in Canada that's held up and validated and supported is the one that allows access to the land to continue so that resource extraction can continue in those territories without benefiting the people whose land it actually is.

There's an economic basis and drive that underpins this. The people who are in resistance are those that get in the way of that flow; they get in the way of the ideas that are created to facilitate, enable, and maintain access to the territory and its resources. Those that simply want to remain themselves in their homeland practicing their culture and guided by their spirituality are in the way. That is something that the Canadian state cannot grasp in its current construction. There's no capacity for Canadian governments to relate to true Indigenous governments. There's no capacity of the Canadian state to access and understand and relate to Indigenous culture and on the land and in relation to each other in the way that it is supposed to be operating. So when we talk about reconciliation we have to think about it and turn it around. Again, it's not us reconciling ourselves to colonization: I hope that through this brief history and analysis of Canada you can see there's significant problems in Canada and the way that it is constructing its relationship to Native people.

Reconciliation has to be Canadians reconciling to the fact that they're in an unjust position in relation to the land and Indigenous people. What do you do about it? Reconciliation is problematic. Recognition is problematic. And then there's resistance.

Kahnawà:ke: Not One More Inch of Land

We're all familiar with the term resistance when looking at politics in different parts of the world. In this territory Onkwehónweh have been in a position of resistance for a long time. For Kahnawà:ke in the period between the early 1800s and the construction of the St. Lawrence Seaway in the 1950s, our people were in a position of basically being controlled by the government and the Catholic Church. In the colonial era they suffered population losses and loss of economic and military power to the point where we were in a position of dependence.

In the 1950s Kahnawa'kehró:non, the people in Kahnawà:ke, experienced a significant historical trauma: the harm done to us through the construction of the St. Lawrence Seaway. It's only recently that our community and people have started to actually discuss what happened, to look back and consider the impact of the seaway construction on our people psychologically, culturally, and otherwise. My cousin Ron is here, and there might be some other people in the room who are affected similar to the ways our family was impacted. We had a grandfather and grandmother who lived in a certain area; they had a culture, they had land, they had connection to the river, and they had community and so forth. There was settlement and there was community all along the river, from the present day around where the church is, all the way to Candiac, up to the border of the reserve there, and that was all taken away. Straight up expropriation after they were promised that it wouldn't happen. Government officials literally came to Kahnawà:ke, smoked a peace pipe, and then went away and broke the promise. They came in force. This was in the mid-1950s. Nobody really resisted, not the kind of resistance you saw in the '70s and the '80s and certainly not in 1990. Why was that? Not everyone agrees with me, but I would argue it's because our people were in a position of dependency and trust. They trusted the treaties. If you read the documents of the history of the seaway, they appeal to the treaties, to international law, and to the goodness of that society. So the people said: "How could you do this? You made treaties. Look at our historical role. How could you turn against that?" Nobody at that point in the '50s was in a position to say, "We're going to resist in ways that are necessary to prevent it from happening." And that's something for Kahnawa'kehró:non to revisit and look at. That is also the history of our people, just as much as we have a proud history of resistance. The RCMP came in and removed people; they took old women from their houses while people watched: there were skirmishes here and there, but there was no mass resistance.

What happened after was that people in Kahnawà:ke were in shock. Their community was in disarray. It took a while for it to set in, that this is what happened, and we began to feel the effects. Kahnawa'kehró:non developed a culture where resistance was something that could be put forward, that somebody could say, "That's never going to happen again. Not one more inch of land will ever be taken." Everybody from Kahnawà:ke knows that phrase – not one more inch of land. So if you want to look at 1990 and the idea of Indigenous resistance, specifically in Mohawk territory, in Kahnawà:ke, you can't start in April 1990 to explain July – you go back further. To the 1970s, the rise of Red Power and the revitalization of Native consciousness that paralleled Black Power and other social resistance movements. To the 1950s and before, when Native people basically trusted the larger society and that trust was abused. In Kahnawà:ke, trust was a strategy that was going to get you killed as a Nation. If you continued to trust and if you continued to allow them to do what they wanted to do in relation to the land, you wouldn't exist anymore. Without a land-base we wouldn't have a culture, we wouldn't have a language, and we wouldn't be a community. We're done. People reacted very strongly to any incursion after that. And that's really at the foundation, I think, of the reaction throughout the 1980s and to 1990 and even today in terms of people's hypersensitivity in regard to land.

Resisting as Resurgents

Resistance itself is always against something – it's against that intrusion, it's against those forces that are coming in and trying to do harm, so you're pushing back. By definition that's resistance. But when you're in a position of resistance for so long, you can neglect the things that actually keep you alive as a people. You're always focused outward, taking what's necessary to fight and pushing back. You don't have the time or the energy, the people are not there, to do the things that keep a community strong.

The idea of Indigenous Resurgence is something that comes into play that counters some of these problems with recognition, reconciliation, and resistance. When we talk about Resurgence, first of all, I wanted to make it clear that it's not negating the utility of all of these other things. It's not saying that resistance is no longer necessary. It's not saying that there's absolutely no value to reconciliation. It's saying that we need to focus on what is at the core of our existence. The core of our existence is maintaining the fire that is our Nation. It's our language, it's our ceremony, it's our culture, and beyond the traditional aspects of it, it's our relationship to each other. It's our bonds of communities, the things we do together. It's the trust that we have. Maintaining that and keeping that strong is the thing we need to do in order to exist as Onkwehónweh.

And it's all about the land. The fact is that you have this in a particular territory, in relation to particular plants and animals and spirits and so forth; this is what defines you as a group of people that can be called Mohawk, and defines Mohawk homeland; generalized across Indigenous people, it's those things you need to do in order to maintain yourselves. Resurgence is really the focus on that. It's taking the idea of resistance and looking at it as something that's necessary at certain times but not structuring your personality, your community, your culture to be in resistance all the time, to define yourself that way. It's shifting the focus to say that what we need to do in order to accomplish the anticolonial objective is to look at the fundamental harm being disconnected from the land, which leads to all of these other harms. Let's connect ourselves to the land. Let's begin to relate to the land and our homeland in the way that our Ancestors did and re-experience that, reinvigorate it, regenerate that culture. It means recognizing that a lot of the things that are wrong, not from white society's perspective, but the things that we experience as wrong in our communities, the gaps that we feel, the problems that we feel, come from not having that relationship or not being able to have that relationship because of contamination, pollution, settlement of other people on our territory. It means focusing on that reconnection.

I want to emphasize that it's not some kind of romantic vision, of saying, go back to the land and everything will be all right. No. What it's saying is that you can't have any imagining of a solution that means anything for Indigenous people at the spiritual level or at the level of cultural strengthening unless there is an attachment to land and unless there is an embodiment in the individual and the collectivity of the ancestral knowledge that came through our generations and that really define us as people. So we can't really just be average people living in a certain defined territory without any connection to the spiritual power and the knowledge that we have as Indigenous people and to the responsibilities that we have as Onkwehónweh in that territory that comes through our ceremonies and our language.

That's what Indigenous Resurgence is. It's saying that white society has to accommodate Native people living in that way, on their territory, growing the strength of their culture, through the strengthening of their families, the relearning of the language, the learning of all of the things that made them strong, our Ancestors strong. It's going to continue to grow, and it's going to butt up against a limited vision that Canadians have of Natives. It's going to butt up against the idea of the Indian reserve first of all, the territorial boundary; it's going to butt up against the image the Canadian government has of Natives. It turns the tables on the Canadian government, and it forces them to react to us as opposed to us having to react to them.

Indigenous Resurgence is an attractive idea for a lot of younger people because the prospects of a career, whether as an activist or just living your life as a Native person in a resistance mode or through recognition politics or in a reconciliation framework, it's somewhat depressing. You could spend your whole career negotiating a land claim. You could spend your whole career negotiating a self-government agreement. Even if you get recognition of it, so what? How does it fundamentally affect the lives of people? Are your children or your grandchildren going to have a better life, a more Native life than you because of that? Theoretically that's the argument for doing these things, but you can look across the country and see it's not the case. In all of these regions that have comprehensive land claims agreements, I run into people of a younger generation all the time who say, "It's not doing us any good as Native people. Maybe we have better standards of living in terms of comfort, but we're losing our language. Our communities are not the same. We're losing our Indianness as it comes down the line."

Indigenous Resurgence as a way of resisting colonization is an opportunity to pass that struggle on, but it also offers young people a vision where they can make real changes in the lives of themselves and their kids in order to make them more Native. The alternative is struggling in a way which is really kind of a trap that gathers all the bright minds and the educated people and people with energy and says, "No, no here, come to this classroom, come to this courtroom, do this," and you spend your whole career doing that, and you enrich yourself in the process, there's no doubt about that, but what does it do for the opportunities of the kids to be like their Ancestors? This idea of Indigenous Resurgence is a turning around of the question in a number of different ways.

That's what I'm going to leave you to consider as an alternative to reconciliation. What is Indigenous Resurgence, and how am I a part of it? Because it's not only Indigenous people: it's also the relationship. The founding premise of Canada was the breaking of the original agreement that allowed white people to be here and to set themselves up in this territory, this particular territory right at the Lachine Rapids where we're standing right now. That's where the French people came and that's where the Mohawks welcomed them, and that's where they saved them with medicines and they brought them back to life and they allowed this country to begin. Now, it's not just an Indian story. It's not just a Native story. It's a story of everybody. How are you part of Indigenous Resurgence? How are you going to make this country a different place, one that is fitting with a vision of justice as opposed to this recolonization vision that we call reconciliation?

I'm going to finish there. Niawen kowa. I look forward to discussion.

Blockade Fire, Kahnawà:ke, 2020

When our people unify, that is when we find our power.

FROM RED POWER TO RESURGENCE

Adapted from an address to the *Then and Now: 1968–2018 Conference*, Institute for the Humanities, Simon Fraser University, November 2, 2018.

The audience for this talk was mainly made up of people who were seasoned veteran activists and senior scholars of radical social and political movements – leftists, socialists, and anarchists. The conference focused on the history and transformation of political activism generally in North America since the watershed years of the late 1960s. For my part, being asked to reflect on Indigenous movements in that era, I decided to trace the heritage of rooted resistance by Indigenous people in North America and show how Indigenous politics had always been an expression of our people's determination to preserve our independent Nationhood and traditional cultures and recover our lost lands. Heavy on my mind as I delivered this talk was the realization that this struggle has been abandoned by many within our Nations. Since the design of the reconciliation agenda by the Canadian government in the 1990s, we have been living through an historical moment where the goals of our ancestral struggle have been undermined by the emergence of an entire strata of comprador Indigenous elites within institutions of higher education, the legal profession, national and regional Indigenous organizations, and even many community governments, who are not committed to struggle or sacrifice in any form, and for whom advancing colonial goals and the assimilation of our people culturally, politically, and spiritually into the Canadian mainstream is a personal commitment and political objective. I used the opportunity of being among comrades to show how this era is an aberration, and to tell them about the alternative to cooptation: the liberatory and transformational potential of Indigenous Resurgence.

What is it to be in struggle as an Indigenous person in Canada? It's much more than just following a chronology of the development of the Indigenous movement. What is really important is defining what it is that we're trying to achieve as Indigenous Peoples. We have many transformational visions of society – utopian visions, socialist visions, anarchist visions. I'd like to add to the conversation a unique element in outlining the Indigenous vision of what it is to be in struggle, and the Indigenous vision going forward.

I'm also interested in the linkage between how other visions, other movements have been enriched by engagement with Indigenous communities and Indigenous struggles. In this moment of resistance to the Trans Mountain pipeline there is allyship, but if you go back a decade or more, you find not only lack of connection but also some animosity and some conflict between environmental movements and Indigenous movements.[1] In 1998 I gave a talk in Australia about Indigenous ethics at a conference on environmental ethics. Arne Næss[2] was sitting in the front row, and when I mentioned that Indigenous Peoples were at odds with environmental movements because those movements didn't take into account Indigenous rights and sovereignty, he literally jumped out of a seat and ran toward me. Now I'm a bigger guy and he's a smaller guy, but he came at me and banged on my chest to make the emphatic point in front of a whole conference that this was not environmentalism – not in the way that deep ecologists know it. They know and I know that if it's ever going to mean anything, environmentalism has to take into account Indigenous rights and Indigenous sovereignty. And so right there I knew we had something to build on.

You can look at the really strong transformations that have taken place in regard to connections and building a movement – when we come together and respect the true roots of resistance in this land, there is transformational potential of all of the movements. It's taken us a long time to get here. Everybody has their own issues and concerns – war, nuclear threats, suppression of women's rights – all of these battles have been fought and movements have been organized to fight these battles. But transforming Canada from a settler-colonial state to a country that is good for everyone is going to take the coming together of all these movements. The rootedness of these movements going forward is through Indigenous philosophies and Indigenous principles of resistance and ways of life. That's the commitment that I hold and bring to this work. In the past I've shared different commitments – toward Nationhood, toward resistance, toward a lot of different things. But like many other people I've come to recognize the power in this coming together, as we've learned more from our own people, and as we have re-rooted into the powers of Indigenous teachings. And so in tracing this history, I'm tracing a historical trajectory of the development not only of a powerful movement in Canada and its potential but also a coming to the realization that as Onkwehónweh, the Original People, we have our own power rooted in our own philosophies and ways of existence.

To describe this history of struggle and the vision going forward I'm going to talk about "the Four Rs" – Revolution and Resistance, which are more historical; Reconciliation, which is the contemporary condition; and Indigenous Resurgence, which is the future.

A Revolution in Consciousness

Looking at the Indigenous movement as we conceptualize it today is to think of it as a coherent thing that links Indigenous Peoples, but it is in itself a modern construction. Previous to colonization, previous to the contemporary era, before modernity, Indigenous Peoples were Nations in and of themselves. Like "Aboriginal issues," it's similar to how people think about Indigenous people or even Indigenous Nationhood as a single thing. We have to remind people that no, those things are made up of very distinct groups of people, distinct political, social, and cultural entities. Today we can speak about Indigeneity as a singularity because of colonization, because of the fact that we are in resistance to a force that affects us all in relatively the same way. But the Royal Commission on Aboriginal Peoples [RCAP] found that before colonization there was great diversity: over sixty distinct groups of people living in the area of what is now Canada, groups that had unique languages, cultural practices, histories, and land bases. This multiplicity of Nations is now simply referred to as Indigenous Peoples, Aboriginal Peoples, although within our communities, and anyone who studies these issues, we know that this diversity hasn't gone away. These Nations are still here, and they're still salient features of any discussion of politics or society or culture. But we also have to recognize that there is a commonality of experience and a focus to our purpose. And so over time the idea of being Indigenous has emerged, and it has become real.

Using the word *Indigenous* in the way that I'm using it now used to be contentious. In the 1990s when I talked about the concept of Indigeneity I remember getting shouted down by people of an older generation from Native communities and rightly so – they said, "You're attacking our Nations, you're undermining our Nations when you say that." That degree of contention still exists intellectually over the value of framing the struggle as an Indigenous struggle, versus rooting yourself in your own Nationhood as a Mohawk or a Gitxsan or a Mi'gmaw. So I don't want to give the impression that I'm blowing through these complexities and moving on to a new conception of Indigeneity. But my assertion is that clearly there is a consciousness, there is a set of political relationships and increasingly there is language, culture, kinship, and all of the makings of an ethnic national identity that you can identify at one level as being Indigenous. And so there's a coming together of Onkwehónweh.

I feel that my Onkwehónweh identity is a nested identity. In Kahnawà:ke, it's my family or clan. If I go to a conference in Buffalo, which is Haudenosaunee, I'm Mohawk. If I go to Trent University, I'm a Mohawk, no doubt about it, I'm Kahnawà:ke Mohawk. When I'm here in Vancouver, I'm a

Mohawk. If I go to Australia, I'm a Canadian Indigenous person. I am all of those things, and they are all just as real. "Indigenous" then, as part of my nested identity, exists at the level of the commonality of all these Nationhoods that are in struggle against colonization.

Thinking of our identities in this way is something that's really new for our people, although there were precedents and examples of activism at the international level. For example, in the 1920s Chief Deskaheh, a Haudenosaunee Cayuga Chief, went to the League of Nations to advocate for the recognition of our sovereignty as the Six Nations.[3] There have been times when the struggles of the collectivity of our people have been represented in a unified way. But it wasn't until the 1960s and '70s that we really began to see the coming together of a consciousness of Indigeneity. This new shared awareness was also emerging in Latin America and Australia and New Zealand during the era of decolonization. It helped to radicalize people and remake identities on many different axes. Indigenous Peoples were reading newspapers and watching the TV like everyone else, and these events and ideas came into their lives.

My own political consciousness was awakened in 1973. At the time it was called an "Indian" consciousness – an *Indigenous* consciousness – and directly influenced by the civil rights movement in the United States, especially the Black Power element of the liberation struggle of African Americans. This directly influenced the development of not only a consciousness but also a strategy and a strategic vision on how to confront oppression in our societies. During this time of Indigenous consciousness and struggle an element of redefining and re-conceptualizing identity was at play.

Part of the colonization of our Peoples was in the creation of a negative self-image. Nowadays we're familiar with thinking about how colonization is constructed and implemented and maintained, and following the line taken by anti-colonial writers like Frantz Fanon and Albert Memmi, we realize that this negative self-conception is essential, it's the foundation of colonization, it's basic. Indigenous Peoples in this country had come to think of themselves in that way: the breaking of that notion of what it is to be an Indian, and the freeing of people to explore and to develop and to recreate themselves in their own languages, using their own culture on their own land, was a significant part of what we called Red Power in that era. If you go outside the Longhouse where Deskaheh is buried, there is a marker that explains what he was fighting for, and it's very simple – what we want is to be able to be free to live by our culture, to worship our gods in our own land. That's what we are in struggle for – to be ourselves, to be authentic. It's not only a struggle against the power put on top of us; it's the struggle to empower our authentic selves.

Resistance Rising

If you want to trace militant resistance on the part of Indigenous Peoples, you have to trace it through the rise of Warrior Societies.[4] The main thrust of our activism and our politics was the organization of forces in order to confront the mechanics of colonization and the powers that were imposing colonization in our communities most directly. It was groups like the Warrior Societies and the American Indian Movement (AIM) that confronted the most present features of colonization. I mentioned my own political awakening in 1973. At that time in Kahnawà:ke where I grew up there were a series of riots involving the Mohawk Warrior Society, which had been influenced by AIM. It had been trained by and directly took its inspiration directly from Black Power. My own family was involved and people throughout the community were involved in this Red Power sensibility of having to confront not only what it is to be an Indigenous person but also to confront in revolutionary ways, through resistance, those forces that were keeping so many of our people back in that colonial mentality, in that colonial set of existences. Band councils were burned, people were evicted, all kinds of tactics and strategies that we're all familiar with in all of these movements all over the world, were used. That was an agenda that was put forward.

This aspect of the movement, which began in the 1960s and continued on through the 1970s, reached a watershed moment for Canada in 1990 when the Mohawk Nation and Quebec confronted each other face-to-face during the Oka Crisis. I'm sharing my own experience because that's where I grew up and so that's what I remember the most, but there were occupations, land defenses and land-based activism throughout the period – the Mi'kmaw, the Anicinabe Park Occupation in Kenora in 1974 that included the Ojibway Warrior Society and AIM; the Gitxsan and other Nations in northern British Columbia in the 1980s. There was resistance throughout the country. But the 1990 standoff is the most representative moment of Indigenous resistance in Canada: even today we see the Mohawk Warrior flag at political actions. It's come to symbolize resistance against oppressive measures by the state, resistance to illegal occupation, stolen lands, disregard of treaties, and so forth. All this can be traced to the resistance of the Warrior Societies to that most present feature of colonization, and an attempt to move that power away.

This hasn't ended, but energy shifts. The dominant experience moves over to new opportunities and develops. But even as we speak today, the Manuel sisters – George Manuel's granddaughters, Art Manuel's daughters – are the ones leading the resistance in Canada, both in terms of ideology and actual on-the-ground action, and this continues.[5] There are people still doing it in this way. They're committed to that resistance mentality and resistance posture in relation to the Canadian state, as are many Indigenous Peoples.

The False Promises of Recognition

After Oka, which had such a huge impact across the country, major shifts started to occur, building on the momentum that had been developing since the 1960s. We see the development of an approach that attempts to resolve the disconnection between two incompatible ideas in Canada. On one hand, we have the fact of the continuing existence of Indigenous Peoples, the fact that Indigenous Peoples were here before Europeans arrived, the fact that we have Nations and culture and rights, and on the other hand, we have the idea of the Canadian state and Canadian settler civilization, the idea that the European occupation and control of this territory is legitimate. How do you reconcile these opposing ideas?

In the past the attempts to reconcile these two opposing realities were coercive: get rid of the Natives, move the

Natives, control the Natives. But beginning in 1970 with the Supreme Court of Canada's decision on the Calder case, Indigenous Peoples were now successfully challenging the Canadian state within its own judicial realm.[6] And so starting in the 1970s, and especially into the 1980s and into the 1990s, there is a shift from on-the-ground resistance and political resistance to activism within the legal realm – you have legal activism. From 1982 on, with the repatriation of the Constitution you have a situation where for the first time, reluctantly, in Canadian law, in the highest law of the land, there is a recognition of the idea of Aboriginal rights and title to the land. The government's response to this legal activism was to create a framework for recognizing Aboriginal rights. The idea of legal recognition emerged, and the Canadian government developed an approach to reconciling Indigenous sovereignty with Canadian sovereignty. But underlying the court decisions and negotiations over self-government was the premise that the only place for Indigenous Peoples was *within* the governmental structure of Canada. Modern treaties like the Nisga'a treaty in British Columbia are emblematic of this approach.[7]

I've spent so many talks and written so many pages criticizing the doctrine of Aboriginal rights and title that I'll just boil down my critique into a one-minute version, which is that – and I believe this reflects the consensus among Indigenous Peoples who are active politically and who are organized around this identity of Indigeneity – which is that the doctrine of Aboriginal rights and title does not allow for the full exercise of Indigenous Nationhood and culture. Canada recognizes Indigenous sovereignty, it recognizes Indigenous existences, and it recognizes Indigenous cultural practices and so forth *only to the extent* that they don't fundamentally contradict core Canadian values. And of course, most Canadians support this and accept that notion. But from an Indigenous perspective, especially someone who is coming from an era of resistance, where the idea is to preserve your land, preserve your cultural practice, restore your Nationhood, and get control over your territory and future, the idea that you're going to get recognized to the extent that it doesn't contradict the ongoing colonial project is a bit disappointing. And so my critique is always centered on that. And I would say that boils down to what we're going to see coming forward.

Here's a bold prediction on my part: the Supreme Court decision, when applied to the Trans Mountain pipeline issue, means that Aboriginal rights and title may be infringed, even when they're proven to exist, if the courts find development is in the interest of the national economy and the society as a whole.[8] It says that right in the major decision, the *Delgamuukw* decision, which has been brought forward many times in legal reasoning on other cases and is emblematic of the recognition framework approach.[9] And so that's what is an Achilles' heel or a fatal flaw in the doctrine of Aboriginal rights and title: going to court is essentially a stalling tactic – it requires years of legal wrangling and millions of dollars to delay the inevitable, in the hopes that meanwhile politics shifts, economic changes, and so forth will make these things undesirable going forward. But as an Indigenous Nationhood principle, the idea of Aboriginal rights and title is severely limited. But that has been the thrust of our movement since at least the 1980s and into the 1990s, and it continues.

Like with the Resistance movement I mentioned before, we have the Manuel sisters who are still fighting hard on the ground. And with this Recognition-Reconciliation approach, we have an industry; we have a whole structure built around the ongoing project of recognizing Aboriginal rights and title. In Canada today that's where the bulk of activity takes place in regard to the relationship between the Indigenous Peoples and the Canadian state. You could point to that whole complex of negotiating self-government agreements, taxation agreements and basically taking the colonial structure and trying to reform it in a way that is minimally acceptable to the bulk of Aboriginal and Canadian people. And it's a huge project that's ongoing. That's recognition. And from this pursuit of legal *recognition* comes reconciliation, the current dominant political condition and approach.

Reconciliation with People, Not Nations

I trace the origins of the reconciliation discourse to the Royal Commission on Aboriginal Peoples that was in place from 1992 to 1996. It was a large-scale rethinking of policy and law and history and offered an incredibly complex set of recommendations about the relationship between Canadian society and Onkwehónweh. The idea was *not* reconciliation in the sense of reconciling the existence of Indigenous Nations with the Canadian settler state. What emerged out of that process was an idea of finding a reconciliation pathway with those specific individuals who had been harmed by policies and programs of the Canadian state in the past. It was hard to identify at first because we were talking about so many different things. But I think with historical perspective you begin to see more clearly that we had RCAP, followed by the Residential School Settlement Agreement, the Residential School apology from Prime Minister Stephen Harper in 2008, and then you see the Truth and Reconciliation Commission (TRC) and then the TRC report.[10] You see a honing of the perspective that colonial injustice was an injustice done to *people*, not *Peoples*. And this is a key difference in legal language and political language.

People are individuals, *Peoples* are collectivities. Focus from the legal and the political perspective has been on the individual citizen. It resulted from the activism of individuals who had been harmed. There were people who had been harmed in residential school, who bore that shame for so many years, and who had the courage to stand up – at the Alberni Residential School, for example, and all over Canada – to stand up and say, this is the true history of Canada.[11] This is what we've endured. That psychological aspect was important in reconciliation, and that's why I will never stand up and broadly criticize reconciliation. Reconciliation is absolutely necessary because of the harm done to people. While harm to individuals needs to be addressed, it's not enough to simply focus on the individual experience. It is Peoples, collectivities, that we really need to talk about. Reconciliation needs to be more than a process to provide restitution for those people that suffered sexual, physical, emotional abuse from priests and nuns at residential school. It's also the loss of language. It's also the loss of culture. It's multigenerational. It was part of a larger-scale process to remove the original inhabitants from these territories so that capitalism could come in and exploit it. If you don't talk about those things, then it's not reconciliation. It's recolonization.

For a few years I was very angry about this, and I thought reconciliation was a sell-out. But in dialoguing – and this is the currency of reconciliation, it is dialogue – and in taking it seriously in dialoguing with people in Canada, I have come to understand that there is still potential moving forward, even in the concept of reconciliation, because most people misunderstand it. There are very few people for whom reconciliation is an agenda, a way to limit justice for Indigenous Peoples. If this is the agenda, it's wrong. Powerful people benefiting from the land, usually ensconced in government or corporate positions, may have those agendas. But for a lot of people, it's just a mistake in understanding. If it's a mistake, we can continue to engage, we can educate, we can dialogue, and we can enhance people's understanding and expand the notion of what reconciliation is. If it's an agenda, then we defer to our other strategies of resistance. And so it's not either/or. For an Indigenous activist, for a person envisioning Indigenous resistance, we have to have a multiplicity of approaches because, as I've come to learn, there's no "monolith," no one thing to dismantle. I was joking this morning that I used to think it was *all* white people. As a Mohawk growing up, you're like, it's white people and that's it. And of course, I've learned in the job that I do, and the circles that I travel, and the friendships that I have, in the political activism that I've engaged in, that there is no monolith.

In outlining these three things – revolution, resistance, and reconciliation – and in particular looking at the fundamental critique of the current framework of reconciliation, and in putting this vision of Indigenous Resurgence forward, I hope Indigenous activists going into the future can be more effective in understanding and navigating the particular locations, issues, and segments of society. What posture do I take? How do I relate to them? How am I most effective? Because it is an issue of justice, but it's also an issue of survival.

Resurgence Is Survival

How do we survive? Indigenous Peoples, more than any other in this land, are affected in a fundamental way. Not only is our individual survival affected in so many ways, but more profoundly, the existence of our cultures and our Nations and our languages is threatened. We have to acknowledge that. And so envisioning our future, it's really incumbent on the thinkers and the activists to put that profundity – the survival of Indigenous Peoples into the future – right at the core. This is the survival of the coming generations. If we don't figure out a way to defeat colonization, to address the injustices, there won't be a Mohawk Nation. It's not a matter of the quality of existence of the Mohawks there won't be any. And there won't be Gitxsan and there won't be any Mi'kmaw. This is a qualitative difference in the struggles that we have here. If people recognize that aspect and take it on, especially in relation to environmental concerns, and the idea of the planet and its ability to sustain us, if we put that survival principal into our movements we will have a lot more ability to draw a lot more people to a lot more effective action.

One way is to reframe all of these things into a new conception of what it is to be in struggle. And here's where the resurgence comes in. This idea has grown out of these other three experiences of earlier struggle. We've been involved in resistance. We've been involved in governmental and legal activism. We've been involved in trying to do our best with the reconciliation framework. And to me, just like Oka is emblematic of the revolutionary strategy, and the *Delgamuukw* decision is emblematic of the legal strategy of recognition, and the TRC report is emblematic of reconciliation, Idle No More is really the emblem of Indigenous Resurgence so far because what it did is really show for this generation of activists and this generation of thinkers both its potential and its limits.

Idle No More showed how powerful we are, but it also showed the obstacles we face in our continuing empowerment and in making transformational change. Idle No More was a challenge, but it didn't transform the system in the way that we had hoped it would. And so when I talk about Resurgence, I'm talking about a present, but I'm also talking about a future vision. It's just developing. What are the elements of Indigenous Resurgence that distinguishes it from these other aspects: the focus on dialogue and creating a good relationship between Native people and Canadian society; reconciling the legal inconsistencies between Indigenous sovereignty; confronting the obvious injustices and oppressions, and so forth? It is really this: How do we re-root ourselves in our existence as Indigenous people so that we can regain our authenticity in our lives and pass that legacy on to the next generation?

When we talk about what Indigenous Resurgence is right now, we're really talking about reframing a pathway for people to recover that Indigenous authenticity and then to act on it. It's community-based, it's land-based, and it's relationship-based. For me it harkens back to an old revolutionary Red Power type of spirit. I feel like we're getting it right, we're doing it more right than they did back in the 1960s and '70s. This isn't to say we're doing it all right – but we're getting better. We have to work on not being afraid to make mistakes, be bold, take chances, learn as we go – all those sorts of things in building a movement are important. That's how we can talk about what Indigenous Resurgence is now – we've tried, and we've made mistakes, and we've learned.

It's community-based, much more so than the routes of getting involved in legal struggles or occupying the offices of the BC Treaty Commission or things like that. It's re-rooting yourself in your own community, and that's where the activism is taking place, at the community level and the family level. And it's taking place at the relationship and at the personal level. It's taking the idea of colonization – and this is building off Indigenous feminist critiques and queer theory – to move the idea of what it is to be in struggle down to the root and the most intimate connections of colonialism to ourselves. This is a challenging and exciting time because it forces us to examine our very insides. It's easy to be revolutionary when you're looking outside, very difficult to be revolutionary emotionally when you're looking in the mirror. And so this is the moment we're in.

And it's land-based. It's really about land and water and here's where the connection to the environmental movement comes in. It's not about gaining governmental power. It's not about retaking the Indian structures and making them our own as we envisioned in the past. It's about creating a healthy environment, protecting the lands and waters – and this is profoundly Indigenous – it is looking at *all* our relations in a serious way. If we look at our conception of who we are as Indigenous people, there's no distinction between human beings and other elements of the natural world. The animals, the waters, the land, the bugs, the trees, from an Indigenous sensibility, we are in a web of relationships that place us in no hierarchical position relative to anything else. You have a responsibility to do now, as an Indigenous person with the power that you have and the skills that you have, to do what those things did for our people for thousands of years. We were naked and vulnerable, and they provided us life with their own bodies and everything that they gave us. Now they're under threat. What's our responsibility? That's what we have to ask ourselves. And that's the thing that Indigenous Resurgence does: it is putting Indigenous teachings with contemporary intelligence and applying them again. It's transformational. It's family-centered, it's community-centered, it's relationship-centered, but it is oriented toward transformation of those relationships to reflect what anybody here, I think, would agree are terms of justice, and in that way it goes beyond Indigenous values and the Indigenous sense of what goodness is in terms of a relationship and the way people experience life.

That's probably the most difficult journey for a lot of us because the impacts of colonization have been so profound. And it's the decolonizing as well. So it doesn't let go of the spirit of resistance and it has and does these things that root us in this way of struggle. The difference between a Resurgence attitude and, say, a resistance approach, is it doesn't seek to cause confrontation. What it does is it roots itself in a place. It lives Indigenously and defends itself from intrusions. That's where the decolonization comes in. It's a matter of focus. Do we structure our movement to go and confront, or do we do our Indigeneity on our land and pass it on to our future generations and resist when people come in to try to stop that? It's a subtle shift but a very important one because it puts the priority on reclaiming, renaming, and representing ourselves in our own land according to our own teachings. Idle No More was a strong reflection of that. But even in the five years that have passed since then, it's very different and I think much stronger. You have much stronger rootedness of this idea of reclaiming our own existence and redefining our own existence as Indigenous people and standing on that and developing political associations, relationships, movements, strategies, and tactics to make that real and to have other people respect that.

To stand on our own authentic Indigeneity and to demand respect is really what Indigenous Resurgence is all about. I think that it's a powerful movement. And I think that the more people inside Indigenous communities and outside of Indigenous communities, whoever is concerned with justice, know about it, the more they're drawn to it, because I don't think that Indigenous Peoples are the only ones who see limitations to reconciliation, recognition, and resistance. So I think that we have a really strong basis for moving together and working together to defeat those forces. And I look forward to the dialogue and continuing conversation and hopefully work in the political realm on the ground with anybody who's concerned with these issues as well.

Mercier Bridge, Kahnawà:ke, July 11, 2020

We will always have the honor to protect our people, land, and rights according to our treaties.

REBUILDING THE FIRE: IN CONVERSATION WITH PAMELA PALMATER

Adapted from an interview on Pamela Palmater's *Warrior Life* podcast, episode 25, July 5, 2019.

Pam Palmater has become one of the leading voices for Indigenous people in Canada and is a true force for Indigenous Nationhood in the work she does as an academic, advocate, and media personality. We have been comrades and friends for many years, and I was honored to be asked to be a guest on her podcast, which features conversations with Indigenous people from diverse cultural and political backgrounds who share a commitment to breathing life into the ancestral vision of their Nations and confronting colonialism in an uncompromising way. At the time of the conversation I had been reflecting on lessons learned over the course of my career as word warrior, foremost in my mind being the price that must be paid and the lessons that must be learned for a person in leadership to be able to stay strong, relevant, and useful to their Nation.

PAM PALMATER: *Hello warriors! This is a show about living the warrior life, a lifestyle that focuses on decolonizing our minds, bodies, and spirits but at the same time revitalizing our culture, traditions, and practices. It's also about asserting, living, and defending our sovereignty all over Turtle Island. Today we have with us a Mohawk warrior who has impacted the lives of Native warriors all over Turtle Island, Dr. Taiaiake Alfred. I have to admit that I have read all of his books, watched most of his public lectures and read his journal articles. Because I'm such a huge fan, and for my own doctoral work and the research that I do, his three books, have had a real impact on me.*

Taiaiake, I've always used your writings as a guidepost to make sure that I'm on the right path when it comes to things like Native sovereignty, independence, Nationhood, and protecting our territories. Welcome, Taiaiake, could you please introduce yourself.

TAIAIAKE ALFRED: Thank you for the introduction and your good words, Pam, I'm so honored to be on your show and so good to hear about the impact of my work in your life and your work. I was born and raised in Kahnawà:ke, Mohawk territory, and I really root myself in that identity and the culture and the ideas that make up what it is to be a Mohawk, Kahnawà:ke. The way I see my work and my career, it's always been an effort on my part to represent what that means to the best of my ability: making the best use of the talents that I've been given by the Creator to go out into the world on a level of what it is to be Kanien'kehaka, a Mohawk person, and to bring the message that our people were given and the lessons that our people have learned about how to survive in this world of colonialism and how to bring the fight of our people to the people and situations that are oppressing us, and to help clarify in the minds of Onkwehónweh what's going on, what they need to do, and what the strategies are, and what the ideas are that they could bring into effect in their personal lives and the lives of their Nations in order to make sure there's still Indigenous Nations in the future. And that's not guaranteed. That's what we were always taught: it's not guaranteed. We have to fight for our survival, and we have to do the things culturally, spiritually, physically, and politically to make sure that the generations that are coming up out of the Earth understand what it is to be Onkwehónweh and that they have the chance to live out that life. And so if I think about my career, whether it's in writing and academics, in politics or community, organizing different movements, that's what it's been all about for me. And, looking back over the thirty-two years I've been at this, there's a lot to reflect on and there's a lot of lessons learned and I really appreciate the chance to talk about that with you.

PP: *I feel really fortunate to share the people I've learned from with the next generations that are coming up because this next generation seems really hungry to know more, to do more and to resist this ongoing oppression. Sometimes I think we take for granted that because, oh, the government has issued a statement saying they recognize our rights or there's a new human rights instrument or something, people think, okay, well we're good. We don't have to worry about that anymore. But in fact, it's always been about us fighting for it and then fighting to keep whatever it is that we do establish. Could* *you talk about what this fight involves, because if you listen to the government – and that's the education source for most Canadians, through the media – it seems like everything's getting better. Everyone focuses on jobs and education and social integration into the Canadian public, and that is the so-called goal for Native people. Can you talk about this fight, and what's really at the root of it? What are we missing in the national dialogue?*

TA: The problem we're facing now is the one that our people have faced all along, but it's really coming to the fore now, and it's more of a challenge than ever: to preserve our basic connection to our homelands in order to remain who we are as collectivities. We're at a place in history where governments have realized that despite all their efforts, it's very difficult to eliminate a race of people and to wipe out the whole notion of Nations that have pre-existed them for tens of thousands of years, that have such a long history in this land, and have cultures and basically a love for their own existence. It's very difficult to do that outright. And so they're trying a different strategy now – assimilation and integration. They're not coming at the effort to eliminate our collective existence in a blunt way, as they have in the past; they're actually enticing us to eliminate ourselves. And so they're offering us the advantages, as they see it, the benefits as they're described, and the enticements of the comfort of an existence which doesn't involve constant battle and constant struggle and which shares some of the material wealth of the conquest of our Nations with us. If it stopped there, that's not a bad thing. We deserve to have the wealth of our land impact our lives in positive ways. But the problem that we're facing today is that there's a big string attached to that, which is that, in order to access these benefits we have to agree to surrender the fundamentals about who we are as a collectivity, which is our presence in this land as autonomous Nations of people: our ancestral ties to this land, our sovereignty, our governance, our autonomy, and, basically, our Nationhood. All the things you talk and write about all the time, Pam, these are the things that our Ancestors fought for, and these are the things that really make us Onkwehónweh, Indigenous people. It's not the fact that we have a nice car, a job that pays the bills, equal access to health care and drinking water and all that stuff – those are things that everybody should have. But the thing that makes us Native is the fact that we have this special connection and we have control over our own territory. We are the ones as Indigenous people, as Onkwehónweh, whose culture governs the way that this land is used, which is to say the relationship between human beings and the natural environment on this continent.

That's what they're trying to break, that's what they're trying to take away – the special connection to our territory, to our land, the special responsibilities we have to make sure that our culture and our ideas and our ethics govern the relation between humans and the natural environment. Right now, their strategy is to make us believe that we're not special, that we're just like everyone else, and that we start to embrace the ideas that the Europeans brought over here in order to create material wealth. And that's simply not possible in the Indigenous values framework that set out the things that define a good human life. They want us to give up on that.

PP: *That's what I really appreciate about your writing. You make it very clear that this isn't a choice between abject poverty and suffering or Native independence. That we are entitled to all of the wealth that we always had before, and we're entitled to the good life as we choose it. But what makes us Native is that we're also autonomous, sovereign Nations, Peoples, and we're connected to the land and it's our territory and we should be the ones governing this territory. And I think it's putting those two things together because what really concerns me is, and I'm going to bring up a political topic, is the Assembly of First Nations (AFN) who started out as the National Indian Brotherhood in a good way as a form of resistance but has now morphed into probably the biggest voice box for Canadian government. And the motto seems to be "Close the gap! Make us like Canadians! Close the gap! Welcome us into your economy. Close the ..." It's always about closing the gap to make us like Canadians and very little talk about land and sovereignty.*

TA: I think that we're caught in this trap. You use the example of the AFN, and I think that to a certain extent, just to be completely blunt, it seems like the AFN is reflecting a feeling that's unfortunately shared among a lot of Indigenous people – that it's not worth fighting for anymore. We all want economic development, so to speak. Everybody wants a comfortable life, feed their kids, go on vacation, and all that kind of stuff. That's a modern type of existence that we all deserve. But the criticism that I have, and that I agree with you on, is that if it comes at the expense of our Nationhood, at the expense of further surrendering the very thing that makes us Onkwehónweh, then I think we need to fight. We need to fight legally, politically, and as our Nations have shown, even physically to defend those very things. It seems like people have lost sight of the nature of the compromises that are being made and the eventual impact of those compromises on our continuing existence. And, that is clearly a facet of our political life today where this effort to close the gap, so to speak, is coming at the expense of the foundation of who we are as a people.

I'm all for closing the gap. If the Canadian government was coming at that question, with a good heart and a good mind and saying, "Let's close the gap and let's also respect the fact that you're a Nation of people who pre-existed us and we want to have a Nation-to-Nation relationship founded on respect," that's great. We could be into that kind of a process with integrity. But if they're coming at it saying, "Let's close the gap, but only if you surrender who you are fundamentally and become a Canadian," no, I don't agree with that. And I know there's a lot of Indigenous people who don't agree with that either. And I think you're right to point out that's there's a younger generation coming up that sees a flaw in that logic, and they're craving something more authentic and rooted in the ancestral vision as far as their movement goes.

PP: *All of these young kids who saw Idle No More, they saw our resistance across the land in various ways. You see this mounting resistance to the Trans Mountain Pipeline that's happening.*[1] *You see sort of a new development. We've always* *had individual First Nations here and there, individuals who have supported the federal government or provincial governments for whatever reasons. We have to admit that we are all colonized people, and dealing with oppression is very difficult, and sometimes you're making very, very difficult choices between two difficult scenarios. However, there are some times when colonization has such an impact on us over time that even with the Trans Mountain Pipeline, I think if this was twenty or thirty years ago, you would have seen more of a unanimous position against this pipeline and in support of the sovereign Nations that live in the territory who will be impacted. Whereas now you kind of see this development where there are some First Nations outside of the area who are now, "Well, let's make this a business, let's put in a proposal," and totally counter the First Nations on the ground who are saying, "Hey, wait, we don't want this, and we don't care if it's the Canadian government imposing it or First Nations imposing it. It's our territory." It's really complex, it's really difficult. This is how colonization works. I understand all of that. But when governments try to use First Nations to essentially silence the voice of impacted First Nations, I'm wondering what you think about these kinds of developments.*

TA: It's a refinement actually of the age-old strategy of divide and rule. We've been facing this from the beginning, this playing off one against the other. But I think that what's happened in recent years is that federal and provincial governments have really hit upon an effective development of their strategy of divide and rule, which in my mind seemed to emerge out of the whole set of debates around self-government and the imposition of policies on taxation and so forth where they identified, in quotes, "champions." They identified certain Indigenous leaders and people within communities who, on one hand, represented truly Indigenous people but, on the other hand, had either been convinced or enticed or in their own mind came to the conclusion that the assimilative pathway was the best thing for Indigenous Peoples, to give them the benefit of the doubt. So they identified these people as champions, and it started with the taxation and with the land management regime. And I think that they found it to be very effective in countering opposition in legal, political, and media terms, and in swaying the Canadian public – which is really the only one that matters for Canadian governments. By saying that there are Indigenous leaders who support this, there's a rationale behind their decision and that they're using it to much greater effect now on much higher-stakes issues like the pipeline. It's a general phenomenon in my mind, and it's their newest turn in the divide-and-rule strategy. It's happening in politics and academia and law and everywhere – to divide and rule by identifying people who are amenable to the government agenda and demonizing or marginalizing everyone else who has a more rooted, and therefore more problematic position, from the government's perspective. It's working quite effectively in their mind. And I think we just need to recognize it for what it is and recognize that the people who are behind the positivity and supporting government agendas and plans and visions and reconciliation frameworks and so forth are all going to be supported financially and legally. And when it comes down to it, with the physical force of the state against the truly rooted Indigenous perspectives.

PP: *You're raising one of the things that concerned me the most: "the Revolution won't be funded." We know as Native people that any advances we've ever made in defending our territories and rights have always come on the backs of our sacrifices. From the very earliest forms of resistance we didn't have bands of lawyers and we didn't have tons of money and we didn't have major PR campaigns, and even Idle No More was an organic growth of grassroots Indigenous resistance that wasn't particularly funded. We face the same kinds of oppression and challenges. They just adapt to new forms. We have a scenario now where "divide and conquer" will, in fact, be funded. We've got this scenario in the west where you have the BC government willing to spend millions of dollars on lawyers and defense funds and law enforcement and PR to give voice to those particular Indigenous leaders who have, for whatever reason, decided to support the government agenda. Whereas we know what's facing the Indigenous resistors on the ground. It's facing law enforcement. It's going to involve trying to fund ourselves and support ourselves in many different ways.*

And what I like most about some of the things that you've talked about in public, and one time I went out to BC to be part of a warrior resistance training camp for some of your students, is that even though we have to be honest about how these challenges are very significant and we can't ignore them, you are also very positive with a plan, you are saying, "But our Ancestors did it. That's the job that we've inherited and here's some things we can do going forward." And you talked about this kind of circle where it's not just the warriors on the ground that are doing the work, but there's all the things that are encircling them that provide support and feed to that. Because we all have our own skills and we all take part in resistance in different ways. It's making sure that we're all together, wrapping our arms around each other, doing support in different ways. I'm just wondering if you could talk about that a little bit because I found that so inspiring.

TA: Oh, well, thanks, that was a good memory you invoked. The circle idea is something I used to use in teaching and in speaking in communities about the idea of where do we stand in relation to the struggle of our Ancestors. It was in response to the feeling that I heard from a lot of people who are getting involved in this struggle in the 2000s that because they were born outside of their community, or they were adopted out, or they were in foster care, or they just grew up in an Indigenous family that wasn't cultured in an Indigenous way for various reasons, they felt like they were outside of the circle. I used to hear that a lot, you're outside the circle.

I talked to some people here in Kahnawà:ke and somebody gave me a story about the fire of our Ancestors, which I believe is a really profound teaching, looking back on it. There was a whole metaphor developed about what constitutes our Nationhood and our existence as people. *Kahwá:tsire* means all our fires are connected, and it works in Mohawk particularly because in the words for fire and family, the root is the same. So, kahwá:tsire: all our fires are connected. The whole idea is that colonialism broke through the original ring of protectors that allowed our fire to be strong and to continue, and all those forces of colonization – the racism, the capitalism, the misogyny, all that kind of stuff – broke through and weakened us by taking away the ability of that fire to sustain itself and to continue to be strong. And so the effort that we're part of now is rebuilding that fire. That's what this idea of Indigenous Resurgence comes from. Rebuilding the fire. You're gathering the embers again, you're picking up all those pieces of wood that used to be burning, metaphorically speaking – our language, our ceremonies, our history, our governance, all those kinds of things. And you're putting them back inside the circle and you're reconstituting that circle. That's what traditional governance is. It's our Clan Mothers and our Chiefs and our laws and our traditions reconstituting, linking arms together and protecting that fire.

The thing that I added to that is, it's not 1700 and it's not even 1800 or 1900, where that's enough. Even if we reconstitute that fire, it was broken once by colonialism and it will likely be broken again. Now, even if we do have our language revitalization and restore traditional governments and teach our kids our history, all of those forces that almost destroyed our Nations earlier on are still here, and they're stronger than ever. And so what we need is another circle around that one. When I wrote *Wasáse*, that's what I was talking about. We had this jokey phrase, the *Wasáse* zone, around the fire, but it's kind of the thing that I'm thinking about, where you need a new circle of protectors around our Nationhood. And that's where all these people who are otherwise thinking of themselves as outside the circle exist.

It's true they're outside the circle. If you're a Mohawk born in Vancouver or if you're a Cree born in Montreal, you're not directly living in the territory of your people. If you're like me and weren't taught Mohawk, you're missing something. And so you could go down the line with all of these things that supposedly take us outside the circle. But in this new way of thinking about it, there's a wider circle and we're all part of it. And this weakness of our existence is actually something that we might think of as a strength. If we're born outside, we know the system better than people who are born inside. We have more experience with it. We speak English very well, we go to white schools, we know the enemies, so to speak. And so there's a utility for us, there's a usefulness for us. And the real problem is, and has been, that all of the people in that zone don't have anyone to be accountable to in the struggle to restore the fire of our Nations. And that's what Indigenous Resurgence addresses. It looks at it and says, all these people living out there should be warriors for our Nations and we need to create pathways for them home, in terms of knowing who they are, welcome them back ceremonially, ritually, identity-wise, and to create an accountability structure for when we're doing the work that we do outside of the first circle of our Nations, outside of the intimate space of our Nations, when we're out here in white society and white institutions battling for our people and our Ancestors in the generations to come, that we answer to our own Ancestors, our own ancestral ways and to the people that live here in our community. That's what we have to recreate. That's Indigenous governance in the twenty-first century. And if we do that, we've just expanded the circle of our warriors and our Nations exponentially. And we've also given the people who live outside the comfort and security and the strength of a community that's not the community of white or immigrant peoples which we all are forced to adopt when we live outside. The basic question is, "Do you answer to your Ancestors and the culture and the traditions of your people? Or do you answer to your employer who happens to be a white university or white institution or white government or all of your friends out there who are not Indigenous?"

These are really fundamental things in conceptualizing who we are in terms of our identity, and it's really important for us to think about this as a framework for our movement. And I think that the Government of Canada understands this very, very well. They probably watch my YouTube videos and read my stuff and understand that there's something powerful in this passing down of Indigenous wisdom and that they need to disrupt it. They need to keep that connection from being made and they need to work in very serious and brutal ways to make sure that those of us that are supposedly outside of that circle remain there and that there's no unity. And that people answer to outside ideas and concepts, European ideas – capitalism, racism, patriarchy – all this stuff that they answer to, rather than to our ancestral teachings. And so all of us who are caught up in colonization and reflect all those things in our lives, we don't find our way back to the circle that is the foundation of our Nations; we don't recover who we are and become part of that community and become a warrior for the matriarchies that are the foundation of our Nations. Instead, we become warriors for other causes that come from Europe.

PP: *That message really inspired me because we, as academics or people that work with First Nations, we learn from the people that we work with, we do research, and sometimes we think, okay, well this is the answer. But then there's these light bulb moments. You are talking about this circle and specifically the circle of people who were born outside of it through no fault of their own. Colonization has made us think that we're all at fault if we don't know our language, or if we don't live in our home reserve, or if we don't know the ceremonies, like it's all our fault. And that guilt carries this idea that we can't connect because we're somehow not authentic and there's nothing that we can do. And for years and years and years I've had Native students come to me and say, "I want to be part of the resistance. I know it's important, but I was raised in foster care. I was taken away from my parents. I don't know my parents, I don't know my family and I don't feel like I belong in that community." You're tapping into the people who have been most impacted by colonization and oppression and forced out of our circle, and saying that there is a place for you, and that you actually have things that you can offer to this resistance, whether it's knowing the language or knowing the colonial laws or knowing the enemy in a way of how can we resist it in multiple forms. That's really inspiring to me because then it's all of us. We're not just talking about a small number of people. We've now holding our arms around our whole family, which is so much bigger. There's lots of people that we need to bring home. I think about all of the people that are* *languishing in prison or the kids that are living on the streets and feel like they have no purpose and they're so disconnected. Your message is "You already are connected, by virtue of who you are and you don't need any other qualification." And you can join this circle and be welcomed back and share what you know and we can share what we know.*

I just really, really, really like this concept of being welcomed back ceremonially because so many people feel so disconnected. I think that's the government's best weapon, that they know that this dynamic exists, because they created it. And if they can continue to foster divisions, and continue to make our people feel bad internally, and continue to create conditions such that we take it out on ourselves, we hurt ourselves, we hurt our family members or we engage in some of the worst kinds of harm, where there's high rates of suicide, and all of this is about disconnecting us from ourselves and our people. And I really appreciate that message because of all these people that are in that circle who want to learn more and be part of it. And I think it's incumbent upon the rest of us to make sure that everybody's inspired and see that there's a different way, that it's not just about having a job and a car, that in fact we're fighting for so much more for our Ancestors. And I really appreciate hearing that message from you because you're part of Kahnawà:ke and you've always been a leader in Indigenous academics and resistance. There are lots of young people who would say, "Where do I fit in all of this?" And you've just said where they all fit. So I really appreciate that.

I know you've done some work in the southern part of Turtle Island in the United States with some of our brother and sister tribal governments. Is the same phenomenon playing out down there in the same way? Is this the kind of message that we should be sharing with our brothers and sisters in the southern part of Turtle Island?

TA: That's an interesting question that I've thought about quite a bit because I have done a lot of work in the so-called United States. I find that the problems are the same in terms of the way people are feeling about this basic issue of disconnection from the land and the kind of alienation and the psychological and the psycho-physical effects of that on their lives. So there's physical impacts in terms of diseases and physical afflictions that come from living an unhealthy existence and being disconnected from our Ancestors' ways. And then there's the psychological impact as well, which affects us in terms of not living out our true vision of ourselves as to who we are. That's unfortunately very common all across North America: in almost every Native community you visit, you recognize it. And to a certain extent it's a good thing in that it feels like home everywhere you go. But the negative part is that we're all in our homes dealing with the same problems. And I think that the way to resolve it, in my mind it's the same answer. But while it's the same answer, the way to enact it and to breathe life into it is different because there's different laws, there's a different political system, there's different constraints, and there's different opportunities. There's opportunities and challenges they have down there that we don't have here, and vice versa. I guess the way to think about it is, it's the same goal with the same vision but has to be adapted to a legal and political environment that is very different to the one in Canada. And so if you're going to do this kind of work down in the States, you have to learn that way of relating to governance and the laws and the policies and the kind of strategies that you've developed coming out of that are different than the ones that you use here.

PP: *Yes, I noticed the same thing. When I started working with some of the Native governments down there, I just assumed they were in a better position because they have some degree of recognition of their sovereignty vis-à-vis the individual states. I thought their issues would be different, but when I started working with them, it's literally all the same. It's just, as you said, a very different political context or legal context and dynamic. But the core concerns of communities and the core concerns of the people who are living away from communities are all the same. They're about protecting our land and autonomy and our identity and for future generations. I was really struck by that. In some of the limited work that I've done with Indigenous Peoples at the United Nations, I hear the same thing from Native Hawaiians and Samoans and Native people from New Zealand and Australia – that on a more global level, they have some of the very same issues, having suffered from colonization, and they just have a different political and legal context.*

So I really like how you can breathe life into that, your concept of this circle, regardless of what the context is, so long as we adapt for the context.

Another thing I got out of your writings, especially your books, but also in this warrior camp that we had (which I wish was everywhere all the time) was this idea that there's a personal dynamic to sovereignty and autonomy and Native identity. The collective is this primary sovereign idea, but as individuals we are also responsible and accountable to our

Ancestors for how we live our lives as individuals – not just necessarily in the fight for sovereignty and land, but how we take care of our own health and our own spirituality and well-being. And I'm wondering if you can talk a little bit about the idea that we also need to be acting as sovereign individuals.

TA: That's one thing that I learned starting investigating this whole idea of warriorhood. Basically I started in 2000 and did research and interviews and traveled all over the place talking to people about this idea of the warrior, and that evolved into *Wasáse*. The one thing that was very, very clear was that you can't build a strong movement on weak people. We can't ever achieve our liberatory goals unless we're constantly working at strengthening ourselves as well. And so, looking back, I'm still proud of that book because it kind of anticipated a lot of the issues and discussions and conflicts and challenges that came afterwards and are happening today in terms of looking at our own individual colonization. The basic point is that we have to be honestly and authentically looking at where we stand in relation to colonialism, how we embody colonial behaviors and ideas and attitudes. And every single one of us, including me, embodies colonial ideas. The first step is recognizing that and then taking the steps necessary to try to understand and then change and transform ourselves using the teachings of our Ancestors and the support of our communities to be able to embody more of our ancestral vision than the colonial teachings and experiences that we've all been shaped by. I think it's still hard for some people to acknowledge that because it's such a personal, intimate, and very emotionally fraught process. We barely survived, and then we go and ask people to reflect on their problematic behaviors and weaknesses. That's asking a lot of some people, but I believe it's absolutely necessary. And if you can't do it on your own, then having people around you to be able to talk to you and look at you in a supportive way and say, "This is where we're at, this is where you're at and this is where we need to change." That's what those gatherings that you were mentioning were all about. They were about political strategy, but they were also about building a network of support for people to work their own way through their own colonization and be able to strengthen themselves as leaders. It was called the Indigenous Leadership Forum, and there was a reason for that: it was trying to create the circle of accountability and this circle of support for people to move through all of these challenges.

Thinking about where we've come from, if I look at where I've come from in my life, from the kind of community I was raised in, the kind of values I was given, the kind of language I spoke, the kind of ideas I had about all kinds of issues – politics, gender, relationships, physicality, physical health, all these things – these have evolved over time in relation to this constant effort to relate myself to my Ancestors and to find a truer way of being a Mohawk. And so this process in my mind never stops, because the colonization is very deep in our communities and it's constantly throwing new things at us. So we need these kinds of relationships in these circles in order to continue to evolve as leaders, and to be truer to the vision of our Ancestors, and not to reflect the negative. And by negative, I mean things that are harmful to our cause of Indigenous Nationhood and all of the values of peace, power, and righteousness that we have embedded in our culture. If we're going to become people who are able to recognize the things that we do and say that impact that negatively, and change and evolve to a higher standard of leadership, then I think that we need those circles and we need the active process. And it's a difficult thing. It's a challenging thing. It's a painful thing, in a lot of ways, but it's absolutely necessary. And I think that I hit on that in *Wasáse*, but the actual living of it is a very daunting thing and you have to be very committed to the struggle to stay at it. It's easy to run away and it's easy to take solace in the comfort of the bourgeois existence.

PP: *The bougie Native existence.*

TA: Yes, the easy outs that are afforded people, especially if you're privileged. If you happen to be a highly educated person you have the privilege of escape into those circles and not being held to account by community members for your disconnection. If you're a male, you have the privilege of escape into male patriarchal circles and not have to be held to account by women. And so on and so on. And so there's a lot of ways for every one of us to escape. To be committed to the struggle, staying in it and continuing to learn from the struggle, is something that a warrior does – they don't run away from the challenge. To me it's one of the essential aspects of what it is to be a warrior, especially today when our culture is so confused and our people are so affected by colonial behaviors and ideas.

PP: *To me as an individual that was really impactful because there's certain parts of warrior living that are easier than others. You can speak out on issues and advocate, you can help your community. But then you have to turn inward and say, "Oh wait, am I living a warrior life? How's my nutrition? Am I just living on sugar and processed foods and all of the things that are going to make me live a shorter, unhealthier life, a life that I won't have the strength to keep up the fight in the future? And what about my physicality? Am I keeping up? Am I treating my body the way a warrior should treat their body so that we'll live 120 years and be strong warriors so that we can keep up the fight and we have this huge collective? Or am I myself contributing to the colonization of myself and making myself weaker and weaker and weaker, whether it's health or spirituality or relationships?"*

I like how the way you think about warriorhood is in a holistic way, holistic in the sense of individual and collective, holistic in the sense of those that perceive themselves to be inside and outside the circle. And, no matter where we are on Turtle Island, I think we have to really think about warriorhood that way and push out all of these horrible colonial ideas that the government would say, oh, here's what a good Native is versus the so-called bad Natives. And that you've really shared a lot with us today. I wanted to share with my listeners some of your really strong wisdom and knowledge. You're sharing what you've learned and you're sharing how you think about being accountable to our Ancestors. And I think that is the support group. Sometimes we can't all be together. Not everyone has the privilege to be able to meet you in Kahnawà:ke and talk with your community and say, "Okay, what are we doing?" So we have to use this social media platform as another gathering place to bring all of our warriors together and weed out, decolonize all of these of oppressive thoughts and oppressive ideologies and challenges that the government and media and corporations and society as a whole really put on us. This isn't just a government issue. It's a whole of society issue. And with the rise of white nationalism and lots of other hate groups, I think it's even more important on us to bring our circle together and bring all our warriors together and show these youth we have a path forward and it'll be a much healthier, stronger path. We just have to commit to it, no matter how hard it is. And so I want to thank you so much for all of your work, Taiaiake, for inspiring so many people, for learning over time and evolving and adapting. Our views change over time and our practices change over time. And I appreciate the humbleness and that you can acknowledge that we're not in the same place we were twenty years ago. Our minds change, our practices change, and that's part of it. That's decolonization, how we improve ourselves over time. So I really appreciate that.

TA: It's been an honor and I'll come back anytime.

Tekakwitha Island, Kahnawà:ke, 2020.

Take me to the river to feel the harmony of Heaven and Earth.

RONÓN:KWE

Adapted from an interview on Ian MacKenzie's *The Mythic Masculine* podcast, episode 34, January 19, 2021.

This conversation with Settler Ally journalist and filmmaker Ian MacKenzie for his series of podcasts delving into the ways in which versions of masculinity are produced and transformed in different places and cultures gave me the opportunity to trace my own manhood journey from youth to maturity and reflect back on the ideas and thoughts about what it is to carry the responsibilities of a Ronón:kwe, a Mohawk man, as they evolved over the years.

IAN MACKENZIE: *You joined the military when you were eighteen or so, and I'm curious to approach this question around masculinities: What was it in your upbringing that maybe put forth a model or idea or sense of masculinity so that you wanted* *to join the military? In some ways it tends to be a very masculine place. For you growing up, what was it that influenced you, that drew you to choose that role or that function?*

TAIAIAKE ALFRED: I think in some ways it's kind of a universal experience, in all societies, that happens to everyone … a situation where every young boy growing up has to find a way to prove himself. There's a menu of options in the culture that you grew up in. For the culture that I grew up in, in order to manifest your manhood and your masculinity the menu was dominated by ironwork, high steel iron work. Most of the men in my community, including my father and all his friends and all my relatives and grandfathers, did high steel ironwork. That's one model. That's one thing you could do, not only to satisfy the basic requirements of manhood as it was constructed at the time in terms of providing for a family and contributing to the community economically and so forth but also to gain the esteem and the recognition of moving from boyhood to manhood. There was that. There was the sport of lacrosse, which our Haudenosaunee people invented and which is very significant in the cultural life of our community. So proving yourself by playing lacrosse and your exploits around that game. Then there's the military. It's different now because the military of course doesn't distinguish on gender anymore, but at the time I was growing up and when I joined – this was early 1980s – it was still gendered male primarily and almost exclusively.

Those were the three models. Of course, there were people – rarely – who did not follow one of those pathways and had other jobs. It was emerging in the 1980s that you could take part in higher education, and you could do other things. But I think it's fair to say that in the late '70s and early '80s in a place like Kahnawà:ke, those were the three ways that you engaged with a masculinity and a model of what it was to be a man. My father did not want me to be an ironworker. He refused to sponsor me and let me enter that trade. He wanted me to do something different. I wasn't a very good lacrosse player at the time. One thing I had as an option to pursue was the military.

That's an interesting question too, to kind of go back into your seventeen-year-old mind and figure out what was driving you at the time. All I can do to try to answer that question is to try to recall the imagery and the experiences that stayed with me. I think it was definitely, in my mind at the time, a pathway for validation as a man. There are all these kinds of smaller motivations about wanting to travel and not having money, growing up on a reserve, not having the financial means. A lot of non-Indigenous young people have parents to sponsor them to go to Europe for a year or to go to college and take trips and things. We didn't have that. So for me, there was that adventure element. There was the cool factor. You're seventeen years old; it's pretty hard to beat the United States Marines for coolness in that era. But I also have to say, I used to dream about it as a teenage boy. I don't know, it might've been GI Joe, comics, it might've been movies, it might have been the *World Book Encyclopedia,* looking at the pictures. To me, the United States Marines represented the epitome of a man at the time.... I was drawn to that.

IM: *It comes to me as this sense of longing or desire to step into the role of the warrior, archetypically or iconically, this younger boy view of the Marine as the coolest expression of the warrior that you could see or had access to. I know in your work, you've talked about the warrior and the role of warrior in Indigenous communities. What did you learn during your time in the Marines? How did it map on to what you thought it was or what it wasn't? How did your sense of the warrior change?*

TA: I think you're right to point to the motivational factor, being wanting to explore and touch that idea of a warrior and be one. The main lesson that I have, after all these years thinking about it, is that I have realized that what it is to be a warrior is really to endure suffering. To have courage, to persevere, and to do what's necessary to fulfill the responsibilities you have to that community. And so of course my "community" in quotes has changed. When you're a United States Marine you're protecting the Empire. So there was a lot of respect in the Marine Corps, not only for people who were super-skilled, or all buffed out and strong, but you got respect for your Esprit de Corps. You got respect whether you were *Gung Ho*, whether you had the fighting spirit, and whether you were brave, whether you were crazy brave.

For me it's shifted over time, but the essence of that is who's willing to put themselves forward to stand in the way of danger, to have the courage to fight through their fear, to do what needs to be done to protect the core of their community and what they believe in? So to me, I kind of found that through experience in the Marine

Corps. I have kept that idea of being ready to stand up and do what's necessary, whatever the consequences.

I think this is very consistent, from what I've learned from reading and from talking to people, with Indigenous teachings on warriorhood. There's no Mohawk word for a "warrior"; it translates to *Rotiskenhrakete* – "those that carry the burden of peace." So the way I looked at it was over time, I came to understand warrior in a different, deeper, more expanded way by going further into the teachings in my own culture. What I found was that I had to let go of a lot of ideas around soldiering or warriorhood that came from that imperial shock troop experience that I had when I was young. But the core of warriorhood is the same in all cultures when it's practiced, I think, in its essence, and when it's practiced properly: it's that willingness to suffer, willingness to go to the extreme, to die, and to kill, which is, in a lot of ways, harder than dying, I think. To kill for the People. Who the people are, that changes over time for us Indigenous people. As I became more and more decolonized, I saw myself more rooted in this understanding of my people as being my Indigenous Nation in the resurgence of our being, as opposed to being just part of the larger society as an ethnic person who happened to be Native American.

IM: *In her book* The Chalice and the Blade *Riane Eisler talks about this recognition of "dominator culture" – she uses that lens as opposed to patriarchy, which can miss this deeper layer of a culture of domination. For example, the army or the police or these other sorts of warrior roles in an imperial culture end up being used for furthering domination. It's just such* *a different energy than what you just described as a warrior carrying the burden of peace; I can actually see them almost as inverse. The expressions may be similar – needing to use force when necessary and needing to kill – but the reason or orientation is very different, if it's for the nation state versus actual people that you know, a community you're protecting. That's a very powerful distinction, especially for men who may not have that sense that there are other possibilities.*

TA: The issue I think we're still grappling with is when you are in combat, whether or not that's on a battlefield, or on a sports field, or on the street if you're a cop, is to what degree and what kinds of dominator skills are still necessary in order to survive? So, you grew up in certain environments, or you put yourself in certain situations like I did in the Marine Corps, you do need those dominator skills. You need to know how to fight; you need to know how to pull the trigger. You have to have that kind of mental sharpness and emotional hardness to be able to do stuff like that. A lot of the discussion is around how to leave that on the battlefield, how to leave that on the street, or leave that on the court, so to speak. But I think what we're finding now is that it's really hard to do that. What we're finding out about cop culture and the domestic relations they have, and you certainly find it in the military, and you find that with team sports as well, the ideas that you have that are ingrained in you that you need to be successful, never mind just to survive, but to be successful in that environment, it's hard to leave those behind when you're not in contest. So that's a big problem. They get ingrained in you, even though you're not a violent person, you're not a person who intends to do harm or wants to do harm or has any motivation to do that, it's hard to switch on and off. So the attitudes stay there.

That's the beauty, I think, of Indigenous teachings on warriorhood. The key difference in the idea and practice of warriorhood among our people in Haudenosaunee or Iroquois communities at least is that the warrior is operating within the context of women's power and decision-making and a balance between men and women. There's no separation. It's not like it's just all men. When I was in the military, and I think it's still the case that although there are a lot of women and other genders in the US military now, it's still very much a man's world and a man's game. When you have men telling other men what to do and men trying to impress other men in a physical and social space that's completely male, that's different than operating as a warrior where you have women watching over you with the ability to determine the decisions in that community. I think that's key in understanding the difference between mainstream and Indigenous concepts of warriorhood.

IM: *I appreciate this sense of sourcing of what it means to be a good warrior, to be a good man, because I feel like modern culture is dogged by a kind of lostness in that it doesn't know where to source its sense of what's meaningful. I hear you saying, "In the Mohawk tradition, this is the way we did it." Could you speak more about that need to actually be in relationship to a place or to an actual specific cosmology in a way to have any sense of what is meaningful?*

TA: I think that in terms of being an Indigenous person and in terms of masculinity, we're all unfortunately subject to not only the struggle that every man goes through in trying to find himself and work out a way that is satisfying and ethical and useful and good but also doing that in a colonial context where it's not only that; it's also this pressing need to defend ourselves from the assault of colonialism, psychologically, physically, spiritually and also from the erasure of any kind of positive, healthy, useful-to-our-own-community notion of what it is to be a man. It's not that way now because, of course, we put work into it and we've had some movement where young boys now have other ideas to integrate into their own notions. But when we were growing up it was still a very colonized reality and the process of surviving and empowering and living out your masculinity in that environment is very messy. That's for a person that has a strong sense of self and intelligence and the mental strength to be able to get through that. You can imagine for all the people that by no fault of their own don't possess those things and fall victim to the worst teachings of colonialism on what it is to be a man.

There is really no other way in my mind to realize what it is to be a father, an uncle, a brother, a partner, a good man, as a Mohawk, as a Haudenosaunee person, as a Onkwehónweh, other than tracing the roots back to the central teachings of what it is to be part of a family. What is it in terms of a set of responsibilities? What kind of roles and responsibilities do people have who are male gendered in this environment? What I've found is that there isn't really a set of teachings on masculinity: it's about how to be a good human being.

It's about people serving different roles based on the gifts and the talents and the particularities of their birth. The fact that you're a man versus a woman or another gender, these are things you have to consider, but the framework for thinking about goodness is the same for all of us. It's how do you serve the community? How do you live out the spiritual aspect of your existence? How are you a good human being? And so to me, that's been essential insight: there's no way to be a good man and a good woman. It's how to be a good human being.

As a man, in a physical sense, in a cultural sense, and at this moment in history, how do I manifest the responsibilities that I have? In our culture, the teachings are the only way. You have to immerse yourselves in the mythology. You have to put yourself in a vulnerable position, to have people look at you and teach you in various ways, through words, through actions, through criticism, through holding you to account to teaching you by example, all of these different things. It's this active process of decolonizing your mind and your way of being with the objective of tracing that root back to the center of the community, where we believe our Ancestors had a really good way of living amongst themselves that promoted the values that we all share as human beings. According to accounts of people who encountered them and through our own oral histories, the Ancestors were very satisfied people. They were very happy people. They were very healthy people. To trace our root back to how to be part of that family, what contributions do we need to make to ensure that it is their lived reality of future generations? That's the real question: What is it to be a good human being?

IM: *When I speak to Indigenous Peoples about how they orient around these questions, in ceremony and different tasks in the community, they say, well, there are different roles, but they're not in opposition. I see that as a fundamentally different orientation from a lot of the modern mainstream discourse on gender.*

TA: I think what you're talking about is reflected in the central story of the founding of the Haudenosaunee Confederacy. It's a long story and has many elements to it but one aspect of it reflects our conversation right here. In the story, in the teaching we have, there are all kinds of people and there are all kinds of examples of how to be a human and how to be a man and how to be a woman. It's not a story of defeating or overcoming or molding these diverse ways of being into a perfect way of being a Mohawk or Onkwehónweh. It's about the harmonization and the unification of these into a whole, which in its diversity represents a power of being that is something worth preserving in the world.

There's the Peacemaker in our story who comes with a message to our people because our people had descended into civil war, chaos, cannibalism. This is the story of the Haudenosaunee before the Peacemaker. He comes into our world and he encounters a warrior who is willing to listen: Hiawatha. Hiawatha means "he's awakened." Here you have a warrior who's the Chief of a village living out this reality which nobody wants to live anymore, but they're caught in this cycle of violence and they don't know how to come out of it.

The Peacemaker comes and Hiawatha is the first one to listen and give this message respect. He suffers for it. He loses his daughters and he suffers all kinds of things. There's also a woman in the story, Jigonsaseh, she is a person who is aiding the warriors. The message is brought to her, she accepts it, and she stops assisting the warriors with their battles and becomes the first Clan Mother who's going to advise and guide the Chiefs in their decision-making. You also have the War Chief who refuses to accept the message: he and his boys challenge the Peacemaker to prove what he's saying, because they don't believe him, and if they let their guard down, who's to say that these other Nations are not going to come in and try to kill them while they're sleeping? So you have all these stories woven together. There comes a point where the head sorcerer of the whole territory, Tadodaho, who is evil-minded, twisted, with snakes for hair, a great Medicine Man who can do great harm to the land and the people, comes in. They all come and bring all of their unique realities and powers to this person and convince him to smooth out his hair and become part of the Great Peace, and they make him the head Chief for doing so.

The thing that strikes me is that in the essential mythology of the Haudenosaunee you have an acknowledgment of all of these different types of people and characters and instincts and necessities and roles. They don't get rid of the warrior. They don't get rid of Tadodaho. They're all harmonized for peace and so the message is very different from "The One Right Way" of Christian cultures where there's one way, there's one truth, "the only way through it is through me." We all know the kind of refrains from Christian mythology and the way it's been translated into Western European cultures: "I am the way, the truth and the light" and that's it. I think that the genius of our way is that we recognize that in any human society you're going to have all these things; the one thing that is absolutely necessary in the thing we struggle for, the thing we strive for, is this balance and this harmonization of diversity, and so we accept these different ways and roles, not only in their reality but the necessity of them. We need people to protect, we need people to do these other roles and so forth, but what are they subsuming themselves to? The chance for the next generation and two and three and four and five generations to live in peace amongst each other is the thing that they're asked to sacrifice for.

Beaver Dam, Kahnawà:ke, 2022

In spite of the loss and the harms, there is still such beauty in our land and lives.

ROOTED RESPONSIBILITY

Adapted from an interview with Syracuse University professor Hugh Burnam for his PhD research.

Among the generation of Indigenous scholars and activists coming up in our movement, there are many who speak our Indigenous languages, who are more culturally knowledgeable and informed about the effects of intergenerational traumas, and who are committed to manifesting our Ancestral ways in their lives, to a much greater degree than among people of my own generation, and especially within our Haudenosaunee communities. I felt privileged to have the opportunity for an intergenerational dialogue with one such person, Hugh Burnam, when he interviewed me as part of his research into Haudenosaunee masculinities and our people's experiences with institutions of higher education.

HUGH BURNAM: *Where did you find mentorship during your education experience?*

TAIAIAKE ALFRED: There were a lot of people in Kahnawà:ke who encouraged me to do what I did, and be the way I am, and the ways I relate to my community and my responsibility. My dad's family, they're pretty militant. They're a radical warrior society crowd and there was always this kind of responsibility to contribute to the struggle. My mother's family owned a business and they're really community-grounded people, not as political, but more along the lines of, you've got to help the people of Kahnawà:ke. So, I always thought about my education in that sense.

There was a family friend, Mary Two-Axe Earley. She was one of the first people who stood for Haudenosaunee women's rights, the ones who married out and lost their status and were fighting to get their recognition back as Mohawks. She encouraged me to get an education and to use it for the Mohawk people. The people I worked for in Kahnawà:ke were very influential. Billy Two Rivers was a prominent controversial guy in his younger days, a professional wrestler and very flamboyant. He came back from Europe to focus on politics, he was our first intergovernmental relations guy on the band council side, I worked for him. Our recently deceased former Grand Chief, Joe Norton, influenced me. Arnold Goodleaf, who worked for Indian Affairs in Ottawa for many years and then came back, he was my direct supervisor.[1] I learned a lot from him about politics, how to work in this environment, and to achieve things in the political realm.

I've named people who hadn't gone through higher education but who understood the value of it and always encouraged and supported me. They always pushed me to move forward, and I attribute that to their own good sense as Mohawks to say, we could use people that are educated. But they also grounded me in a lot of different ways, through teaching and joking, that need to stay connected and humble and answerable to the people. I think they understood that people who go to university tend to get disconnected and start answering to people outside the community. They made sure that didn't happen to me. And so, right from the beginning, it's been part of who I am, and I've always been willing to make the sacrifice – to alienate people on the outside to stand with my community. I don't think a lot of people in the university environment understand the importance of doing that to fulfill your responsibilities, but it was taught to me early on.

HB: *You've said some Indigenous people in university settings don't always necessarily understand their responsibilities.*

TA: It happens as you rise in any organizational hierarchy in mainstream society – could be arts or government or business. In university, as you make that journey from undergraduate student to graduate student to professor to being a manager or administrator, you become more and more part of the organization. The reward is security, money, validation, status, but there's also a cost. They expect your loyalty. The more responsibility they give you, the more they expect you to carry out their mandate, answer to their values, and represent the institution. But universities are part of the colonial structure and still in a colonial relationship to our communities, so it's a very difficult position to be in. My life as an academic has been always colored by that tension. I never for one minute questioned my responsibility of choosing to side with the community, even when it went against the mandate of the university.

I'll give you two examples. One was supporting the Land Back movement. It's a big hashtag now, but twenty years ago in British Columbia it was militant. The Warrior Societies and militant youth were involved, they were ruffling feathers, pissing people off … they were doing things that would bring them – and me – into the realm of criminality in the eyes of mainstream Canada and the people who run the university. My instinct and also my reasoned positionality was, I'm a senior professor in this university, but I'm Onkwehón-weh first. I never came to the university just for the job. I came to act as an agent of Indigenous Nationhood; and this is the right thing to do. It caused me lots of trouble.

The second example involved my own community's ideas about membership. In Kahnawà:ke the rule is, if you marry a non-Native, that non-Native person can't live on the reserve and your rights are impacted. Like most people in the community, I have all kinds of complicated and subtle views around that, but nobody supports white people coming to live on the reserve, and very few people do it. Somebody brought a legal action against the community because of the membership rules. The community asked me, as a Mohawk historian and scholar, to be its expert witness as part of its defense against the legal action. It wasn't just the band council – everybody's like, "Nobody should tell us who our members are except us." So, what do you do, right? For me, again, no question. I did it.

Some university people started saying all kinds of things about that, but there are other ways of thinking about answerability. It's not only to these power structures that demand certain things about you that are colonial. It's the whole idea of what it is to be Onkwehónweh – what's the true Indigenous perspective, what's valued? In the university there are people who look at my community's membership ideas as backwards, misogynist, racist, and so forth, and so anybody who stands up and defends them is labeled that way. I knew this going into it, and I think that if you're not truly committed to your responsibilities as part of that community, you would be scared off. But for me, there was no question. When your own community's views go against the consensus of Indigenous academia, it's a very subtle and in many ways more difficult choice to make. Indigenous academia is influenced by all kinds of discourses – human rights, feminism – they all have merit. But when they prevent you from actually supporting your community when it needs you, to me all that theory goes out the window. Our community was under legal assault and I needed to help out. So, that's another example: are you willing to burn all your bridges and be tarred and feathered by Indigenous academics when you stand up for your people? I have to say yes.

HB: *One of the things I had running through my head when you were giving your examples is the way that the university seems to affect Indigenous communities, especially since we have many Indigenous scholars coming back to our communities. But with that education comes influences from the outside world. We've known the outside world for 500 years; we can't pretend we exist in a vacuum. In what ways would you say the university influences Indigenous communities?*

TA: University brings influences in so many different ways, both negative and positive. I've seen some really good people who engage in the university and get educated to whatever level and then commit back to working with Indigenous people, whether it's in an urban environment or on a rez, foregoing the benefits of a career on the outside. I've seen the negative example of people who get caught up in social or political or intellectual circles that actually transform their understanding of themselves and their responsibilities and their own community. They bring those outside perspectives and ideas back to the community, not with a constructive intent, but with the intent to kind of fix the community, to bring in an agenda determined from the outside. I think that's where the problem lies: if there's no real engagement or real accountability to the community, but instead it's like an effort to fix the community, that's where people get into trouble.

I think for a lot of academics, their Indigenous identity is built on the clout, the respect, the validation they've got in the university. Good for them for doing that. But then you have to go back and take the position of a youngster in a debate or in a community context where people are like, "You don't know shit – just sit and listen." They have to stand up with their own being, not their credentials. It's a daunting task. If you grew up there and if you love the place, it's no problem. I'm used to getting told off, my whole life I've been put in my place by people there. For all its faults, for however messed up it is sometimes, for all of the things that you know are wrong with it, you have that love for your community, and that puts you in a position of humility. It puts you in a position of wanting to seriously commit to helping those people on their own terms and being part of a community, not standing apart, not standing above, not standing outside lecturing or giving ideas or thinking you know better. I aspire to do that. But it's difficult for some people to go from being respected as an expert and having all the people, students and academic administrators, kind of bow down to you as an Indigenous expert, to then go home and have to earn your way, your voice. I think what matters to a lot of Indigenous academics are the bourgeois rewards of being an academic. They don't want to put the work into going into a community and having to go through all that stuff in order to have a voice and be respected in the community.

HB: *When you say community, you mean your people's community. It's different to people talking about community in the context of a university.*

TA: Do you remember the talk I gave on Indigenous masculinity at the NAISA [Native American and Indigenous Studies Association] conference in Honolulu in 2016? That was the genesis of the hatred that some Indigenous feminists have toward me, because the crux of what I said in response to an audience question about community accountabilities was: this is not a community. This is a bunch of people with self-centered motives working in a white system to get paid and to move up, and there's no accountability or answerability. I said my accountability is to the Kahnawakerò:non, the people of Kahnawà:ke. But for most of the room, those academic groups and organizations and conferences, that's their community, and they were insulted by the fact that I dismissed it. I think what they heard was, you're not a real Native, but what I mean is, you're certainly not a real Native academic if you haven't engaged in real community where people come together on Indigenous terms, whether it's rez-based or in an urban context. I think that's a hard thing for people to swallow who only put the effort into building themselves up in an academic environment.

HB: *Although that was a quick interaction, I sat with it for a long time. It changed the way I thought about issues of masculinity, definitions of feminism, and what it might mean for different groups of people. I'm interested in the way my community views equality or equity, not what's been co-opted from the outside. While we can learn and listen to people who bring in new ideas, there's this struggle, this kind of tension. What are your thoughts on these ideas or definitions of gender?*

TA: It's a huge question. I think we experienced in that very moment a genesis of conflict between two completely different perspectives and a whole a set of engagements that have gone off in different ways, some positive in terms of leading people to do better research or have deeper insights and a lot negative, just because of the colonial context that we live in and how people are functioning in academic contexts without a stable, solid understanding of who they are. There's all kinds of turmoil: intergenerational traumas, experience traumas, unprocessed guilt and hatred, all kinds of harms. Unfortunately, in the first phase of this whole Indigenous Nationhood movement, that wasn't put up front. These discussions haven't been happening in a context that's supported by culture or by even basic safety nets for people who have experienced trauma: they have reactions and issues that that are not related to ideas, but that are more visceral and cause them to say and do things and react to people in a certain way.

It's hard to believe now given where we're at, but outside of some feminist circles there was no mainstream discussion about these masculinity issues when I decided to stick my neck out and start talking about them around 2013. I saw it as an act of leadership to say, okay, I'm a man of some privilege and power in the university who's achieved something within this structure, and now the structure and my role are getting critiqued and criticized, and I don't have a vocabulary. I don't fully understand. I don't believe I've done anything wrong, but obviously there are problems because some people are pointing them out. So let's start talking about masculinity. I'm going to talk about men and boys and raising men and masculinity. Even though I'm a beginner on questions framed using gender analyses, I'm going to start trying. I knew it was going to cause a firestorm when we started talking about these unprocessed issues – all the suppressed rage and hurt that we were giving an opening, and a face, and an embodiment. I was willing to be that person, to show some leadership and to follow up with what happens because of it. But the sad thing for me was that it wasn't taken as a dialogue or an attempt to learn or work together in the context of a concept of Indigenous Nationhood. It was taken as an attempt to kind of usurp women's roles in bringing light to things that were wrong or to put a cap on it or to cover it. In fact it was the furthest thing from that as far as my own motivations.

I think most people who identify as feminist want reconciliation between men and women and people of other genders. They want the wholeness to be restored, peace, they want things to get better. But there is this little fringe within that group with an ideological perspective that men in power are a threat, that any man in power is there by virtue of patriarchy, has misogynistic intent, and should be taken out. And that small element dominated because they were more vocal, more active, and more passionate. I was willing to make a stand and pay the price because, however ugly and painful, it is what needed to be done. I didn't come up in gender studies, so I didn't understand, initially, everything they were talking about, what they meant by masculinity. I've learned a lot from listening to people and reading the literature, and now I've come to understand it from a critical perspective.

Masculinity was defined in negative terms and that needed to happen. That was the first phase, where the ugliness was exposed and the negativity was brought to the front. The people that led that were defined by a very strong critical version of feminism and their intent is not to rebuild our communities or families or to make their brothers or sons or uncles better. That wasn't their goal. I think now we're seeing this kind of energy playing itself out. It's not leading to harmonization and reunification. The problems that we're identifying are not going away. It's not making things better. I don't have a lot of time for people whose main objective is only to punish or who say they want to bring down the patriarchy without putting that goal in the context of patriarchy being situated within colonialism and the need to strengthen our families and rebuild our Nations. After all this time, I'll still stand by the idea that any theory or analysis of gender that doesn't feed into the restoration of the strength of our culture, and our repositioning ourselves on our land and the restoration of our traditional government systems is at best a distraction and at worst a column of whiteness into our communities.

HB: *You had built a very successful Indigenous Governance program and around 2015 it came under a lot of criticism, and you left it. Can you tell me what happened from your perspective?*

TA: My understanding has evolved to the point now where I can understand it in its complexity, but back then, it was some students saying it was a "violent" environment. I remember thinking to myself, what are they talking about? As far as I know, no one's ever been injured or assaulted or had any kind of experience in any way close to that. But the decolonizing method that I had put into practice in the program was now being identified as problematic. The method, basically, was to point out someone's flaws and weaknesses, ask them to explain them, hold them to a standard of behavior, tell them that this is what it is to be Indigenous, and you need to work to achieve that. If you don't put the work into it, you're letting your Nation down. That was the message. I've been completely open about that and stand by that. That's what we were asked to do and that's what we were doing. People came from all over the world to get that experience and education.

Over time the concept of harm changed. People's emotional state, the psychological effects of their interactions with other students and my teaching methods, the negative self-perceptions they started to feel, all these sorts of things are now seen as forms of harm. University programs all over the country were following a trend toward creating environments where students were insulated from these experiences. And in Indigenous education they started promoting a reconciliatory healing outlook and model. When this started happening, I said, "I don't think the point of education should be to make people feel good." When this became clear to me, I chose to stand by the things I had said and done – though of course I was sorry for causing anyone to truly suffer or be harmed. But tough love was our way, and for twenty years I was held up as a hero for doing things that all of a sudden became harm, and I was villainized by some of the very people and I had taught and mentored and who had held me up.

I had to check myself, in my own mind. I was like: I can probably learn a few things about sensitivity, but I'm not changing my views; I don't believe in reconciliation; I don't believe in this new no-standards model of education; I didn't get into education to make the ground fertile for white people to come in and learn and appropriate our culture and our ways; and I didn't come to teach white kids about Onkwehónweh. For twenty-plus years I did what I believed to be necessary to train leaders who are strong enough to go out into the real world and fight off white power and to Indigenize the university. I was great at motivating and mobilizing people to get things done on campus, and sometimes that was in the mode of a bulldozer using First Nations leaders and students to push university administrators where they did not want to go. But in the end I realized that people were right when they said that the ground had shifted. Because of criticisms by a few students of our program for it being a toxic environment that didn't welcome all perspectives, people in university circles weren't willing to defend it anymore. People started to believe that both I, and the program that reflected my ideas and methods, were too radical, too militant, too exclusionary, too tough, and causing harm to students.

My whole time in academia, I took the advice of Vine Deloria Jr. seriously. He told me once that it was our responsibility as Indigenous intellectuals to work our way into the system, get the White Man to trust us, and then turn on them. It's funny, but it's no joke! That's my experience, that was my commitment. But after years of conflict within academia, I realized it was time to begin the next phase of the journey because obviously my understanding of what education is, what kind of leadership we need, how to confront colonial mentalities, masculinity, decolonization, are no longer valued in the academic environment, which is focused on reconciliatory goals and creating inclusive healing spaces. I realized that I needed to understand myself again in the context of my own community. I needed to live and put myself in that community. So I went back to Kahnawà:ke, where for the past five years I've put a lot of mental and spiritual energy into critiquing my own ways. I've learned a lot and come to some realizations about the things we did wrong in the program. It's not a criticism of what we did, but in today's language, it was not "trauma-informed" education. We weren't told, we weren't trained, and we didn't have that vocabulary. We were doing decolonization with a wartime mentality. People suffered and fell by the way if they couldn't cut it. It was like going to try out for a lacrosse team. You get cut, you get cut. Except in a university, they can come back and file a human rights complaint.

HB: *The gossip and the rumors, that's one thing I was trying to feel out. What is the truth? I came to you because I wanted to understand more about the truth from your perspective. Otherwise, there's a loose end that's missing. People said, don't talk to Taiaiake, because of his views on things. I've been wading through a lot of silence. That's really what I wanted to understand.*

TA: It's a political thing. Someone told me, when people weren't standing up to defend the program, that in academia, I'm "iconic" – he said, you've got to understand, they don't see you as a human, they see you as this icon, this thing, and you'll never change. It doesn't matter what you are as a person. That's the most frustrating thing to me. They're not willing to really understand the full reality and to bring an element of truth, which is very important. It's different if you're in an environment where your public persona doesn't really connect with you personally. But in our communities, it's different. Everybody knows everybody. People know me, they know my family, and it harms them when people were playing this political game to pull me down. I think that method of disciplining or attacking me as a symbol of what they see as an unjust power, it's going to backfire because it's not true. People can see it doesn't match up. Being the subject of it, I live my life, I am who I am. But I can't take the lies. I would threaten to sue anybody who lied about me in print, I would come back at them hard, and so they stopped doing that, now they just do it gossipy. It's a careerist kind of move in academia. It's not like I'm some sort of demon, for them to say, don't talk to him. Why not? I don't understand that part of it.

HB: *In what ways do you hold yourself accountable? In what ways have you changed?*

TA: Around 2017, I encountered an educator on sexual violence and gender issues at the university who came in and did seminars and education, and we worked one on one. I'd have to really point to them as one of the people who taught me a lot. They were always very critical of the program on two counts. One, they are nonbinary and two, Métis. And so, on the nonbinary thing, I was just ignorant, I didn't understand the vocabulary or anything. So, things would happen where I'd say, hey, ladies, and they would say, "Fuck you, I'm not a lady, don't call me that." We'd have a discussion and there would be a learning moment. We had those kinds of encounters. The other aspect of it was the Métis part. After about three years of working through these gender issues, they said in a talking circle, "You've harmed a lot of us and you need to acknowledge that." And I'm like, "what? I'm really sorry to hear that, I can't recall any time where I've done anything to you like that." And they said, "No, it's your words." That's the first time I realized harm could mean something other than the intent to go and hurt somebody, either with violent words or physically. They said, "Remember that speech you gave about Métis rights and how the concept of Métis emerged from colonialism and is an ally of colonialism? That's causing me harm because I respect what you have to say." And I'm like, wow. That hit me. I responded by saying, "you should critique it like we critique our Indigeneity, as potentially colonial. Métis should not just stand on the idea that they're Métis and therefore Indigenous and have the same rights, because it emerged in a colonial context." It seems like an obvious point to me. But the first part of the phrase got repeated over and over on social media. That's when I realized my words have more impact than the average person's. I'm not seen as just another guy, they're really paying attention to what I say. That could be a blessing, but it also could be a negative thing. I have to really watch what I say. So, yes, I worked it out with them, I apologized and explained what I believed. Yes,

I dismissed some First Nations, some Native people, some Métis. Anybody who's phony or false, anybody who was not fighting for our Nations and our land, I would dismiss them. But to my friend, I said, "Not *you*. I can see and deal with you as an Indigenous person." The response was, "Well, you never made that clear. So, when you dismissed Métis, I thought that was me this whole time."

My realization about harm kind of started there. We had a long talk and they went through some of the basics when it came to gender relations and sexualized violence. My generation, people used to think that harm was putting your hands on somebody or degrading them with your words. But I've come to understand the pyramid structure of rape culture, patriarchy, where what animates and allows the people who do those harms is this broader base of casual, everyday sexism. And so, in that realm, there's objectifying, casual misogyny, locker room talk, being insensitive to people's feelings, not caring, pornography. We worked through all those things in the circle sessions we did. To me, that's been a central understanding: how casual misogyny or maleness is a support for the ones that do the kind of more severe forms of harm. When I said, "I've done harm," – yes, I've objectified women, I've been insensitive, I've done a lot of those kind of things. I put that out there, I want to acknowledge it. It's an act of leadership. We all exist in this world where men are enabled to take advantage of this whole structure. And I've been a participant – I was a Marine. I played lacrosse, I did all these things, I've been enmeshed in all of that. And I realize now that my ideas and my words and my behaviors caused harm. This person had felt bad for years because of what I said. And that really hurt me to know that. I never intended that, so it really made me think about being more sensitive, more careful, listening more, paying more attention to cues, verbal and nonverbal, and also being more humble in terms of what my entitlements are. Am I entitled to basically have people serve me and build me up ego-wise? That is part of patriarchy and we took it for granted.

So, that's the second part of your question. What have I done, what am I doing? Being aware of this, thinking through it, recognizing it in myself when I'm able to, and if not, taking seriously what people say and thinking about it and making the changes so I'm not being part of that foundation that supports bad behaviors that hurt people. We can't avoid doing harm. We do harm all the time and that's another thing I learned. They said something like, "You might think I've got it all figured out, but I probably harmed someone today. Don't be afraid of acknowledging that you're harming because we're human and we all do it. The value is in recognizing it: don't run away when people bring it forward. Take it on. Take it seriously and try to deal with it." That was a big learning moment for me.

HB: *I think our men have to learn a lot about being enmeshed in patriarchy. That's the transformational part – it sounds like the dialogue you had has made you aware of the things that you did and said and empowered you to deal with it, work through it. Is it difficult to say that kind of stuff?*

TA: It was at first, it was really hard when we started having our circle discussions. You're opening yourself up, you're admitting weakness and you're humbling yourself. But the more you do it, the easier it gets. To me, that's an indication of how confident you are in the rightness of it. You understand it to be true and you're able to talk about it in words that make sense and connect with other people. And I think that when you get to that point, it becomes easier to articulate. I've been speaking for more than thirty years, so I can say before now, I probably would have been not at my best talking about this, but now I think I could talk about it in any context and be able to take whatever comes back because I believe it to be true. And I think it's an honest self-reflection.

HB: *My last question is, for us coming up, Mohawk men and Haudenosaunee men and for the younger boys coming in, what would you like to say to them based on your experiences and where you are now?*

TA: That's a big question. I would say to keep in mind that your families and your Ancestors need you to be at your best, and that we all have it in us to be a good man, a good person, and a strong Onkwehónweh. And we've had that taken away from us, we've had that minimized, we've had that assaulted by all kinds of factors, but that's no reason to stop the journey of strengthening yourselves. It's not enough to do it for yourself. You need to do it because our Nations and our families are depending on us to be strong and to be good and to have ourselves together. And I think that's an important thing to consider. The answers are not out there in an academic context, they're not in theory, they're not in hip-hop or country music. They're within our own culture and community. And that may even seem like a truism or trite, but I'm one of those people that can stand up and verify that the more you know about your culture, the more you know about the teachings and the language, even if you're not fluent – I'm not – the more time and energy you dedicate to putting together a sense of yourself as a man in the context of that culture, the stronger you'll be and the better you'll be for your partner, your kids, and your Ancestors. It's a battle worth fighting because to just go along with what's expected of us, there are too many pathways that are harmful, that take us out of relevancy as a good person for our Nation and our community. And so, we have to really be conscious in putting effort into thinking of ourselves in that cultural context.

Wampum, Kahnawà:ke, 2023

We are taught to be Onkwehón:weh by our Ancestors, who speak to us through sacred ceremonies out on the land and in dreams.

YOU CAN'T DECOLONIZE COLONIZATION

Adapted from an interview by Robyn Pebeahsy and Ricardo Saenz on the *Decolonized Buffalo* podcast, episode 116, September 16, 2022.

This interview, originally conceived of as opportunity to explain the concept of reconciliation to an audience of Indigenous Peoples and settler allies in the United States, widened to give me the opportunity to engage on some of the contemporary controversies and issues facing Indigenous Nationhood and decolonization activists today and to thus think of Indigenous Resurgence in the context of not only its origins but also its future: What does it offer young people who must think their way through our present challenges and into Indigenous futures for themselves, for generations to come, and for the land?

Reconciliation – The Highest Evolution of Colonialism

RICARDO SAENZ: *So the first topic we would like to talk to you about is reconciliation. This is a word that doesn't get used as much in the United States. What is it? What does it mean within Indigenous politics in Canada?*

TA: The idea of reconciliation is founded on the recognition of the fact that Canada is a settler colonial state, and this has been a long time coming. This is, of course, the reality of our people since the inception of the country, since the first set of relationships went sour, since treaties were broken, and since the settler societies began to establish themselves and develop over the past three hundred years into a form of government, an economy, and a culture that we have now. It has been the work of many Indigenous people and non-Indigenous allies for generations to get Canadian society, the people, the cultural institutions, and the government, to recognize that they are a colonial enterprise and to address it. People have worked on resistance – physically and in terms of territory, political, legal, and cultural resistance and in the realm of ideas, bringing the truth of history, bringing the truth of the experience of our people, bringing the truth of the motivations and the actions of the government of Canada toward the land and toward the people. It has resulted in the recognition of the fact that history can't be escaped: Indigenous people are not going to just accede to the idea that is grounded in the mythology of Canada as a peaceful enterprise.

In the last twenty or thirty years, some people root reconciliation in the work of the Royal Commission on Aboriginal Peoples [RCAP] in 1992–6. In the Canadian and British tradition when there's a substantial issue society is facing, a Royal Commission is formed where they bring scholars and political leaders and people together to identify a problem and solutions. The RCAP determined that there were substantial problems that were going to continue to undermine the health and well-being of Indigenous Peoples and impede Canada in its development and maturation as a country. This was set on the table in the public discourse, and ever since then the Canadian government and Canadian society have been coming to grips with this. Over the years, it's developed this approach to decolonization called reconciliation, which is basically the idea that we have two experiences, two groups of people that have been subject to history and we need to bring them together, to reconcile the conflict and to move forward together. Anybody who was brought up in the Christian tradition will recognize a lot of the language and the instinct: forgiveness, truth telling, confession, redemption. It's basically a Christian concept applied to politics. Many of us have been critical of this approach and the essence of this idea of decolonization, framed around reconciliation, as opposed to other ideas in a more radical tradition around decolonization.

But this is the era that we're living in. Since the 1990s and the RCAP, this has developed into an actual agenda around the idea of reconciliation: it's a declaration now and a statement openly from the Government of Canada that we are reconciling. So there are public institutions, there's money, it's worked its way into the culture and public discourse and even into individual people's sense of themselves as Canadians, that we're in an era of reconciliation, so there's a whole lot of activities in the personal, the political, and the cultural realms. It's something that really shapes the whole lived experience of an Indigenous person in Canada today, whether you agree with it or not, whether you are on board with some of the reconciliation agendas or whether you're opposed to it, it is the big thing in Canada these days.

ROBYN PEBEAHSY: *In the US we're not even close to even saying the word reconciliation. We're not even close to the word acknowledgment. I feel that if that word were to come up, it would never happen, there would never be reconciliation. There's just too much history. There's just too much anger and hurt and trauma. I'm not confident that it could happen. Maybe that's just me being emotional rather than seeing it as a process. But for me as a non-trusting person toward the government, living on the rez, it's kind of like, okay, it's just going to be words, there's not going to be any actions. So I'd love to hear what this process has been for you and how you feel about reconciliation yourself. Not from an academic perspective necessarily, but how does it make you feel?*

TA: I don't think you're being untrusting, I think you're just being real. What you've expressed is what I feel and what the vast majority of Native people living in communities feel. A major criticism of reconciliation I've had is that it's a strategy that the Canadian government is using to try to deflect responsibility away from the more serious aspects of what decolonization is and should be. When this whole reconciliation thing first started as an official platform of the Canadian government, I wrote an article arguing that restitution needs to come before reconciliation.[1] I've given speeches explaining how reconciliation is recolonization. I've been playing around with this whole idea for a long time: that reconciliation is this conscious invention of a moderate response to shield

Canadians from the true responsibility they have, which is rooted in the theft of land; the crimes they committed against our children; their destruction, consciously and systematically, of our systems of governance in our communities; and the war they declared on our Nations – every Indigenous community is roiling from this still. There's anger and there's trauma that manifests in all kinds of different ways. In my view, the only real solution – and I think this reflects older versions of what Indigenous leaders put forward as their vision of decolonization – is the restoration and recognition of our traditional governments, payment of restitution for the harms that were committed, and the restoration of our land base – our land back.

Those of us that are rooted in that life, the politics around Nationhood and the lived experience of people being in resistance to colonization, that's in our bones – that's what we're fighting for. But the opportunity for reconciliation was there because of the disconnection of a lot of Indigenous people from their own culture, from their own communities, from the ideas that are essential to Indigenous Nationhood. There was an opportunity there, and the Canada government sensed they could take advantage of people who are Indigenous but who are not committed to the struggle in the same way that people who grew up and who were engrained with that mentality. They created a moderate version of what decolonization is, a non-contentious version; they've funded it very well and created all sorts of incentives for people to come into the realm of reconciliation. It comes with the caveat that it all leads to the integration of Indigenous Peoples as full Canadian citizens, not liberation from the Canadian state into a restoration of a Nation-to-Nation relationship between, for example, the Mohawk, the Anishinaabe, and the Cree, and the Canadian state. Nationhood was sacrificed under the incentive of increased opportunities career-wise, in terms of integration into different institutions, monetary incentives and so forth, for Indigenous people who are committed to Indigeneity, to making life better for Indigenous Peoples, no doubt, but not to Nationhood.

That crucial difference is the essence of what makes it a colonial project. Reconciliation is the highest evolution of colonialism because it offers the most educated, the highest-achieving individuals who identify as Indigenous, the opportunity to maintain themselves in terms of their identity as Indigenous people, but foregoing their affiliation and commitment and defense of our Nationhood in order to take their place within Canadian society. And it's a brilliant strategy. It's working incredibly well in Canada today. Most of the academics, most of the cultural leaders, and more and more political leaders in our communities are drawn to this framing of what decolonization is, in contrast to the framing that you had prior to the 1990s, which was strictly about Nationhood, land recovery, reparations, and based on treaties. So they must attack the notion of Nation-to-Nation. They attack the notion of our existence being a collective existence within Nations distinct from Canada. They use academic cultural power to do that. And now they're reaping the reward of it and have generations of leaders who see themselves as Indigenous individuals within the Canadian sphere, not as Indigenous individuals representing their Nationhood against Canada and the crimes it committed against our collectivities.[2] For some people it's kind of a subtle difference, but if you live or grew up with that experience as an Indigenous person, you can sense right away when someone is representing their own individuality versus their tribal or their Nation-based existence. My critiques have all been around that. From the beginning of this era of reconciliation, I was one of the first people to speak out against it and to get blowback and to go to battle and to engage on that and to have to make choices and sacrifices on that.

We have a situation in Canada today where intellectuals, if you operate in the realm of any official institution in an official capacity, whether it's a university, a government agency, a federally or provincially funded organization, there's no way out of reconciliation. You will have to embrace and abide by what reconciliation is as an agenda or else you just will not have a job, you will not get funded, you will not be allowed to participate. And so the way it is for anybody that maintains that strong Nationhood perspective, you have to operate independently or in the realm of the community that still maintains itself in that identity as a Nation. And luckily, there are a number of those in Canada where people can work and make their contributions and that is a fact, but the hegemony is reconciliation.

Decolonizing Is about What Kind of People We Are

RS: *There's a conversation within the US left – communists and socialists – and they say that the moment the US becomes communist or socialist, it won't be a settler state anymore. But the way they envision liberation for us is the same scenario at this point right now when it comes to the relationship between the settler state and the sovereign Native Nations: it's guardian/ward. I tell them no, that's not decolonization, that's not liberation. I think we have to think past the settler state. What does decolonization mean to you? How do you envision decolonization?*

TA: I've come to think about the answer to that question in many different ways over the years. I think decolonization has a number of facets to it, and it's more of a way of framing or thinking about your posture in relation to the settler state. If you identified Canada as a colonizer state in the 1990s you would be in a radical position of critique and action: because it was such a colonial reality, pointing at it was a radical act. We've come to a position now where the Prime Minister himself is up there giving speeches saying that we're a colonial state and we need to reconcile – so now, to say that you're decolonizing is nothing. The government has co-opted decolonization. Every university is still controlled by white people, but they say they are decolonizing, so what does it mean? It's language, it's rhetoric, and it means nothing.

For me, I look at what people are doing. It's a good question you asked. What does it mean to be decolonizing? Are you still challenging and confronting the essence of the injustice that makes Canada what it is and keeps our Nations from having our own laws, our own government, in our own territory, and our own freedom to govern our own land? In one sense that's a fundamental definition of decolonization. For example, the Mohawks have a territory that we never surrendered; we weren't ever defeated in war. We negotiated treaties to allow access and sharing, which were broken, which were fraudulently abrogated, and so forth. By sheer force of numbers the settler society comes to be able to impose its false or invented interpretation of the treaty. So having our land back, our laws and institutions and power governing that land, is fundamental.

And importantly, here's the other aspect that I've come to learn over time: having our people come to understand themselves as Onkwehónweh through the lens of our own cultures and teachings, our own identity shaped and formed out of the foundations of our own teaching and culture and language, as opposed to Christianity or Western ideas of individualism or liberalism or even communism or Marxism, whatever it is. Not to say that we can't evolve and learn and take in new ideas, but our identity framed within our own culture. And I think that's the missing piece today. People are very good at critiquing the settler state in economic terms, political terms, historical analyses, and so forth. We're all very good at that in the intellectual realm, in academia, we're able to do that. But the idea of personal decolonization and learning how colonialism has shaped you as an individual, your behaviors and ideas, and what it's taken away from you and what you need to re-instill that level of colonization and decolonization I think is the key. What I've learned is, you can have successes in the realm of decolonizing in economic or political terms, but if you're not embodying the values and principles from within your own culture, it's a replication of the victory of the colonial state in shaping you in such a way to serve its own interests. So that to me is the whole interplay. There has to be a political agenda, there has to be a political movement, and there has to be the means to generate economic self-sufficiency. And then there has to be that personal decolonization, which is the realm of culture and spirit, to be able to re-instill that in the generations of people coming up. What it is to be Mohawk or Cree or Anishinaabe or Yakama? In the end it's about what kind of people we are and how we are relating to the land and to each other. And that's almost the hardest thing to do. We're finding out that decolonization is all of these things.

Our Land Is Our Identity: Try Explaining That to General Motors

RS: *Can you talk about what land and territory mean to communities? I think that's what's missing for non-Natives who say, you know, these Native people are not working the land. They don't see our relationship to the land is much more than economic. Can you talk about that?*

TA: My sense of the land has deepened because of the work I've been doing for about eighteen years now on what's called Natural Resource Damages Assessment (NRDA). It's a legal process actually in the United States, where tribal groups come with a claim against people who have polluted and contaminated the natural environment and thus disrupted their relationship to their natural environment within their territory. Most of the work that I do is researching and listening to people in tribal communities, talking about what the land means to them, what their cultural relationship is, both in terms of teachings and ceremony but also in practice, in a very pragmatic way. What kinds of things did they used to do on the land and in the water to maintain themselves? I'm listening to all this and trying to understand the harm that has come because of pollution and contamination and alienation, because of those things, and then thinking about restoration, about how Indigenous people see or define what restoration is – what is cultural restoration?

So yes, you're right to point to the fact that there's a big difference between this and the way that people who are coming from a Western mentality basically see the land. The milieu I've been operating in is lawyers for resource companies, federal government agencies, representatives of the general public, and so forth. They see land as a resource for exploiting, for generating money, when you come right down to it. They may love the land – a rancher may love their land – but it's because it makes money, they can use it in order to generate some sort of economic gain.

I'm not going to say Indigenous people don't have that, of course. We use the land to support ourselves, we use the land as a resource, but I've kind of come to understand it in a much deeper way: it's also our identity. We see the elements of the natural environment – the plants, the animals, the rocks, everything in the natural environment – as a relation of ours. Our identity and our existence as Indigenous Peoples is formed within that whole set of relationships. And so a mountain is not just a mountain full of gold. It has agency, to use an academic term. It is a person in the same way the human community is. The fish, the sturgeon in the river, they're not just resources that can be calculated in terms of their nutrient value or calories or money and how much people will pay for them. There is a relationship there that is essential to being Onkwehónweh that you must respect. There's reciprocity: the plants, the animals, the natural environment, give something to us, we give something to them. And if that relationship is harmed or is not there or is disregarded or forgotten, we are less Onkwehónweh. We're less human. We don't exist independently. We can't just go anywhere. We can't just think about human beings. We have to think about ourselves in the context of those relationships. And so land is one element of this whole set of relationships in any analysis, whether it's Western or Indigenous. But when you look at it from an Indigenous perspective, the land includes all of these other things. And it's this whole complex set of reciprocities that must be respected. There are spiritual and psychophysical consequences to disregarding or disrespecting those relationships that within Western culture, science-based Western culture especially, there is no appreciation for.

One of the main challenges in the work that I've done in the NRDA context is to convey that. Can you imagine trying to convey that to a lawyer for Monsanto or General Motors? And my own personal challenge in the work that I do is to be able to be that translator, to take that understanding and to respect it because I live it, but then to put my foot into the realm of a legal or corporate engagement with corporate or financial entities and bring that forth because the tribal groups have chosen to do that. Come into their realm to talk to them and try to get them to appreciate that perspective and somehow put a value on that so that they can be open to some form of justice for what they've done. Usually that translates, you know, sad to say, into putting a money value on all this and having them think about considering compensating the tribal group for the harm they've done. And the tribal group comes up with an idea about how to use that money in order to develop pathways for youth to once again experience life as an Indigenous person in the natural environment. So it's a very on-the-ground engagement between land and territory, and I am very thankful for having been drawn into that realm because it is the real world.

You know, we talk about different ideas about land and territory from Indigenous and Western perspectives. Well, operating in the context that I'm describing here, it's right where you have the strongest representatives of Western mentalities: Hanford Nuclear Reservation, General Motors, Teck Cominco mines, Monsanto – entities that generate their extreme wealth and generate extreme wealth for American society based on a mentality guided by Western science. Indigenous Peoples' perspectives and understandings in a courtroom or sitting at a negotiating table confront this atomistic, materialistic view of the natural environment as a resource. So it's academic and it's scholarly, but I feel I've been lucky to be able to engage on the ground, right at that level in terms of battling to have that perspective valued and to have it prevail in terms of defining what justice is in certain areas.

Accountability, or, How Can I Tell When I'm Being Co-opted?

RP: *What you're speaking of is the eternal struggle since contact: you're trying to get people not from here to realize that this place and your relationship to it is more important than the money that they're trying to get out of it. And that turns into the Indian problem, which is what we call it here in United States – you know, the problem is we're still in the way of this "progress." One of the things that's hard to have others grasp is that the violation of these unwritten laws always results in something catastrophic. You're trying to get all these resources from our Earth, not necessarily our land but the Earth, and sure you're making money, but you end up having to pay this bigger price in order to achieve that, which is not only the deterioration of your soul as a human and your connection to the Earth but, there are also economic costs – like the Oka Crisis, it costs money to defend your right, to call in the military to do it.*

I wanted to ask about accountability. I feel like one of the things you're talking about in terms of reciprocity is accountability, to the land but also to your community. Why is that important, how does that help in Resurgence, which I feel is like re-Indigenizing how we're going to approach things. I feel like accountability is a big part of that.

TA: That's another huge theme. Because, as you just articulated very well, when you're coming into this work or any work as an Indigenous person, from a community, answering to that community is the most important thing. Maintaining your relationships in your Nation is crucial. It's not something that you can take lightly or disregard because your whole identity and your whole being is rooted in having those relationships respected and honored. And that's so different compared to someone operating in the context of an institution outside of the Native context where your answerability is institutional. I'll even deepen the critique to those people who have their own personal lives intertwined with the non-Native society, where not only are they institutionally accountable in a job sense, but they're personally accountable to non-Native society and their own personal life. I'll just use myself as an example. I tried to do the work in a university context for so many years, and having my own accountability maintained in my own community was a conscious decision that I made – to be able to write what I wrote, to talk about what I wrote, to think about my ideas in a very open way that was transparent and accountable in terms of answerable in my own community. I was conscious of this in making my choices in terms of personal relationships and everything else I did, which were all shaped by this effort to serve my community as best I could and remain accountable to Indigenous realities and Indigenous communities and people. This brought me into conflict almost constantly when I was operating in non-Native institutional contexts because I didn't feel like I was answerable at all to the institutional powers that were the structure of my job, my position. You're always in a position of contention as long as you're decolonizing. How can you tell when you're decolonizing? It's because someone's institutional power in a colonial institution is pushing you back, trying to silence you, or manipulate or prevent you from achieving your objectives.

I remember giving advice to students who would ask, How can I tell when I'm being co-opted? Well, if they're patting you on the back, if your boss is patting you on the back and smiling and opening the way for you in the institution, you're probably co-opted. If you go back home and people are looking at you sideways and don't want to hear what you have to say and are very critical of what you have to say then yeah, that's a pretty good sign right there.

But you can flip it around too. I'd rather go to an Indigenous community and be a hero and be hated by the people in institutional power any day. And I always made that choice. And the only way to really test your position is to maintain those relationships: go into the Native community, talk about your ideas. Be involved. Immerse yourself. Go into the institution, continue to talk about your ideas and don't moderate them: see what the response is. Be willing to pay the price in terms of walking away, or conflict and things like that. I find it's not very common these days in academia. I had a lot of conflicts, and one of the reasons I left was because it was made abundantly clear to me that the space for the type of decolonizing work that I wanted to do, and the posture that I had as an individual in relation to that white power and the people in that milieu, was not tenable anymore.

They closed up that space.

To me it's a sign that the colonial institutions, at least in Canadian society, have been very successful in co-opting the Indigenous elite into that realm such that there is now a critical mass of people who are co-opted and who are amenable to the colonial agenda, a.k.a. reconciliation. People who come at it from a community perspective, who are willing to confront and defend strong Indigenous-rooted perspectives and articulate them, there's pushback against them, and in a lot of cases, the door to those institutions is shut. And that's the situation we're facing now in Canada. I sense that it's the same in the US because there's an academic culture that's emerged and I don't think you could have a Vine Deloria today that's prominent. You couldn't have a Beatrice Medicine. You couldn't have me. At one point I was angry about losing that space. We were defeated but not really – it just sheds light on the reality and points to the fact that the work we need to do and the rightful place of a person doing decolonizing work is in our communities, not in non-Indigenous institutions. We thought we could decolonize, we thought we could Indigenize the academy, as the phrase went, but you can't decolonize colonization. We've come to realize that these institutions are pillars of the colonial society and within them it is Indigenous people addressing some concerns. I'm not casting aspersions on their motivations, and they may have some impact. But participating in and enabling the continuation of one of the pillars of colonial society is not decolonization.

I think we were starting to come to the realization now that there are hard limits to decolonizing in a cooperative way. The elements of decolonization that are cultural or educational, we found the hard limit to that. You can educate people about their culture, their identity, you can talk about history and so forth but not to the extent where it means white people giving up control and not to the extent where it means altering the basic power relations between Indigenous people and white institutions of power in this society. And if you're all about that, then you have to go back into your community and work to empower your community to go and fight to take power back into the political, legal, or physical realm. And I think that my own experience in engaging with non-Indigenous institutions for many years has taught me that lesson and that's what I'm all about now.

Online Influence versus Doing the Work

RS: *As you're talking about this, I wanted to ask you about your journey within academia and talking about these subjects. I'm pretty sure you become frustrated when it comes to challenging institutions because I've had issues myself with universities, talking about fake Natives or taking up spaces, and talking about this within leftist spaces. When it comes to online conversations or conversations in your different communities about decolonization, do you think they're going down the right path? Or do you think it's stale?*

TA: I've been engaged with social media from the beginning, but it's become something where I think the conversation is not reflected in the reality. But it's not only social media: it's the whole culture and how everyone is able to create personas and senses of themselves and even convince themselves that they're making contributions to the movement via social media as opposed to doing things that actually have an effect in the community. And unfortunately, social media is a capitalist enterprise, and it rewards people for that. So people are rewarded financially, they get social clout, and so forth. But when you look at who's doing work that's transforming Indigenous communities – I'm not going to write off everyone who has a large social media presence because some of them do both – but for the most part, when you go into Indigenous communities, you see people who are raising the kids, you see people who are taking in five of their relative's kids, even though they already raised their own, keeping them healthy, keeping them fed. You see people building houses, you see people doing the healing work, people doing medicines, all this stuff. There's no internet clout for that; they don't have 50,000 followers telling them how awesome they are every day for raising four foster kids. But somebody can put on fancy regalia, and dance on a TikTok and all of a sudden they're getting paid thousands of dollars to give speeches about what it is to be Indigenous, what it is to decolonize. That's bullshit. When we're talking about decolonizing in the realm of liberation, when we're talking about community building and Nation building, this kind of conversation/discourse/

social media/media presence is bullshit. It means nothing. You can have a social media presence, but it should reflect the work that you're doing. It should be oriented toward engaging with a wider public from the platform that's rooted in community. Unfortunately we all know often that's not the case. Most of the so-called activists these days who think and believe that because they've been rewarded with esteem and financially, just for doing the things they get recognition for, that that's enough. There's very little connection to the important things from the Indigenous perspective.

I see the value in what some people do, who do both. I'm very supportive and I admire Thosh Collins and Chelsey Luger and their organization Well For Culture.[3] I think that's a good model: they're rooted in their community and personally embody a lot of these things and they have a huge media presence, and they take advantage of that. It's a source of income for them. That's just one example of how you can do both.

There are people who do beading who are rooted in the communities, and they happen to also promote it. But there's also a lot of people doing beading who just discovered that they were Native last week and copied somebody on YouTube on how to make earrings. And it's exactly because they are assimilated and are able to negotiate white spaces and have white connections that they become more prominent than the person who taught them how to do the beading. To me that's wrong.

RP: *Thank you. Thank you. I'm a beader.* [laughter]

TA: My girlfriend is too. Just because of that experience, surveying the landscape of beading, I've seen this play out and it seems to be so prominent. And it's also in dance, I think – the way that people portray themselves in terms of their regalia and is it entertainment? Is it performativity? Or is it actually a cultural intervention? It's just that people don't always seem to have a consciousness like we have here, right? That's not to say you shouldn't get on TikTok and do dances in certain public spaces. Hey, if it's an intervention driven by a political consciousness that's disrupting something and leading to some positivity for Indigenous Nationhood, awesome. But if you're just doing it to make money and get recognition for yourself and you're disconnected from any kind of national struggle, then I don't support that. And I think it's actually a detriment to our movement.

On Gatekeeping, Pretendians, and Ethnic Fraud

RP: *Thank you so much for bringing it into that realm, because I've seen a lot of this firsthand. A lot of it is very similar to what you're saying about academia; it's similar to and is connected to the accountability aspect. I'm not thinking of anyone in particular, but I do see that there are Natives who can thrive in those environments because the reciprocity and the accountability isn't as daunting in those spaces. I went to the University of Washington, I know what it's like: you get praise for stuff that you do, and it's nice, and you can always stay in that realm but it's almost like* The Matrix *– you can stay here in the university, swallow the blue pill.*

Or you can go back to your community and stay accountable to your community, which is harder, but it's far more rewarding, and it definitely helps feed your identity and your stance in your identity. And this is something that's discussed a lot on this podcast, the reconnection, reconnecting people. Social media definitely has those same rewards that academia does. If you give this something up, or if you show this, you get the rewards: the likes, the "Oh, I've never seen that, it's really awesome!" And it is, I agree it is really awesome, but I wouldn't share that, you know, because my aunt who is also on social media, would be like, "Why did you share that design? Why did you do this?" That accountability part is there, which is also important to the development of who we are.

I know that Rick has been accused a few times of being like a gatekeeper, and it's just like, look, even if you're extremely rooted in your community and in your culture, you're gatekeeped. Those of us who are connected – I live on the rez – I get gatekeeped on certain things. At the end, the gates are there for a reason. It's like you have to get to that next level, you have to prove that you're in that next level. It's hard to explain to those who are assimilated or who are trying to decolonize: when you're in that process it's going to feel like you're hitting wall after wall, but it's that way for a reason. It's not that I'm trying to gatekeep you or because I just don't want you here. No, it's that you have to prove that accountability. And you have to prove that hey, this is what I'm really for, I'm for our people.

TA: Yeah, I agree with everything you said. It's sort of like having a high standard as an Indigenous person, what you're calling a gatekeeper. Is it gatekeeping to say that if you claim to be a Mohawk, you should be able to prove it, like you should be able to talk about or demonstrate who your family is and who your relatives are? And are you a member of a community? Do they consider you a member? Is that gatekeeping or is that just fact checking?

I used to get in trouble for years in academic environments by standing against what's now called "Pretendians." It wasn't called that at the time, it was called ethnic fraud. We had an organization, a few professors, back in the '90s, that stood against ethnic fraud, which is basically people falsely claiming Indigenous identity to get jobs and fellowships. Now it's out of control because institutions have implemented policies based on self-identification. To those of us who have come from an Indigenous perspective – tribal in the US or First Nations in Canada – it's laughable from the beginning. Like Robyn just said, you get gatekeeped in your own communities: what clan are you? What part of the clan? What family are you? That's normal to have to answer those questions, that's part of being Native. You show up, someone says, "Where are you from? Who's your parents? Who's your grandparents?" That's all natural, to be able to demonstrate that connectivity to the community. But then the universities attack that, which to me is a conscious attacking of Indigenous Nationhood and an imposition of individualism, of unrooted atomistic individualism, which by default puts you into the American or Canadian context as a capitalist consumer citizen which says that anybody can claim to be Indigenous and you're not allowed to confront them. And you're not allowed to challenge them. It's the *law*. And so right now institutions in Canada are confronting this huge problem where people have been given free rein to self-identify and have taken up all kinds of space and leadership positions. It's so bad that even the people holding them accountable probably wouldn't pass the test in Native communities, but they at least have a conscience about lying. It's so funny to see people who are the gatekeepers in Canadian academia not being able to pass the test in a Native community themselves. But you're like, go for it. You know, good. At least you have a conscience. At least you're calling out the total liars.

RP: *Maybe they're like, I can't pass it. You're not going to pass it either*. [Laughter]

TA: Exactly. But it's come to the point now where it's so ridiculous that people, just on the basis of truth versus lie, just on the basis of it being completely counterfactual, are calling people out. It's not come to the point where anybody is advocating, as far as I know, in art circles or in Canadian academia, for a nation-based definition, or Indigenous Nations controlling access to positions designated Indigenous within mainstream institutions. I don't think anybody is advocating turning over control to, say, Kahnawà:ke for who gets hired to McGill or Concordia – which to me is the way it should be because it's on our territory and they're operating in terms of representing what it is to be Indigenous, so we should have a say, if not control – but no one's advocating for that. They're simply saying that somebody who says that they have an Indigenous ancestor, it needs to be true. I mean, that's a pretty low bar. And in spite of that, there's so many people in academia who are failing the test, which shows you how bad it was up until two years ago.

The Baseline Is the Treaties

RS: *There's this conversation in the US from people saying their ancestors the Europeans worked the land for 200 or 300 years, so now they're Indigenous. They call it indigenization. I think it's really dangerous rhetoric from my point of view, that they're indigenizing themselves using colonization as a tool, when really they're squatters. Could you talk about the dangers of this kind of claim or process?*

TA: To me that's easy. It's just patently false. Here's an equivalency – could you argue that all the possessions of the British Museum from the day they were stolen from all over the world, that they're British because they've been integrated into the British Museum and the British have had them for 300 years? Stolen property is still stolen property: does time change that fact?

I do understand that they may have developed a connection to the land and a sense of themselves that is now distinct from their European origins. But that doesn't take away the fact that there's a fundamental injustice at the root that needs to be addressed. Our Ancestors addressed that fundamental problem through treaty. There are treaties everywhere. The treaties just need to be honored and respected. Before the 1990s that was the whole rhetoric of the Indigenous Nationhood movement: honor the treaties. It's not like we need to invent anything new. The treaties are there, and white people should be happy that we're just talking about the treaties, because the treaties themselves are compromises. If our Ancestors had it their way, I'm sure they would just have liked to kill off all the white people to begin with, but they couldn't. So they made treaties because they had to coexist, and so coexistence is the underlying premise and objective – harmonious coexistence is the underlying premise of our treaties, and that's respectful of the historical fact. If you want to argue with someone on the fact that the United States Army defeated certain Indigenous Nations in battle and therefore blah, blah, blah, well, the treaty reflects that. The treaties were signed in the historical context of the aftermath of armed conflict between the US government, the Canadian government, and Indigenous Nations. And so the baseline should be the treaty. And if that is the case, then the weight of the argument from the other side disappears. Their ancestors, their government, designed the treaty process, negotiated the treaty, and signed a promise on those terms that recognize the fact that our people are the original inhabitants, that this was our land, that they are newcomers, and therefore have been granted rights through the treaty. I don't see how any person with European ancestors, from Germany, from England, can claim to be Indigenous. How can you claim to be Indigenous? There's a place where that language, German, English, is Indigenous. You can trace your lineage back to that place. Onkwehónweh, granted, we have some mixture, racially speaking, but Indigenous people can all trace our ancestry to here. And unless you can trace your lineage back to this land here, you're a colonizer and the only legitimacy you have is through treaty. To me, that's a simple relationship. They should be happy that we're talking treaty because otherwise they're just illegitimate invaders and over the course of history, if we continue to think about them that way, things may turn against them. Whereas if they have a treaty then they do have a legitimacy here and they have a place and our people granted them that place. And that's the way I combat that argument.

I used to come at it a little bit differently. More dismissive: You have no right to be here. But the Elders in our community and my own reading of our treaties and treaty history brought me to a place now where it's more of a grudging recognition of the legitimacy that was granted to these societies through treaty. And I think I understand now why our Elders were so strong on the agenda of honoring the treaties: look at the signs they're waving when they're occupying Alcatraz and the Department of Indian Affairs and on the marches they had in the 1960s and 1970s – honor the treaties. Simple. We've gotten away from that now and we have an agenda that is much more about integration in the institutions of American and Canadian society, and I think it kind of confuses people into thinking Indigenous people are just another ethnic group, and if they can be Indigenous, why can't we? Some historian from the University of Washington says, "Oh, this tribe has only been here for 400 years, so now we're equal, right?" Those are the kinds of arguments you get into when you get away from Nationhood, from treaty, when you get away from your rooted Indigenous perspective and start arguing in terms of the settler society as another group within that society. It's a no-win situation for us, and that's what they want us to do, because then we just become part of that larger group and the weight of numbers drowns us out even if we're right. So we shouldn't play that game, although we are playing that game now to our detriment.

RP: *Thank you so much for bringing in that view of treaty rights. I'm always trying to find new ways to look at our own sovereignty and treaty. Here on the Yakama rez, I feel like we're very politically astute and very vocal. We've often taken cases to Superior Court to reaffirm our treaty rights. And I feel fortunate that we win the majority of the cases because of that treaty and because of the way that we view our treaty and our rights through that lens.*

I've been back here on the rez for eight years so I'm talking from experience – it's a hard perspective to take when you don't live here because you grapple with your Nationhood almost every day when you live in the cities and you're kind of disconnected. You're always hit with this rhetoric of like, No, we're the United States and ***we're*** *recognizing* ***you****. But the way you're saying it is, no,* ***we*** *as a people, our own Nation, we recognize* ***you*** *as the United States. And that brings the legitimacy of our relationship upfront. Learning about the formation of treaties is something that I find really interesting. Working with the Colville Tribes in Washington state, I just learned that they weren't necessarily a treaty tribe to begin with, whereas the Yakama Nation has the 1855 treaty, we met with the governor and we sat down and even that whole meeting is contentious to bring up; but there was no formal treaty process with the Colville and some other tribes that were kind of after the whole treaty era. I find it interesting how it plays out. I've* *seen some articles where even Yakama was like, "No, we're treaty tribes, we get precedence over these non-treaty tribes." I never thought we would play that card because I didn't know we have non-treaty tribes, I only know there were tribes who were recognized later. But when you're talking about the relationship through recognition – I recognize you now and this is our relationship – what does that look like if you don't have that process? What kind of agreement is that? So thank you again, for kind of like rearranging my thoughts on what that looks like. It's something I really want to look into further.*

The Simple Answer

RP: *I wanted to bring up that I remember your lecture when you were at the University of Washington, and it was something that stuck with me. It was in 2004, 2005. We all went as a First Nations club, and there was this girl who I didn't really like, we were always butting heads. You know, I was from the rez and she was from the city, all these things. So, she asked you a question. She asked you, how do you keep from being jaded? And it was just a simple question, but I did kind of see her as jaded. That really woke me up. And then your answer was a really great answer. You told her that to stop from being jaded toward your Indigenous communities or toward your Indigenous Peoples, you have to love all Indigenous people. And I was like, wow, like, okay, so it was like a double answer for her and for me, because you know, I thought I didn't like her. I have friends who are still friends with her, and she talks about that lecture too and how that answer changed her perspective. So I just wanted to say thank you and share that story with you. You have a lot of weight, you know, even the most simple sentences.*

AFTERWORD: WA'TKWANONHWERÁ:TON: *"GRATITUDE AND ACKNOWLEDGMENT TO YOU ALL . . . "*

by Taiaiake Alfred

This book is a chronicle of the evolution of an idea in my head and feeling in my heart called Indigenous Resurgence, something that I have been doing my best to breathe life into and share with the world for thirty years. I am very proud of the speeches and interviews presented in these pages, of the role I have played in our movement, and in the lasting salience and strength of my political analyses and core messages. These were all informed and shaped by the teachings of my Ancestors before me and by the lived experiences and wisdom shared with me by family, friends, community, and colleagues.

Writing the closing words of this book offers me an opportunity to say some things that have been weighing on my mind for some time. Looking back at the words, strategies, and tactics I used as a public intellectual, educator, and activist over these years, I have come to see that I did not always appreciate the overarching importance of inclusion and unity, and I did not always embody the values of humility and respect. In our struggle to decolonize and in our resistance, we all have a role to play in the resurgence of our Nations and have much to learn from each other, and everyone's voice needs to be heard, valued, and respected. Yet, some of the things I said were dismissive, insulting, and even hurtful to people I disagreed with. Indigenous feminists, in particular, found my words and methods hypermasculine and sexist. At first, I did not see this and was defensive in the face of their criticism, but I am listening, and I am learning. I see now that I was wrong to ignore feminist and LGBTQIA+ perspectives for so long and to rely mainly on the perspectives of men rooted in traditional notions of masculinity to inform and shape my outlook. I have gained deeper insight into the nature and dynamics of colonization in recent years by taking seriously and engaging with these criticisms of my work, and I am grateful for the strength and courage of those who pushed back against my ideas and held me to a higher standard. Their criticisms were the catalyst of a necessary transformation, leading me to a deeper appreciation of the need to take better care of all my relationships.

The words in these pages are markers of who and where I was on my journey at the time; they were spoken sincerely and reflect the context and trajectory of our movement as well as the dynamics of my struggle to decolonize my mind in the same way that I call on others to do. It has been an arduous and difficult journey to hold myself to account while at the same time fighting hard and constantly for our righteous cause. Indigenous Resurgence is not an either–or process:

we can and must put the work into the never-ending task of decolonizing ourselves while empowering the movement.

It is too easy for even anti-colonial men to fall into the trap of normalizing everyday injustices, power imbalances, and modeling the oppressive behaviors of colonial patriarchy. In this, we can end up becoming tools of oppression ourselves. And with this normalizing comes the sense of entitlement to power, position, favor, and voice. For years, I focused only on enabling and validating voices, and did not value or honor the criticism that was leveled against me and my work. Though the harm people experienced because of me was in the realm of psychological stress and emotional pain, caused by my words, I see that still, I was caught in a cage of colonial masculinity and that I fell short of meeting the expectations of a leader by disregarding and minimizing my impact on others.

Were it not for the strong women around me in these years who opened my eyes to their lived reality in our communities and in our movement, I may not have ever come to see the full truth, or come to understand the essence of Indigenous Resurgence, or what it really means to be on the journey of the body and soul that we call decolonization. In this, I owe a huge debt of gratitude to my love Ashley Seymour, my good friends Mary Teegee, Pam Palmater, and the late Lee Maracle – sometimes their words were hard to hear, but they were necessary and always delivered with love and kindness – and to all the strong and wise Mohawk women I have worked for and learned so much from, especially Barbara Katenies Tarbell, Jessica Teiotsistohkwathe Lazare, Kahsennenhawe Sky-Deer, Winona Polson-Lahache, and Linda Karonhiénhawe Delormier.

Finally, I am immensely grateful for the vision, tenacity, and work ethic of my new friend and comrade Ann Rogers, who has shown me great respect and honored me with her dedication to this project. Our collaboration has stoked the fire of the revolutionary in me, reminded me of the power of solidarity, and strengthened my belief in the transformative potential of the Indigenous Resurgence.

Ever onward toward the Victory, and Decolonization!

It's all about the land.

Taneh toh.

BONUS TRACK: THE FOUR INTUITIONS

Adapted from "Taiaiake Alfred on Canada and Its Indigenous Peoples," *Big Ideas*, TVO Today, April 20, 2003.

Invited to appear on TVOntario's *Big Ideas* program in 2003, this very early taped speech finds Taiaiake stepping into the role of public intellectual to acquaint a naïve non-Native audience with the lies and myths that enable Canada to operate. Sandwiched between an episode with a young Jordan Peterson talking about the fear of the unknown and Bernard Lewis discussing the impact of the very recent 9/11, the building blocks that will become *Wasáse* are already in place as Taiaiake juxtaposes the two opposing systems of thought – Western and Mohawk – that underpin his critique of the fraught settler–Indigenous relationship on Turtle Island. (AR)

Taiaiake Alfred stands on a wooden podium in front of a green chalkboard and addresses an audience in a classroom. He's in his late thirties, clean-shaven, with short black hair. He's wearing a long-sleeved gray and black T-shirt.

What I wanted to focus on today is that if we are human beings committed to justice, our responsibility is to challenge the effect of lies on our own lives, purge ourselves of those lies, and commit ourselves to the truth and then to carry out a set of political decisions and to develop a political strategy and a way of living, a way of life, and a new ethic, that is, a rebellion of the truth against the lie.

I'm from Kahnawà:ke, and especially since the 1990 uprising, people associate us Mohawk with rebellion. There is a certain association of our people, the people of the Eastern Door of the Haudenosaunee, and the communities of Kahnawà:ke and Akwesasne in particular, with acts of rebellion – physical, mental, intellectual. I'm trying to give you a sense of a tone, a sense of an attitude, a posture, with respect to the accepted truths that form the basis of our Onkwehónweh relationship with Canada today. When I use the word *rebellion,* I use it consciously in terms of what the implications of using that word are. And I'd like to leave you at the end, with a sense of what I mean by rebellion. I don't mean a thousand Okas. I mean a much deeper and more profound rebellion against the psychological and spiritual effects of lies on the lives of our people, and inside of our own heads.

The Problem between Canada and Indigenous Peoples

Oftentimes we think about the problem between Canada and Indigenous Peoples as land claims, self-government, problems of injustice, social justice, and so forth, and I think that those are probably good ways of trying to get access into what the real problem is. But when I think about what the problem is facing our people, when I think about why we're even sitting here talking, when I think about why I was involved for fifteen years working with a band council system to try to change the lives of our people, to try to achieve what we thought was justice, I've come to think about it in a different way.

I think the real problem is that our people are living unhealthy lives. They're unhappy, they're dysfunctional, they are not perpetuating the kinds of things in their lives that lead to happiness and peace and good relationships and a sustainable relationship on a respectful basis among themselves, with the Earth and with other Peoples. So I bring it down to a real human level when I think about what the problem is. In the first instance, I think about what are we fighting for? And what we're fighting for is to bring peace and happiness into the lives of Indigenous people, as a starting premise. That may seem obvious, but I think it needs to be said as a reminder to those of us who are involved in making change in this society.

In in the last ten, twenty years or so, our movement's efforts to change Canada and its relationship to Indigenous Peoples have lost sight of that objective. I reflect back on my own experience, when I started in the mid-1980s as a junior researcher, writer, someone just learning about his own community and the dynamics and trying to make a contribution. I remember very distinctly Elders, people in the community, all the people who were holding us accountable to what we were doing in that community, saying, "Well, what you're doing is really to make our lives better." We need justice, they said, and by justice they meant we need to be able to live lives with dignity, that are healthy according to our own laws and our own choices on our own land.

Skennen

There is a very concise definition of *skennen* for our people: peace. It is our objective as we struggle for self-government or the settlement of land claims or economic development and so on. *Skennen* is not simply a lack of violence, a lack of fist fights or rioting in the streets; it is a more profound statement that speaks to a state of affairs and also a state of mind – a spiritual state in a person's makeup and being. *Skennen* means you have peace of mind, you're balanced, you're happy, you're at peace in the world. When we say peace, we mean *skennen*. Every time I go to Six Nations I get different teachings and learn something more about the foundations for *skennen*. What does it take, how do you have to think, what do you have to do? I'm going to be learning for the rest of my life just like everybody else. But the central fact is that the politics, traditionally, for Indigenous Peoples, and my own people, Haudenosaunee, is to achieve that state. Now, of course we fail and we flounder and we go off track and we fight among ourselves. But that's the orienting objective.

On the other hand, the ultimate aim of the Canadian Constitution is "peace, order and good government." "Peace" gets folded into "order and good government" without any real questioning as to what constitutes the basis for social order, and it is this version of peace that Canada promotes through the kinds of institutions, policies, politics, and ways of life that have been instituted and elevated as an ideal within this society.

So when we talk about politics, we run into an immediate problem. We run into the difference between *skennen* as an objective, which brings with it a whole set of assumptions about the basis for that existence, respect, honor, honesty, sharing, all of these things, and the very different objectives of the Canadian state and the policies put forward by the Canadian government today in relation to this problem that it's inherited: the problem of history and the conflict between the needs of Canadian society and the needs of our Peoples.

Even a very progressive mentality within the frame of Canadian government doesn't capture or touch upon the notion that I'm speaking of. The last Throne Speech talks about social justice, and about giving houses, building better houses, fixing the ones that are rotten, giving water, food, jobs, all of these good things, to Native people. Who can argue with that? I certainly can't argue with the fact of Native people having the right to have a material existence that approximates that of the lower middle class in Canada. But is that justice? Is it a foundation of *skennen*? It may be a small step, but it's not sufficient. It is not justice.

Social justice in Canada, meaning the material well-being of Indigenous Peoples, is an important component to the creation of justice from an Indigenous perspective. But from an Onkwehónweh perspective, you're missing three-quarters of the solution if you focus on material well-being. Because you still have to deal with emotions, and you have the intellectual aspects of our being, and you have a bunch of other things that go into making up what a human being is and creating *skennen*.

So what I think is the central problem in Native politics today, and in the relation between Native people and non-Native people, is that even with the progress that the society has made, it's still very narrow in its conception of a solution.

Building policies, putting forward laws, and having the kind of cultural ethic that builds up around the type of solution to the social justice problem perpetuates the larger injustice. That's a harsh thing to say to people who think they're doing good. I understand that. But I believe that we're all human beings with a sense of justice that transcends the differences between us. If we really commit to transcending those differences, then we have to look at justice not colored through our flag, not colored through a set of experiences that our grandparents had in coming over here, not colored through a region where we live, a school we went to, not filtered through and constrained by emotional attachments that we may have.

We have to look at justice and be honest enough and courageous enough to look at ourselves, Native and non-Native people, and see where we are constraining the achievement of justice through the choices, the beliefs, the actions that we take. And I make that point again consciously: both Native and non-Native.

Agreeing on Truth

Canada is founded on lies. What are some of those lies? Well, one of the lies is Crown sovereignty. One of the lies is Crown title. Look at them, legally and in their historical context, and you find some very serious gaps and flaws in those concepts. They are flawed ideas if we apply a concept of truth that is not colored by an emotional attachment to a flag, a region, a religion, or things like that.

What constitutes truth? Let me give you my concept of what truth is. If we're going to talk about truth and use it as a tool to question whether or not our laws and policies and institutions and attitudes are just or not, or right or not, let's look at what truth is. Well, first of all, it needs to be accurate. I believe that accuracy, a factual, empirical accuracy, should be the foundation of whether or not something is truthful. The other criterion is whether it fits a developed concept of what justice is. It ought to be framed within a concept of justice, and it ought to lead to a set of behaviors and actions that promote that sense of justice and create rightness in the world.

Even on the first foundational premise of historical or factual accuracy, we find the notions of Crown sovereignty, Crown title, and institutions that govern the relationship between Canadian people and Native Peoples foundering because they're premised on untruths, they're premised on very uncomfortable facts for people to have to acknowledge here in this country, which imagines itself to be tolerant and not racist. There are serious problems with the assumptions that underlie the founding constitutional premises of this relationship.

Historical accuracy and the loss of memory among both Native and non-Native people, and the manipulation of that loss of memory and the insertion of a false history into the legal development of the institutions that are used to govern our society is a central fact of what this country is all about. In the scholarship about colonization, people like Fanon and Memmi have criticized colonial mentalities and about how central forgetting is – how central obscuring the truth is to building a colonial country. Canadians don't often imagine that that is a part of the development of their own country, but it is, and it's a situation that needs to be rectified before anything can progress. Because in the way of our teaching, you can't have *skennen* until you have understanding. You can't have understanding until it's founded on the truth and on mutual acceptance of what the truth is. We have to have knowledge to have the truth. What we have today in the place of knowledge is the mythology of colonialism. We have a mythology in place of truth. We need to understand the past if we're going to go forward.

The truth is, Indigenous Peoples never surrendered. They never surrendered. They never surrendered the land, they never surrendered their consent to be autonomous Peoples, free Peoples. They never surrendered their identity. They never surrendered. Indigenous Peoples engaged in the relationship with the newcomers to the territory based on these good principles – *skennen* for my people and other ones among all of our other brothers and sisters. And that relationship was the foundation of that society until the epidemic diseases wiped out the military and political power of those founding Peoples. And at that point, another ideology and another set of actions and behaviors and policies and decisions emerged – a whole culture emerged based on the assumption of the demise of the Indian. A colonial arrogance which re-imagined the Indian out of existence. And to the extent that the Indian was on his way out, they created reserves, they created wardship status, they created situations to manage the "Indian problem" until it went away. Meanwhile, the colonial society arrogantly assumed everything that the Indian had. Her land, his power, all of these things.

In Canada in the 1950s Native Peoples and their rights were assumed to be on the way out, fading away – the Vanishing Indian. The colonizer felt secure that what they did was right, that it was historically inevitable. They told themselves, "We're superior, they're losers of history. We have all of the tools necessary to build a great society here and that's what we're going to do. We're going to develop a legal and institutional regime and a culture to support that. We're going to tell ourselves lies. We have to satisfy our own psychology in order to progress."

When this boomerang comes around it runs headlong into the problem of the older fact, which is in fact a fact, which is in fact the truth in a much deeper and more profound sense than the mythologies that have been developed on this false history in order to satisfy psychological needs of colonizing peoples. By the 1960s the Indian comes back, physically, culturally, intellectually. That culture, that society, that power begins to re-emerge. And you come into a social, political, and legal situation where you have a massive disjuncture between the mythology of colonialism that was built up in the 100-year period between the great dying out and the resurgence of the older fact.

Throughout the 1960s and '70s and '80s and into today, this disjuncture begins to manifest in all kinds of different ways. You have the resurgent identity of the Onkwehónweh running up against the idea of the Indian, status Indian, Hollywood Indian, drunken, wearing feathers, running around, undisciplined. I don't have to go through the whole ignoble savage imagery that runs directly against the experience of our people in what a true Onkwehónweh is. The resurgent identity finds its expression in all kinds of cultural expression: powwow, in literature, in art, in music. It is rooted and it's authentic, and it's reflective of that truth. And there's processes in place inside that culture which bring forward that truth into the present, and it runs headlong into a conflict with the colonizer mythology. And what have we got as a result of this confrontation of colonial lie and resurgent truth? What we got is all of the identity crises and all of the identity politics that we have now in our communities.

Empty Land?

The assumption is that this whole Turtle Island is *terra nullius*, without people, empty land. According to the explorers' journals, Jacques Cartier coming down the St. Lawrence saw 40,000 people in all kinds of villages, with animals and cultivation. It was something called civilization. It wasn't *terra nullius* at all. But once those 40,000 people died off and once all those people had no more military, political, and economic power, they were relegated to a little place where they had no ability to express themselves. Then this mythology of *terra nullius* can assert itself and all the colonial racist things we know now as Aboriginal rights and title can emerge.

Aboriginal title. Even the most progressive so-called Supreme Court decisions reflect the colonizer mentality. Now you run up the idea of inherent Indigenous ownership, possession, whatever word you want to use, relationship to land, you run that up against Aboriginal title, and you have a massive disjuncture and you have a massive conflict that's really unresolvable.

For Onkwehón:weh, you have your laws, your systems of social organization, your teachings, your culture, your language, all of these different things. And then you have something called "the Indian Act," which is a manifestation of the colonial prerogative to govern over lesser Peoples, to override the sovereignty and the existence of all those ceremonies, all that knowledge, all that history, and all that culture and all that civilization, and impose a way of life and a set of institutions on Native Peoples.

Whether Native people are talking about their tax exemption or self-government, or land claims, they are not people who are losers of history asking for the beneficence of a superior people. They're human beings with a commitment to preserving their own existence, which is a basic human right. And they're asking non-Native peoples to live like human beings as well, to look at the truth and to look at justice and to take decisions and actions based on the truth and justice, rather than on the need to preserve privilege that was developed out of this injustice perpetuated over the last 150 years.

Looking Forward

If we are going to look forward, we're committed together to fix the situation. I hope by now you sense my own position on this is that it's not really possible to work within the framework of colonialism to solve a colonial problem. I know this is a perennial post-colonial question: Can you use the master's tools to take down the master's house? My answer is no. Simple as that. If your concern is the fundamental problem, then you can't work within the colonial system. You have to have a higher conception of justice and you have to have a higher commitment to making change. A more serious commitment with more serious implications. A more serious commitment to justice, with more serious problems in the short term, as you work towards the longer objective, which is justice.

So when I talk about a rebellion of the truth against the lie, that's what I mean. We have to begin to reject all of those ideas, those falsehoods in our own lives and develop a relationship and a movement to promote that truth and that objective so that it can develop a positive energy on its own and begin to orient the dialogue, begin to orient people's thinking and then begin to orient social and political action. And eventually become the reality that we're living.

From Theory to Practice

People say to me, that's good in theory. What does it mean in real life? Actually they said that to me the other day at Six Nations. What does it mean in real life for me? What do I have to do? I said, well that's a tough question, that's a really tough question. We have to reason through this, thinking through ways to confront this problem. Any people who are looking for freedom, whether it's on an individual basis or it's on a collective basis, all over the world, throughout history, have to realize that there is no independence or freedom without self-sufficiency. That's a starting assumption here if we're going to change the system. The other thing we have to look at is the system of colonial control, all these lies, the way they have wormed their way into our lives, is no longer the type of imperial manipulation and control that it was at one time. There are no Red Coats stationed outside the building here, forcing us to carry an Indian card. There's no army that's going to punish me for not voting for the band council. It's not that kind of obvious physical control.

It's developed and evolved to the point where we are self-colonized. We talk about self-determination: it starts with the self, the first word, self. We're self-colonized at this point. We're the ones who are doing it to ourselves. And this is not some sort of theoretical, intellectual development in my own mind, I know this is from growing up in a Native community. This is from working with Native communities for years and years. I realize it's hard for people to say this who are not themselves Native. It is hard for someone who maybe comes to this realization intellectually, to say, well, yeah, the Natives really are facilitating their own oppression, and what they need to do is stop participating in their colonial system and maybe then there will be some change. It's very difficult in the political environment we live in today to say that. But I have tenure, and I'm Native, so yeah, I'll risk it. I'm telling you that's what I believe is the main problem. And not only in terms of its most superficial representations of us having a band council, accepting money from the government, and not doing anything to develop any kind of self-sufficiency.

I realize there's lots of people doing lots of good trying to help, but in general, it's also in living those lies and the way that we conduct ourselves. And the lies exist to all kinds of varying degrees. Some of the most obvious ones are very clear, but also even on the margins, in terms of, well what kind of lives are we living when we say we want to be traditional, we value Nationhood, we value our traditions, and we value being Anishinaabe or Onkwehónweh, yet we turn around and conduct our lives in full accordance with what's expected of us as Indians under the Indian Act.

So I think that there's certain principles that come out of that kind of realization and analysis. One would be non-participation. We have to withdraw our consent. And here's something that affects the legal, the political, and the spiritual identity. We have to withdraw our consent from that realm, that framework, that whole concept of what it is to be Aboriginal or Indigenous or First Nations as defined and constructed by Canada or in relation to it. That's the first step.

Second step is that we have to be militant pacifists. Pacifist in the Gandhian sense of pacifist. And we have to be militant, though, because if we're not militant, in this day and age, there's so much overwhelming power in the control of the media, information, communications, markets, of what's been referred to as the whole structure of bio-political power, in the world today, that if we're not militant, if we're not assertive, if we're not active in rejecting that one and taking on the other and building new spaces of freedom in our life, it's going to overrun us, it's going to override us. The momentum of that system is such that it has its own weather system now. It's moving and it's almost unstoppable.

But the thing that makes it stoppable is that it's still an organic system. We can look at history and colonialism and its new manifestations, as something that's separated from human agency, that it's this big economic and social trend that comes into our lives and overwhelms us. But it's not, and it never has been. It started with an idea about what power is and someone's greedy desire to impose his will on that other person. And someone's development, very, very skillfully and using the technology of the time, of the means to be able to do that. And then the development of an ethic and a culture around it. The Roman Empire, the European empires, the Euro-American empire, and now we have this globalizing empire here. It's about domination, but it's an idea. It's an idea carried forward by the decisions of men and women every day.

Sir William Johnston is a famous character in Haudenosaunee history. Basically, he's the guy responsible for us losing just about all of our homeland, you know, hats tipped to him, he did a good job in his own realm. But before he was the superintendent of Indian affairs for the British empire in this part of the world, he was an Irishman. He was part of a culture that was different from the English. He was part of something different, his people were different. They had a language, they had a culture, they had a different way of thinking. They were kind of like natural peoples living in their own territory. What happened to him? He was taken and transformed in his mind and in his heart and in the way he behaved and the way he lived his life into a colonizer. That's how it operates. It doesn't operate on these huge historical plains. It operates one on one. People get convinced of the need to serve that objective and those values, and they get unconvinced of the need to protect their culture, their ideas, their family.

In this sense, I'm not only speaking to Indigenous Peoples here, I am speaking to people in the mainstream, in the larger society who serve that imperial objective. Today that's manifesting as all of the criticism that all of the younger people here today are better than I am at leveling at the system: the global capitalist, accumulative, individualistic mainstream culture that we live in. We choose it every day in the way we live our lives and how we spend our money and what we do to get that money and all these sorts of things, as opposed to investing in alternatives. For Indigenous people, it's our traditional cultures. For other people it might be something else. It may be a new ethic, a new philosophy, a new way of living, a new community. But we choose every day to not invest in that, to invest in something else. Colonization comes down to that.

I started off talking about how our communities are not plagued by the lack of a sustainable land base for sustainable economic development or the lack of access to remedies for this and that, blah, blah, blah. They're plagued by the problem of a lack of happiness in their own lives and the lack of ability to live free lives according to an authentic notion of what their culture is. That's what they're plagued by. I'm finishing off by saying colonization isn't all this historical stuff, it's individual people making choices one way or the other.

The Four Intuitions

I'll leave you with four intuitions that I have, because up to this point I've been talking mentalities. Aside from my thoughts, I got a bit of an intuition as to where we should be going to fix the problem in a practical sense. And this came out of discussions at Six Nations and with community people, and this may be more specifically related here to Onkwehónweh than to members of non-Native society, but nonetheless... If we're going to take all this and try to move forward, what do we need to do today, right now, in the next five minutes? I think you look at the four different aspects of a person's life and you can come up with four different insights that have been given to me as a gift from certain people who have shared their time and wisdom with me over the years.

The first one is in the way that we look at the basic essence of what any human being's life is, which is how do we feed ourselves, what do we feed ourselves, and how do we sustain ourselves as physical beings? Right now, we have a situation where most Indigenous Peoples in North America are completely dependent in terms of what they eat, how much they eat, and its quality, on the state, or on markets or on other people. So we have lost the basic essence of self-sufficiency. How can we even go anywhere toward independence and freedom while we're in a situation where, if the power went out and if they closed off our reserve or our communities, we would starve within a week.

I thank my teacher at Cornell University, the renowned scholar Milton Esman, for constantly reminding me of this in my younger days. When I was dreaming philosophically, about freedom and independence, he'd say, "Gerald," – he called me Gerald, he can't pronounce Taiaiake either – "Gerald, what are you going to do for money? What are you going to do for revenue and resources for this?" Tough question. Smart people ask me that all the time. And there are certain answers we can talk about, but safe to say right now, there has to be a basis for self-sufficiency. We have to be able to feed ourselves independently in order to assert any type of program of autonomy from the state. This is a lesson that applies I think, to anybody, and there's all kinds of creative ways to address this. I call this "decolonizing your diet." Never mind the content, which, if you travel among our people, I have to say to my sisters and brothers here today, it's a very dire situation, if you travel among our people. We're very sick people because of what we eat and what we don't do physically and what we do and don't do physically. We have to fix that, whether it's diabetes and all other kinds of things. That's something that's going to threaten our very existence, never mind all this theory. It's going to threaten our very existence. You can't have rights if there's no people to carry those rights forward, so that's a very dire problem.

The second one I believe is just as important because it addresses the psychological state or the emotional state of our people. A criticism leveled at the global empire today is that it's founded on fear. Well, we've been the guinea pigs for that for the past 200 years. The way the media and the government use fear to control people through advertising and media, we've been subject to that for a long time, and it's had a very serious effect on our people. It's been said in other contexts by other people that the other side of fear is freedom, I believe that one.

There's my other slogan: "on the other side of fear is freedom." When we break through the fear. When we acknowledge that we're afraid of change and that maybe we're going to be successful and we're afraid of that. If we acknowledge that there's going to be sacrifices to be made and costs to be paid for progress, and that sometimes, yes, it's going to involve violence, but by sticking to an ethic of nonviolence and by sticking to a militant pacifism, we can tough it out, we can move forward. In fact, it's a price to pay. Once we get over that and we're not fearful anymore, we'll start to achieve freedom. That's just an historical lesson I believe. It's something that I think any movement for justice in the world has faced.

You have to develop a culture and a means to confront fear, and deal with it. But I certainly don't see that right now in the culture of Native politics that I've been working in for the last fifteen years. It's like we're trying to confront the problem with one hand tied behind our back. Well, we're going to fight but only if it's nice. We're going to fight only if they don't hit us; then we're going to go home and you know, think about something else. What about developing a theory to deal with the violence that the state uses against Indigenous people? We have to do that. So on the other side of fear is freedom.

Then we have one from our brothers and sisters in the African American community in the 1970s when they used to say – and this relates to getting out and exerting yourself and asserting yourself – "Free your mind and your ass will follow." I flip that around, say the opposite: "Free your ass and your mind will follow." We've got to get out there and start asserting ourselves on our land. We have to reconnect with the places that we say in our textbooks are sacred. We have to get out there and start using the land and find out what it can teach us.

I've learned so much in the last six years in British Columbia about what it is to live as a Native by going out and doing stuff on the land and talking to people and getting to know and love people who are out there all the time doing that thing, more than I ever could learn about it reading a book or theorizing about it. It's crucially important. So we have to get out there and we have to use this land. This bleeds over into legal strategies as well, political strategies as well, there's all kinds of community building, reconnectedness. There are all kinds of justifications in the law for use and occupancy, and all this kind of stuff that comes from actually getting out there and doing things on the land. It means getting up off the couch and turning the TV off.

And the last one that I'll leave you with has to do with how this takes place. I'll refer to a kind of spiritual conversion, it's a revolution of the spirit. Aun Sung Su Kee said it about Burma. It's one person at a time coming to the realization that in order to have *skennen*, you have to first unify yourself inside of your own mind, inside of your own soul. You have to be in control, stable, strong, healthy inside of yourself, and then that begins to emanate into your family, into your community, into your Nation, then it begins to be something that affects the world.

The slogan for this one is "one warrior at a time." It doesn't happen collectively. It's not like I can pass a law in Kahnawà:ke and say everybody's got to speak Mohawk from now on. Everybody's got to learn the Great Law. Everybody's got to know the Four Ceremonies. Band council resolution, we passed it, there you go. Send it to the minister, get some funding, it's going to happen. Now let's all go to the bar and celebrate, because we did something good for our community. That's a collective type of solution.

Or less flippantly, the Aboriginal Healing Foundation – I'm not picking on these institutions, I'm just saying in terms of the mentality of how this operates. These things do lots of good, but they do it by looking at the problem collectively and thinking about policy solutions and funding it as a policy solution and then giving it to Native or non-Native bureaucrats to manage. Even the way we do education – I'm an administrator, too. The way that we look at making change, we have to rethink this and realize that it happens through the experience of a single person, one person at a time. If you think about the way people are transformed, you don't have to stick within our tradition to do it. For those of you from other traditions, there's just as much teaching and wisdom everywhere in the world. Whether your name's Siddhartha and then you become Buddha or whether you follow Jesus, it's people who go through experiences and who receive wisdom and who touch a profound truth and are changed and then go and spread the message.

If you have followed me in the line of thought that I've laid out for you and you can see that we need to move from a kind of complacency and acceptance of the falsehood of things we call Aboriginal rights, Aboriginal title, even the concept of being Aboriginal. There's a whole ideology around all of those falsehoods that I've laid out and it's called, in my mind, Aboriginalism. And it contrasts the truth of Onkwehónweh. If we criticize it and we follow it through and we look at real strategies for change, I think it's really possible to achieve them, but it means challenging ourselves, it means being very self-conscious about our role in perpetuating these things and being very courageous in looking very deep within ourselves and moving in different directions and making different choices for the betterment of our people, for the betterment of the seven generations to come, and also for the betterment of the world. Because after all, our philosophy is nothing else but a little piece of the wisdom that exists universally in all cultures but is our reflection in this land and among these people of what that truth and wisdom is. So, with that, I'll leave you. In our language, we say *Taneh toh,* which means those are all the words that I have.

Niawen'ko:wa. Thank you very much.

[Long applause.]

A NOTE ON THE SOURCES

The two forms of the original spoken word sources here – orations and dialogues – differ from text in significant ways. Taiaiake follows Onkwehónweh traditions of orality where both speaking and listening are taken seriously: people are brought together as witnesses and participants, as opposed to a more capitalist framing of passive audiences consuming information and entertainment. He also draws on the earlier classical Western traditions of dialoguing as a shared creative experience of, as he says, "learning together in the moment, molding something." To be fully present as the ideas unfold, he speaks on his themes without notes. For this reason Taiaiake says: "Oration is speaking with no net: the individual, secure in their identity, is making themself vulnerable and available to be challenged." The speaker is there to learn from the listener. The process of being in dialogue, as in an interview, is related but with more voices engaging: "It goes beyond an exchange of perspectives to take words seriously and to create something together that elevates knowledge or discourse through this form of engagement and understanding." Participants don't arrive with agendas and arguments they hope to win but with open minds and ideas to share. We thought something like jazz might be a good metaphor: within the discipline of a familiar standard, players take turns to improvise, breaking away from the tune to chase ideas as the others support and contribute to each musical thought, even as they all remain rooted in the main themes.

Reflecting the change in medium from live speech to black-and-white text, the content has been adapted from the following spoken word sources: talks, speeches, interviews, and podcasts that were recorded live and then transcribed and prepared for this collection. Many of them, uploaded to YouTube, have been viewed thousands of times, while others are personal communications. As editor, I went through the transcripts while listening to the original recordings and endeavored to remain true to the words as they were delivered. As to bearing fidelity to the original sources, the material presented here has been edited, sometimes substantially, for clarity, factual accuracy (dates, for example), and conciseness and to avoid too much repetition of general explanations of recurring themes. Where necessary, informational details have been added to the text, and endnotes provide more detail. Over the years, conventions around culturally appropriate terms, capitalization, spelling, etc., have all evolved: *Elements of Indigenous Style: A Guide for Writing by and about Indigenous Peoples* by Gregory Younging

(2018) resolved many of these issues, but how we talk and write about these things is a work in progress.

To read the words, in some cases twenty years after they were first uttered, is a very different but, we believe, worthwhile experience. Rather than trying to capture the ideas around Indigenous Resurgence, we are trying to free them. Readers are enthusiastically encouraged to visit Taiaiake's website at https://taiaiake.net/, where he uploads his latest work, both written and broadcast, and to visit some of the original sources we drew upon for this volume.

Ann Rogers

SOURCE CREDITS

Wasáse Redux

Gregg, Allan. "Taiaiake Alfred on His Indigenous Manifesto." *Allan Gregg in Conversation*, TVO, June 2005. © TVO. Video. https://nationtalk.ca/story/featured-video-of-the-day-native-scholar-be-taiaiake-alfred-on-indigenous-governance.

From Noble Savage to Righteous Warrior

"From Noble Savage to Righteous Warrior: Regenerating and Reinscribing Indigenous Presences." Global Encounters Initiative Symposium, Vancouver, BC, March 6, 2010. Video. https://www.youtube.com/watch?v=8ZfGAqdIJmE&pbjreload=10.

The Psychic Landscape of Contemporary Colonialism

"The Psychic Landscape of Contemporary Colonialism." University of Ottawa, Ontario, November 9, 2011. Video. https://www.youtube.com/watch?feature=player_embedded&v=8n7Cd-kwrw.

Practical Decolonization

"Practical Decolonization." Queen's University, Kingston, ON, April 9, 2012. Video. https://www.youtube.com/watch?v=pq87xqSMrDw.

Warrior Scholarship

Unpublished interview conducted by Aotearoa/New Zealand (Ngāti Porou and Ngāti Uepohatu iwi) scholar Dr. Veronica Tawhai as part of her doctoral research, Victoria, BC, March 18, 2013.

Constitutional Recognition and Colonial Doublespeak

"The Problem with the Constitutional Recognition of Indigenous People." *Drive, ABC Radio National*, November 13, 2013. Radio. https://www.abc.net.au/radionational/programs/drive/the-problem-with-constitutional-recognition-of-indigenous-people/5120732.

On Being and Becoming Indigenous

"Being and Becoming Indigenous: Resurgence Against Contemporary Colonialism." The 2013 Narrm Oration, University of Melbourne, Australia, November 28, 2013. Video. https://www.youtube.com/watch?v=VwJNy-B3lPA.

Reconciliation as Recolonization

"Reconciliation as Recolonization." Concordia University TV, Montreal, Quebec, September 20, 2016. Video. https://www.youtube.com/watch?v=LEiNu7UL7TM.

From Red Power to Resurgence

"Red Power to Reconciliation." Then and Now: 1968–2018 Conference, Institute for the Humanities, Simon Fraser University, Vancouver, BC, November 2, 2018. Video. https://www.youtube.com/watch?v=jV_ohK28PiI.

Rebuilding the Fire: In Conversation with Pamela Palmater

Palmater, Pam. "Mohawk Warrior Taiaiake Alfred on Native Resurgence." *Warrior Life*, episode 25, July 5, 2019. Podcast. https://soundcloud.com/pampalmater.

Ronón:kwe

MacKenzie, Ian. "No Accountability Without Community." *The Mythic Masculine*, episode 34, January 19, 2021. Podcast. https://www.themythicmasculine.com/episodes/taiaiake-alfred.

Rooted Responsibility

Unpublished doctoral research interview by Hugh O Burnam, March 2021.

You Can't Decolonize Colonization

Pebeahsy, Robyn, and Ricardo Saenz. "Reconciliation, Land and Decolonization." *The Decolonized Buffalo*, episode 116, September 16, 2022. Podcast. https://www.podbean.com/media/share/dir-99bd3-152e0a05?utm_campaign=w_share_ep&utm_medium=dlink&utm_source=w_share.

Bonus Track: The Four Intuitions

"Taiaiake Alfred on Canada and Its Indigenous Peoples." *Big Ideas*, TVO Today, April 20, 2003. Video. © TVO. https://www.tvo.org/video/archive/taiaiake-alfred-on-canada-and-its-indigenous-peoples.

NOTES

Introduction by Ann Rogers

1 The quote is from Max Weber's 1919 lecture, "Politics as a Vocation."
2 Ian MacKenzie, "No Accountability Without Community," *The Mythic Masculine*, episode 34, January 19, 2021, podcast, https://www.themythicmasculine.com/episodes/taiaiake-alfred.
3 Unpublished doctoral research interview by Hugh O Burnam, March 2021.
4 MacKenzie, "No Accountability Without Community."
5 Burnam interview.
6 Taiaiake Alfred, "A Critical Reflection on 'From Bad to Worse: Internal Politics in the 1990 Crisis at Kahnawake,' " *Recherches amérindiennes au Québec* L, no. 3 (2020–1): 137–9, translated by Nicole Beaudry, 138.
7 Taiaiake Alfred, "From Bad to Worse: Internal Politics in the 1990 Crisis at Kahnawake," *Northeast Indian Quarterly* 8, no. 1 (Spring 1991): 23–31, 23.
8 Alfred, "A Critical Reflection," 138.
9 Ibid.
10 MacKenzie, "No Accountability Without Community."

11 Gerald R. Alfred, *Heeding the Voices of Our Ancestors: Kahnawake Mohawk Politics and the Rise of Native Nationalism* (Toronto: Oxford University Press, 1995), 3.
12 Taiaiake Alfred, *Peace, Power, Righteousness: An Indigenous Manifesto*, 2nd ed. (Don Mills: Oxford University Press, 2009), 91.
13 Ibid., 117.
14 Ibid., 86.
15 Leanne Betasamosake Simpson, *As We Have Always Done: Indigenous Freedom through Radical Resistance* (Minneapolis: University of Minnesota Press, 2017), 14.
16 Taiaiake Alfred, *Wasáse: Indigenous Pathways of Action and Freedom* (Peterborough: Broadview Press), 27.
17 Interview with author, May 27, 2021, Victoria, BC.
18 Screen captures of Wasáse.org c. March 2005 can be found via the Wayback Machine internet archive at https://web.archive.org/; search http://www.wasase.org/rebellion/index.htm.
19 Taiaiake Alfred and Lana Lowe, "Warrior Societies in Contemporary Indigenous Communities" (Government of Ontario, Ipperwash Inquiry Research Paper: Policing Aboriginal Occupations and Aboriginal/Police Relations, 2005), 2.
20 Alfred, *Wasáse*, 67.
21 BCCLA, *National Security: Curbing the Excess to Protect Freedom and Democracy: A Brief Prepared for the House of Commons Subcommittee on Public Safety and National Security and the Senate Special Committee on the Anti-Terrorism Act*, 2005, https://www.bccla.org/wp-content/uploads/2005/10/2005-BCCLA-Policy-National-Security-Curbing-Excess.pdf.
22 In April 2023 the Assembly of First Nations Special Chiefs Assembly passed a resolution noting that an Indigenous man is four times more likely to be a victim of homicide when compared to Indigenous women and seven times more likely than non-Indigenous males.
23 See, for example, Gloria Galloway, "70 Per Cent of Murdered Aboriginal Women Killed by Indigenous Men: RCMP," *Globe and Mail*, April 9, 2015, https://www.theglobeandmail.com/news/politics/70-per-cent-of-murdered-aboriginal-women-killed-by-indigenous-men-rcmp-confirms/article23868927/; Emma MacIntosh, "We Fact-Checked a Viral Claim About Who's Killing MMIWG: It

Was Wrong," *Canada's National Observer*, June 7, 2019, https://www.nationalobserver.com/2019/06/07/analysis/we-fact-checked-viral-claim-about-whos-killing-mmiwg-it-was-wrong.

24 "Reclaiming Power and Place: the Final Report of the National Inquiry into Missing and Murdered Indigenous Women and Girls," Canada, 2019, Volume 1b, 250.

25 "MascuIndian 2.0," interview with Arthur Kroker for the Pacific Centre for Technology & Culture, University of Victoria, May 1, 2018. Quotes in this section are from the Kroker interview unless otherwise noted.

26 Jorge Barrera, "Enrolment Suspended After Report Finds UVic Indigenous Governance Program Left Students 'Traumatized,' " *CBC News*, April 24, 2018.

27 Daniel Rowe, "Taiaiake Alfred Resigns from University of Victoria's Indigenous Governance Program," *Eastern Door*, March 6, 2019, https://tworowtimes.com/news/national/alfred-resigns-from-indigenous-governance-program/.

28 Interview with author.

29 Brett Forester, "CSIS Weighed Whether Rail Blockades Supporting Wet'suwet'en Could Be Classed as Terrorism," *CBC News*, October 27, 2022, https://www.cbc.ca/news/indigenous/csis-rail-blockades-assess-terrorism-1.6628584.

30 MacKenzie, "No Accountability Without Community."

Wasáse Redux

1 In central Labrador the Mushuau Innu lived a largely nomadic life sustained by caribou until the government permanently settled them in 1967 at Utshimassit (Davis Inlet). The inability to sustain themselves by traditional means had devastating results on the community. In 2002–3, they were moved again to the new community of Natuashish, where problems of addiction, corruption, and anomie persist.

2 The Red Lake Reservation in Minnesota was the site of a school shooting involving a sixteen-year-old boy who killed nine and injured five before killing himself following a shoot-out with police, shortly before this interview was taped.

From Noble Savage to Righteous Warrior

1 Taiaiake is referring to decolonial writers Frantz Fanon (1925–61), best known for *Black Skin, White Masks* (1952) and *The Wretched of the Earth* (1961), and Albert Memmi (1920–2020), whose most famous work is *Colonizer and Colonized* (1957).
2 Taiaiake Alfred, "Our Art Is Our Life: The Power of Marianne Nicolson's Work," in *Border Zones: The Ideas Behind the Exhibit* (Vancouver: Museum of Anthropology, 2010), http://www2.moa.ubc.ca/borderzones/features_nicolson.html.
3 John Ralston Saul, *A Fair Country: Telling Truths About Canada* (Toronto: Viking Press, 2008).
4 The discussion refers to controversies around holding the 2010 Olympics on Indigenous lands. Leaders of the four host First Nations of Lil'wat, Musqueam, Squamish, and Tsleil-Waututh were delayed by demonstrators organized under the No Olympics on Stolen Native Land network.
5 The late Mohawk artist and philosopher Karoniaktajeh designed the flag as a symbol of unity among Native people and as a standard for the Kanién'kehá:ka men of the Rotinonhsón:ni Warrior Society.
6 Louie, a long-serving Chief of the Osoyoos Indian Band in British Columbia, made national headlines with a "politically incorrect" speech he gave that relied on racist stereotypes. See Roy MacGregor, "'Indian Time Doesn't Cut It' for Innovative Chief with On-the-Edge Humour," *Globe & Mail*, September 21, 2006, https://www.theglobeandmail.com/news/national/indian-time-doesnt-cut-it-for-innovative-chief-with-on-the-edge-humour/article1103739/.

The Psychic Landscape of Contemporary Colonialism

1 Andrew Tenakohate Delisle Sr. was elected to the Mohawk Council of Kahnawà:ke in 1960 and became its spokesperson in 1964, a position that evolved into the Grand Chief title. He served on Council until 1982 and remained a community leader and became a founding member of the National Indigenous Council of Elders. He died in 2019.
2 After enormous Indigenous political pressure, Section 35, recognizing "existing Aboriginal and treaty rights" was included

in the new Canadian Constitution, but the content of those rights was not defined. At heart was the issue of whether Aboriginal self-government was an *inherent* right that simply needed to be recognized by the Crown or a *delegated* right – hence the "empty box" to be filled with negotiated agreements. See Russ Diabo, "When Moving Past the *Indian Act* Means Something Worse," *Policy Options*, September 22, 2017, https://policyoptions.irpp.org/magazines/september-2017/when-moving-past-the-indian-act-means-something-worse/.

3 The Dene People's traditional territory includes the Mackenzie River Valley and the Barren Grounds in the so-called Northwest Territories. In the 1970s the federal government mooted building energy pipelines through the region and set up a commission led by Thomas Berger to investigate environmental, economic, and Indigenous impacts. The Berger Report (1977) set new precedents in resource development consultation. Lengthy negotiations and legal battles over land rights continued, with the federal government maintaining that Denedeh rights were extinguished when the Dene signed Treaties 8 and 11 in 1900 and 1922. In 2016 the Deline Dene became the first self-government in the Northwest Territories. Plans to build the pipelines were finally shelved in 2017. Battles over pipeline development on Indigenous lands remain a hallmark of Crown–Indigenous relations.

4 A treaty between the Haudenosaunee and the Dutch in 1613, the Two-Row Wampum is one of the earliest treaties between Indigenous and European peoples. It was understood to be a relationship between two distinct peoples that would require ongoing negotiations based on mutual respect and peaceful coexistence, rather than a settled arrangement.

Warrior Scholarship

1 Taiaiake Alfred, *First Nation Perspectives on Political Identity*, First Nation Citizenship Research & Policy Series (Ottawa: Building Towards Change, June 2009), https://web.archive.org/web/20091218164917/http://www.afn.ca/misc/FN-political-identity.pdf.

On Being and Becoming Indigenous

1 Prime Minister Stephen Harper, "Statement of Apology to Former Students of Indian Residential Schools," June 11, 2008, https://www.rcaanc-cirnac.gc.ca/eng/1100100015644/1571589171655.
2 Anishinabewmowin, Matthew Coon Come vs Women, video, January 13, 2013, https://www.youtube.com/watch?v=YnFQT1-zlBw&t=22s.
3 The January 11 meeting between the Prime Minister and Native delegates led by Assembly of First Nations National Chief Shawn Atleo made plain the deep divisions between grassroots and Native leadership. See for example, Mark Blackburn, "AFN's Fault Lines Magnified by Idle No More Movement, Attawapiskat Chief Spence's Protest," *APTN*, January 15, 2013, https://www.aptnnews.ca/national-news/afns-fault-lines-magnified-by-idle-no-more-movement-attawapiskat-chief-spences-protest/.
4 See note 1 above.

From Red Power to Resurgence

1 The Trans Mountain pipeline system carries crude oil from the Alberta oil sands to the British Columbia coast for transshipment. In 2013 the government approved the Trans Mountain Pipeline Expansion (TMX), a project to add 980 kilometers of pipeline to the existing route. Concerns about the environmental impacts on the lands and seas (through increased tanker traffic), and issues around First Nations consent have led to protracted legal wrangles and civil resistance. The federal government bought the privately held pipeline in 2018.
2 A Norwegian philosopher associated with the Deep Ecology movement that argues that *all* lives have intrinsic value.
3 Chief Deskaheh traveled to the League of Nations in Geneva in 1923 to advocate for recognition of the Six Nations as a sovereign Indigenous Nation when Canada tried to replace the traditional hereditary council with an elected band council. The League refused to hear him, arguing that Canada had jurisdiction over the Six Nations.

4 See Taiaiake Alfred and Lana Lowe's report, "Warrior Societies in Contemporary Indigenous Communities," for the Ipperwash Inquiry in 2005, https://www.attorneygeneral.jus.gov.on.ca/inquiries/ipperwash/policy_part/research/pdf/Alfred_and_Lowe.pdf.

5 The Manuel family, from Secwepemc territory in so-called British Columbia, has been in the forefront of resisting colonization for generations. Twin sisters Kanahus and Mayuk Manuel are activists in the Tiny House Warriors, which has built houses to impede the TMX pipeline from crossing Secwepemc territory. Also known as Kanahus Freedom, Kanahus is the mother of four "Freedom Babies," whose births were not registered with the Canadian authorities. Their father, Arthur Manuel (1951–2017), was an Indigenous leader who took the struggle for rights and lands to the international arena, and the author, with Grand Chief Ronald Derrickson, of *Unsettling Canada: A National Wake Up Call* (2015) and *The Reconciliation Manifesto: Recovering the Land, Rebuilding the Economy* (2017). Their grandfather George Manuel (1921–89), was a Chief of the National Indian Brotherhood, the forerunner of the Assembly of First Nations, and founded and led the World Council of Indigenous Peoples in 1975. He wrote, with Michael Posluns, *The Fourth World: An Indian Reality* (1974).

6 In *R v Calder* 1973 the Supreme Court of Canada recognized the existence of Aboriginal title (ownership) in Canadian law. The case concerned lands historically occupied by the Nisga'a peoples of northwestern British Columbia. The Nisga'a claim itself was narrowly rejected.

7 The Nisga'a Final Agreement is a modern treaty signed in 1998 between the federal and BC governments and the Nisga'a Nation that "settled" an Indigenous land claim.

8 This prediction was correct: In July 2020 the Supreme Court dismissed an appeal from Squamish Nation, Tsleil-Waututh Nation, and Coldwater Indian Band, exhausting all legal options to prevent the pipeline being built.

9 The *Delgamuukw v British Columbia* (1997) case concerned Gitxsan and Wet'suwet'en attempts to establish jurisdiction over 58,000 square kilometres of land and water in northwest British Columbia. The Supreme Court of Canada recognized Aboriginal title as

an ancestral right protected under the Constitution. The case began in 1984, following failed treaty negotiations, and the 1997 decision, although ground-breaking, left the *content* of rights and title unresolved. More legal wrangling is required to establish the content of the specific claim. The 2020 Shutdown Canada blockades across the country were in solidarity with the ongoing efforts of some Wet'suwet'en people and their allies to physically assert control in their traditional territory and stop a controversial pipeline construction project. Both Amnesty International and the United Nations Committee on the Elimination of Racial Discrimination have called for an end to the state's escalating use of force against peaceful Wet'suwet'en land defenders.

10 The Indian Residential Schools Settlement Agreement (2007) was an out-of-court settlement of a class-action lawsuit brought against the Canadian government by survivors of the residential school system. Apart from compensation, the settlement included funding for the establishment of a Truth and Reconciliation Commission (TRC). In its turn, between 2008 and 2015 the TRC collected evidence and stories from more than 6,000 witnesses and issued a report that documented the experiences of more than 150,000 residential school survivors, with a finding of cultural genocide. Its ninety-four "calls to action" constitute the most recent general understanding of "reconciliation" in a Canadian context.

11 The Alberni Residential School on Vancouver Island operated from 1890 to 1973. Examples of the abuse that occurred there include an estimated half of the school population died in 1900 of tuberculosis, nutritional experiments were carried out in the 1940s, and sexual abuse was so prevalent that in a case brought against former school supervisor Arthur Plint in 1995, BC Supreme Court Justice Douglas Hogarth said, "[T]he Indian residential school system was nothing more than institutionalized paedophilia."

Rebuilding the Fire: In Conversation with Pamela Palmater

1 See From Red Power to Resurgence note 1, above.

Rooted Responsibility

1 Arnold Tioronhiate Goodleaf (1950–2000) was a prominent First Nations government administrator, advisor, and strategist. Among his many accomplishments, he served as the founding director of intergovernmental affairs for the Mohawk Council of Kahnawà:ke, was a spokesperson for the Assembly of First Nations and pushed for the establishment of jurisdiction over internet gaming in Kahnawà:ke as an assertion of sovereignty and as an economic driver.

You Can't Decolonize Colonization

1 Taiaiake Alfred, "Restitution Is the Real Pathway to Justice for Indigenous Peoples," in *Response, Responsibility, and Renewal: Canada's Truth and Reconciliation Journey*, ed. Gregory Younging, Jonathan Dewar, and Mike DeGagné (Ottawa: Aboriginal Healing Foundation, 2009), 181–7.

2 A "Nation" in this context is an Indigenous political group that meets the four criteria of Nationhood under customary international law, that is, a permanent population, a definite occupied territory, a government, and the ability to enter into relations with other nations.

3 Well For Culture (www.wellforculture.com) is a grassroots Indigenous health and wellness initiative guided by Ancestral teachings and Indigenous philosophies that has a substantial social media presence.

About the Authors

Ashley Seymour

TAIAIAKE ALFRED is a Kahnawà:ke Mohawk philosopher and political strategist with more than three decades of experience in First Nations governance, political activism, and cultural restoration. After twenty-five years as a university professor, he now works directly with Indigenous nations to help breathe life into their visions of self-determination. He has been awarded a Canada Research Chair, a National Aboriginal Achievement/Indspire Award, and the Native American Journalists Association award for best column writing. He is the author of three highly acclaimed books: *Heeding the Voices of Our Ancestors: Kahnawake Mohawk Politics and the Rise of Native Nationalism*; *Peace, Power, Righteousness: An Indigenous Manifesto*; and *Wasáse: Indigenous Pathways of Action and Freedom*.

ANN ROGERS is a fourth-generation settler on Stz'uminus territory, the author of *Secrecy and Power in the British State: A History of the Official Secrets Act*, and co-author of *Unmanned: Drone Warfare and Global Security*.

Printed and bound by CPI Group (UK) Ltd, Croydon, CR0 4YY

13/04/2025

14656512-0001